Web Design:
A Beginner's Guide

Second Edition

About the Author

Wendy Willard is a designer, consultant, writer, and educator who has been involved in web design for about 15 years. She is the author of *HTML: A Beginner's Guide,* Fourth Edition, and other books. Wendy is a graduate of Art Center College of Design in Pasadena, California.

About the Technical Editor

Kathi McCracken-Dente is a user experience strategist with an expertise in designing for e-commerce, communities, and web applications. Before starting McCracken Design, a web design agency in Oakland, California, she was a designer at frog design, Addwater, and Intuit. Her clients include Yahoo!, Intuit, PowerReviews, and LeapFrog. She is a graduate of Duke University and Art Center College of Design.

Web Design:
A Beginner's Guide

Second Edition

Wendy Willard

New York   Chicago   San Francisco
Lisbon   London   Madrid   Mexico City
Milan   New Delhi   San Juan
Seoul   Singapore   Sydney   Toronto

The McGraw-Hill Companies

Cataloging-in-Publication Data is on file with the Library of Congress

McGraw-Hill books are available at special quantity discounts to use as premiums and sales promotions, or for use in corporate training programs. To contact a representative, please e-mail us at bulksales@mcgraw-hill.com.

Web Design: A Beginner's Guide, Second Edition

1234567890 DOC DOC 109876543210

ISBN 978-0-07-170134-1
MHID   0-07-170134-6

Sponsoring Editor   Roger Stewart

Editorial Supervisor   Patty Mon

Project Editor   LeeAnn Pickrell

Acquisitions Coordinator   Joya Anthony

Technical Editor   Kathi McCracken-Dente

Copy Editor   Lisa Theobald

Proofreader   Martin Benes

Indexer   Rebecca Plunkett

Production Supervisor   George Anderson

Composition   Apollo Publishing

Illustration   Apollo Publishing

Art Director, Cover   Jeff Weeks

Cover Designer   Jeff Weeks

Working as a self-employed web designer has been a fabulous way for me to help support my family while also staying at home with my kids. This book is dedicated to moms everywhere who are finding creative ways to balance their careers and their families.

Contents

Acknowledgments

First, I must thank the folks at McGraw-Hill for letting me update this book. I was thrilled to incorporate years of reader feedback, design exposure, and teaching experience into this new edition.

A special thanks goes to Kathi, my technical editor, fellow Art Center alum, and friend, for giving me the type of feedback I really needed to hear, even while dealing with a new baby and multiple other stressful life events. Kathi, you rock!

Finally, the deadlines involved in finishing a book can often result in some late nights barricaded in the office writing. I'm so blessed to have a family who supports and encourages me in everything I do. Thank you Wyeth, Corinna, and Caeli.

Philippians 4:13

Introduction

When I began work on this book, I performed a search on Amazon for the phrase "web design." I found books on everything from HTML to XML and from web graphics to web usability. What is the beginning reader supposed to think? Where should she begin in this huge list of possibilities? With a beginner's guide, of course.

Web Design: A Beginner's Guide covers a lot of ground in a short amount of time. It is an excellent way to discover everything from HTML to XML and from web graphics to web usability, without having to read a million different books. This book covers all these topics in a succinct fashion, moving you from the beginning to the end to help you understand the process of working on a real web design project.

Who Should Read This Book

Even though this book contains a wealth of information, it is not meant to be the *only* book you'll ever purchase on the topic—just the first. After reading *Web Design: A Beginner's Guide,* you'll be better able to decide how you'd like to proceed in this medium, and you'll know in which facets of the topic you're most interested so you can learn more.

You'll likely get the most from this book if you know a little about the following:

- **Your computer** Can you open, close, and move files around fairly easily? Do you feel comfortable using your current web browser and Internet connection?
- **Design** Do you know what styles, layouts, and so on, appeal to you? Can you express those in terms of color, shape, and texture?
- **HTML** Do you know what it is used for? Have you ever used it to create a basic web page?

If you can't answer in the affirmative to at least two of the preceding questions, you can still use this book as a beginner's guide to web design, but you'll want to pay special attention to the tips, hints, and notes throughout the book. Many of these list resources where you can find additional information about a particular topic, such as graphic design.

What This Book Covers

This book is separated into four major parts: Planning, Designing, Coding, and Going Live. There is an "HTML/CSS Reference Table" included as Appendix A.

Part I: Planning

Part I helps you plan for the typical web development process, first by helping you understand the medium and its related issues and then by thoroughly analyzing the proposed project to create an efficient and effective project plan.

Chapter 1, "Asking the Right Questions," addresses key questions related to starting web design projects and helps you determine the best team for a particular project. This chapter explains the technologies used for typical web development projects and how the site goals and target audience affect a project.

Chapter 2, "Formulating the Answers," helps you answer the questions posed in Chapter 1. Throughout this chapter, I discuss the appropriate documentation for your web project and describe a typical web development proposal. You learn about the technical aspects of the target audience, specifically as they relate to the web project, and the purpose of a site map.

Part II: Designing

Part II moves into the actual design of the web site, focusing on making the site as user-focused as possible and laying the groundwork for good web design. After that, the production of the design is tackled.

Chapter 3, "Anticipating Web-Specific Design Issues," discusses the best design tools for your needs and then moves on to identifying design considerations that are specific to web design. This includes topics such as platforms, code, browsers, bandwidth, and fonts.

Chapter 4, "Laying the Groundwork for Good Design," begins with a few places where you can find inspiration for your web designs. Then you learn to select an appropriate navigation scheme and identify appropriate visual metaphors for your site's navigation. After the navigation is set, it's time to focus on creating a useable layout for the site. Color schemes and images are also discussed as you create design mockups of your site.

Chapter 5, "Preparing for Production," walks you through identifying individual page elements for your web layouts. This chapter also explains the differences among GIF, JPEG, and PNG files and how to add interactivity to design files. Finally, I cover slicing the mockups for page production.

Chapter 6, "Producing the Design," addresses how to save those sliced images from your design application as well as to export whole designs. It also covers saving HTML from design applications and transferring Photoshop files to Flash.

Part III: Coding

Part III integrates the elements produced in Part II into cohesive web pages.

Chapter 7, "Getting Started with the Code," begins the discussion of HTML and cascading style sheets (CSS). This chapter covers creating the file structure for the site, as well as defining the required HTML and CSS code elements and header content for the page.

Chapter 8, "Structuring Content," teaches you to set up appropriate container blocks for content on the page. Then you learn to use HTML to organize content within each container block before adding links and images to define the content.

Chapter 9, "Styling Content," switches gears a bit to work on the style of the page as opposed to its structure. I discuss using HTML tags as selectors to define your styles and then using CSS to customize font characteristics and style links and web forms.

Chapter 10, "Positioning Content," moves back into the structure of the page. First, you learn about CSS box properties and how elements are positioned with CSS. Then I help you recognize the uses of layering and backgrounds in web design.

Chapter 11, "Integrating Dynamic Content," identifies how to embed various types of multimedia files into web pages and how to syndicate with Really Simple Syndication (RSS). This chapter also covers the uses of JavaScript to extend the capabilities of HTML and how blogging software can benefit web designers.

Part IV: Going Live

This part of the book covers the final aspects of a typical web development process: publishing the content and advertising the site.

Chapter 12, "Publishing Content," helps you thoroughly test the web site according to the target audience and then upload the site to the appropriate location. Next, updating the project documentation and preparing the site for maintenance is covered.

Chapter 13, "Advertising Your Site," explains how search engines work and ways to improve your site's ranking in the top search engines. It also discusses the differences between the design of pages to be displayed in web browsers and those displayed in e-mail readers before listing some tips regarding designing for e-mail.

Part I

Planning

Chapter 1

Asking the Right Questions

Key Skills & Concepts

- Understand the key questions related to starting web design projects.
- Determine the best team for a particular web project.
- Identify the technologies used for typical web development projects.
- Understand how the site goals and target audience affect a web project.

*W*eb design. That simple phrase can mean many things to many different people. To a system administrator who's just been given the task of creating or revising the company intranet, it probably means a headache. To a high school junior considering her future, it may be a dream job. Likewise, no two projects you encounter will be the same; each web design project will provide new things to learn and interesting business problems to solve.

So, how can anyone expect to write a single book professing to be the beginner's guide and still have the book fit on a normal bookshelf? No easy feat—that's for sure. This book is meant to be an introduction into the typical process of what it takes to design a section of content to be viewed on the Web (a.k.a. web design). The process itself, however, and nearly everything related to web design, is in a constant state of flux. In fact, some people refer to this process as "shooting an arrow (or, perhaps, many arrows?) at a moving target."

This means you, as the web designer, must keep current on the ever-changing aspects of the Web to aim those arrows best. Over the course of 13 chapters, I give you a cohesive introduction to the tools, technologies, and concepts you need to begin designing web pages that not only look good, but that work. The nature of this business requires that you'll still have much to learn, but I hope to provide you with a solid foundation for your work.

To get started, let's talk about the questions that typically surround the beginning of any web design project. I'll drop back to my high school journalism days to bring out the "five *W*s" (who, what, where, when, and why) plus a little *H* (how) thrown in for good measure. Then, in Chapter 2, I'll delve more specifically into how to answer these questions.

NOTE

Whenever I teach web design, I find it very helpful to move through an actual web site project with students. I typically encourage students to find a local non-profit organization that needs some help with its web site. I encourage you to do the same while working through this book. But for the sake of discussion here, I will frequently refer to several companies I've helped through the process. I hope these real-world examples will help you work through the concepts being taught.

Who

So someone wants you to build a web site. A simple request, right? Not necessarily. As a web designer or developer, you constantly need to juggle the needs of everyone involved, from the client, to the site's users. Often, this means balancing the goals and requirements of the client with the site's design and functionality.

But before you can begin balancing those needs, you need to identify the various team players.

Who Is the Development Team?

When you decide to tackle any web design or development project, one of the most important questions you'll need to ask is who will complete each task? Even if you're working by yourself, you'll likely wear a ton of different hats on any given day: information architect, project manager, account manager, coder, designer, copywriter, tester, coffee maker….

Many of these roles can be easily combined and handled by one person, but typically at least three types of jobs are involved: visual design, technical development, and management. The visual design piece often involves what is commonly referred to as the "front end" of the web site project. This might include the user experience, site layout, colors, fonts, images, copy, navigation, and overall style.

The technical developers work on the site's "back end." If you think of a web site as a house, the technical developers put up the studs to build the walls, while the visual designers apply paint, hang draperies, and arrange the furniture. Both groups work together to develop the "architectural drawings" before a single nail is hammered.

The manager acts as a mediator between the designers and developers, while always focusing on the client's goals and objectives. In some teams, this role is filled by a business analyst or a project manager. This person also might handle the information architect task, which helps determine how the content of the site is presented to the user. For example, an information architect might design what links and choices are presented to the user on each page, what those links are called, and where they take the user upon being clicked.

At the beginning of any web project, you'll need to identify each team role and assign tasks accordingly. To help clarify those roles, let's look at each one a bit closer.

Management Roles

Every project must have a manager of some sort and, in fact, this role typically requires 15 to 25 percent of the overall budget. This person must have a clear understanding of each team member's roles and responsibilities and must be able to communicate effectively with each team member. This means the manager must understand the design process as well as the technical development requirements. The project manager might perform the following tasks within the web development process:

- Develop and maintain good relationships with clients.
- Understand the clients' business goals and objectives, as well as recognize flaws or red flags in meeting those with the project at hand.
- Coordinate kick-off meetings involving all team members and schedule additional meetings as needed throughout the project.
- Identify the site's target audience and seek to ensure that the audience's needs are met.
- Facilitate the development of a user-centric site structure and navigation.
- Create and manage project schedules, budget, and scope, ensuring quality control throughout the project.
- Identify and lead project resources, making sure all team members understand the assigned tasks, deadlines, and deliverables.
- Help educate the client regarding the maintenance of the site.

In addition to traditional project management tasks, the management role may include sales tasks related to bringing in and closing new business, and customer service. In most cases, the manager acts as the primary contact for the client, fielding questions, clarifying goals and tasks, and keeping everyone informed about the project's progress and status.

This role is vital to a project's success. Improper management of any web development project can cost everyone involved a significant amount of time, money, and headaches. Therefore, it's essential that this role be filled with a skilled manager(s) from the point when project needs are established.

Aside from the overall project management, another important aspect of this category is content management. Someone filling the role of content manager may likely complete the following tasks, while working closely with members who fulfill other team roles.

- Identify all pieces of content (whether text or graphically based) to be used for the project.

- Recognize missing or irrelevant content, as it relates to the overall site structure.

- Manage the flow of content between team members (including the client).

The nature of the web means that it's growing and changing every minute. If you think this can lead to nightmarish content-management issues, you're right. For this reason, it's important that strict guidelines be put in place about the site's content management at the start of the project. I discuss how to do that in the section on documentation in Chapter 2.

Visual Design Roles

The creative aspect of a web development project involves designing what's commonly referred to as the *look and feel* of the web site. So in the case of a company's public web site, visual designers style the aspect of the site seen by its visitors, in an effort to achieve the goals of the site. Some key aspects of these roles include the following:

- Understand the client's overall business, to translate a concept of it effectively to web site visitors.

- Understand the client's business goals and objectives, as well as recognize flaws or red flags in meeting those.

- Develop an efficient, user-centered structure and navigation for the site's content.

- Create comprehensive designs (comps or mockups) for key sections/pages/screens of the project, used to gain client sign-off on ideas expressed by the team.

- Write and edit copy as needed.

- Translate comprehensive designs into working prototypes, incorporating the appropriate content as needed.

- Expand or evolve the client's brand as needed for screen-based media.

- Work with technical team members to build the site, using the prototypes.

- Help educate the client regarding maintenance of the site.

- Test the site and revise as necessary.

Technical Roles

The more technical aspects of the project typically pertain to the back end of the web site, which you might consider the "stuff happening behind the scenes" to make the web site function.

For example, suppose your web site requires that visitors register to take advantage of its services. The visual designers will probably design the layout and styling of the registration form, but the technical members will most likely be the ones who actually install the technologies needed to facilitate personalization and registration on the site.

The following list identifies other tasks commonly performed by technical roles on a web team:

- Understand the client's overall business, to translate a picture of it effectively to web site visitors.
- Understand the client's business goals and objectives, as well as recognize flaws or red flags in meeting those within the project.
- Develop an efficient, user-centric design and structure for the technical aspects of the project.
- Design and maintain appropriate databases, servers, testing environments, security procedures, networks, and so on, as necessary.
- Work with creative/editorial team members to build the site, using the prototypes.
- Help educate the client regarding maintenance of the site.
- Test the site; revise as necessary.

Team Dynamics

While one person might possibly try to fulfill all these roles, that scenario is becoming increasingly difficult. This may sound crazy coming from me, a supposed one-woman shop, but here's where I'm coming from on this one.

When I started freelancing, I attempted to market myself as a one-stop web shop, and, for a while, this worked. I started out with smaller projects that required only skills I already had. But, eventually, as my business grew, so did my need to learn new skills to satisfy all my clients' needs.

So I might still officially be a sole proprietorship now, but my web team involves many other web professionals. I might call on the technology experts at various other shops to help fill the role of technology and QA within my web team, and, sometimes, even the project management role as well. Likewise, I am frequently hired to fulfill the design role for teams lacking that particular skill set.

While the smallest web teams might employ a single person within each of the three roles I've identified, many larger teams use many more within each role. As the purpose of a web site continues to evolve way past its original intent (which was marketing only, in most cases), the size of the web team changes.

Who Is the Author?

We've established some key roles on the web development team. But for the end user, perhaps the most obvious question is this: For and about whom is the site created? When someone visits a web site, she undoubtedly wants to find out who it's about. She might be wondering, "Are you an individual? Are you a group of people sitting in cubicles within an office?" After you identify the person or company behind the web site, you must decide what voice the text on the site will use to converse with visitors.

In the case of a personal blog, the answer to the user's question might simply be "Me—an individual." When web sites are authored in the first person, they include statements such as "I am a skilled craftsman." For the most part, first person is used by businesses owned by sole proprietors and personal web sites.

But in the case of a web site speaking for more than one person, the voice behind the site could be stated in a number of different ways. For example, many companies choose to write about the company in the third person, as if the pages were written by someone other than an employee or owner. This might translate into "They are skilled craftsmen." Sites written in the third person tend to read like biographies, which may not be the best if you're trying to win over customers with a friendly and personable web site.

TIP

Third-person narratives work well for news articles, historical accounts, and biographies, but they aren't ideal for friendly conversations with customers.

Other companies prefer a more personal approach, where the site is written by a collective "we," as in "We are skilled craftsmen." Using "we" and "you" makes the viewer feel like he is involved in a conversation, instead of reading a third-party narrative. This typically leads to an engaging, more personal relationship with the visitor.

TIP

Avoid switching from "they" to "we" throughout the site. I recommend picking one voice for the entire site, and sticking with it. (The alternative might be considered an identity crisis.)

Who Is the Target Audience?

Now that we've identified the author of the site, let's flip the coin and consider another "who." In this case, I'm talking about the "who" accessing the web site. If you're creating a site for a business, a group, or an organization, you're most likely targeting people who might buy or use the company's products or services. Even if your site is purely for the purpose of disseminating information, you must be targeting a certain audience.

Knowing your target audience can greatly affect how you design and develop your web site. For example, if you're developing a site for beginners to learn about the Internet, you want to create a site that's extremely easy to use and doesn't stray from standard computer conventions. Talk with the client again to consider the following:

● Determine whether any research exists regarding the user base. This might include demographics, statistics, or other marketing information, such as age, gender, search trends, and favorite web sites. This is easiest if the company has been around for several years and has an established customer base.

● If the site represents a new company or one that doesn't already have information about its customer's demographics, you might check out the competition. If your competition has a successful web site, you can probably learn from them about your target audience.

● If the site targets a wide audience, be sure to visit sites that provide information about online demographics and market research, such as the following:

  ● **www.access-egov.info/learn.cfm?id=demo&xid=MN** Learn the Net: "Online Demographics"

  ● **www.internetnews.com/stats/** Internetnews.com: "Stats"

  ● **www.thecounter.com/stats** Thecounter.com: "Global Statistics"

  ● **www.gvu.gatech.edu/research** GVU Center: "Research"

  ● **www.nielsennetratings.com** Nielsen: "Nielsen NetRatings"

These sites offer detailed information about technical demographics such as browsers, access speeds, hardware, traffic patterns, and site performance, as well as consumer demographics such as advertising trends and purchasing decisions.

TIP

Whenever possible, ask to speak to members of the company's target audience. Then ask about their online usage to determine what they might look for at the company's web site. I like to walk them through a sample usage scenario, asking first how they might try to find the company's web site, and then what they might like to do on that web site.

So what might a target audience list look like? For a summer camp, I might organize the target audience into these main groups:

● Potential campers

● Parents of potential campers

● Potential employees

● Parents/friends of current campers

● Alumni

NOTE

Current campers are left off this list because they are too busy having fun at camp to use the web site!

Ask the Expert

Q: How can I find a competitor's web sites?

A: Here are a few ways to get started:

- Ask the client!
- Look in trade magazines and/or industry newspapers. They commonly have lists of hot web sites for related businesses. Also, visit the magazines and/or newspapers online to see if they have links pages.
- Visit the web site of the industry's association. In other words, if your client is a bed and breakfast on Cape Cod, you might try the local chamber of commerce or the American Automobile Association (AAA) travel desk.
- Visit Google (**www.google.com**) and type **related:***www.yourbusiness.com* where *www.yourbusiness.com* is replaced by the URL of your client's current site or one of a known competitor. This brings up a list of similar sites. For example, searching for **related:www.amazon.com** brings bring up competitors such as Barnes & Nobel and Best Buy.
- Search for the business or a known competitor in a categorized directory such as Yahoo! (**www.yahoo.com**) or Google (**http://directory.google.com**), to find related businesses listed within the same category.
- Look through local and national business yellow pages and other telephone directories to find businesses in similar categories. Because online and printed versions may vary, consider checking both. Popular online directories include **www.bigyellow.com** and **http://yp.yahoo.com**.
- Search for sites with a similar word in the domain name, using **allinurl:** *"text"* in Google. For example, if the business sells gardening tools, you might search for **allinurl: "garden"** to locate all sites with the word "garden" in the domain name, path, or filename (for example, **www.garden.com**, **http://garden.burpee.com**, **www.store.com/gardendept**, and so on).
- Perform a search as if you were a member of your site's target audience. For example, if the site sells handmade children's clothing, try visiting your favorite search engine and searching for "handmade children's clothing" to see what comes up.

Even simple tasks like these help clarify what you can do to meet the audience's needs best. Many people document this type of research in a competitive analysis report, within the project documentation. (I'll discuss the documentation in the "How" section later in this chapter.)

Who Will Maintain the Site?

An often-overlooked question in any development project is "Who will take care of the site after it is launched?" The vast majority of clients I encounter want to have the ability to edit and update the site in-house, using members of their own staff who may or may not have technical web skills. Therefore, it is extremely important to ask this question at the very start of the process.

You might suggest that a maintenance contract be put in place, where you (or your team) will make edits and updates to the site on a regular basis for an hourly fee. Alternatively, you could train someone on the client's team to make changes to the site, or have the client work with a third-party maintenance group.

TIP
Looking for a bit more about maintenance? Refer to Chapter 12 for additional guidance.

So how do you handle clients who want to maintain their own sites but don't know how to edit HTML? The rise of the web content management system (CMS) has paved the way for nontechnical users to edit existing web content and even add new content without "breaking" the site.

TIP
Check out "Web Content Management Style" at http://en.wikipedia.org/wiki/ Web_content_management_system for a more thorough description of web content management systems.

While a technical developer is usually needed to set up a CMS, nontechnical administrators can maintain the site after the CMS is installed and configured. CMSs can be uniquely customized and vastly complex, can cost tens of thousands of dollars to set up, or can be routinely simple using free "install-and-run" software. The most popular CMS tools include the following:

- WordPress (**http://wordpress.org**)
- Movable Type (**www.moveabletype.com**)
- Joomla! (**www.joomla.org**)
- Mambo (**http://mambo-foundation.org**)

This list barely touches the tip of the iceberg. Search for "web content management system" in Google to see an unlimited number of options. If you've never used a CMS, I suggest you start by playing around with one of the listed options, then ask friends and colleagues for additional suggestions.

Why

This may seem like an obvious question (Why build this web site?), but the truth is that not enough people really consider the "whys" of a web site before they start building. For example, just knowing you need a car doesn't get you the right car. You need to evaluate various models to determine the right car to buy. In the same way, it's important that you spend some time evaluating the goals, the "whys," of a site.

Many times, the answers to your questions will come in the form of a Request for Proposal (RFP) from the client. An RFP is a company's way of stating its project needs so that the information is easily broadcast to a variety of potential bidders. Bidders then respond with a written proposal stating how they intend to meet the client company's project needs.

Sometimes clients publish RFPs on their web sites, with a date by which proposals must be submitted. Other times, RFPs are sent to a few select vendors. Regardless of the method by which an RFP is dispersed, most contain the same basic information about the project:

- Description and objectives of the web site
- Budget range
- Background information about the company or organization and the project
- Description of the target audience
- Required components and functionalities
- Available technology in current hosting environment (or a request for hosting to be included as part of the bid)
- Internal personnel responsible for the project
- Methods by which success will be measured
- Proposed timeline
- Details for submitting proposals

Anyone who has been designing web sites for clients for any number of years has witnessed how bad a project can get when the initial requirements were not identified correctly. This all starts with a well-thought-out, quality RFP. As a web professional, it's up to you to get the answers to all your questions up front, to avoid lengthy and costly delays down the road.

Ask the Expert

Q: I didn't receive an RFP from this client because he's a friend of a friend who needs a web site for his new business. How should I proceed?

A: Many businesses send out RFPs when they're ready to receive bids and proposals from developers. An informal version of this document could be a telephone conversation between client and designer, in which the client's needs are discussed. At this point, it's important that you ask as many questions as you can to identify the task at hand as clearly as possible.

Even though the client may be a friend, you still need to get everything down on paper to ensure a smooth development process. In addition to the list you just read, here are a few things you might want to remember while you're trying to assess the client's needs.

- *Get to know the company profile and background.* What are its strengths and weaknesses? Who are its competitors and where do they stand in regard to comparable projects?
- *Get to know the project at hand.* What is the proposed budget and timeline? What business problem(s) should the project address? What are the dependencies? What is the purpose? What is the proposed content? Is security an issue? Can similar projects be used as comparisons? What is the hosting environment?
- *Get to know the targeted users.* Does research exist regarding the client or user base? Can you talk with prospective/current users? What functions should each user group perform at the site?
- *Get to know the contact person(s).* Who are the primary and secondary contacts? Who has sign-off authority? Has the company used consultants on similar projects? What will be the internal decision-making process? Who will be involved in meetings?
- *Get to know the measurement of success.* What is the most important element of the project? What technical guidelines must be met?
- *Get to know the company's brand.* Does the company have a logo? Can the visual design be an extension of a current "look and feel" or must it be a complete redesign?

What Are the Goals?

The biggest part of answering the "Why" question comes from determining the goals of the web site project: Why will people use this web site?

Since the web's inception, millions of new web sites have been created. To compete in such a large market, you and the company must set clear goals for its site. This may mean you have a direct conversation with a client to discuss the site's purpose.

At this point in the process, you need to find answers to a few key questions. For example, before you can understand the goals of the web site, you need to understand the mission and purpose of the company. If the project's RFP doesn't provide the answers to your satisfaction, it's probably best to schedule an information-gathering session with the client. At such an initial planning meeting, you might ask questions like these:

- What is your company's mission?

- What are your company's strengths and weaknesses?

- Whom do you see as competitors?

- Where do you see your business in 90 days, one year, two years?

- What challenges do you see in achieving your business objectives?

- What business objectives/issues should this site address?

- Who are the targeted users?

- What functions do you expect those users to perform?

While this list certainly isn't exhaustive, it should help to get you off to a good start in learning as much as you can about your client and the project. In fact, this is one of my favorite aspects of web design—the part that enables me to learn about so many different businesses and industries.

Ask the Expert

Q: **Do I really need to ask a client all these questions? What if the client has already given me a list of what he wants on the web site?**

A: I have actually won projects simply based on the amount of questions I asked up front. Many, many clients think they know what they want on their web sites, even though they've never considered such simple concepts as who is their target audience. Some of these questions may serve as wake-up calls for clients and enable you to discern between true goals and misguided efforts.

From those initial discussions, you should be able to draw conclusions as to the goals for the web site. You want to include these goals within the documentation for your site and get the client's sign-off to acknowledge approval before continuing. This serves to make sure everyone is on the same page in the process.

A few examples of goals for public web sites might be the following:

- Sell products/services
- Increase public awareness of company/product/service
- Recruit potential employees
- Entertain
- Educate
- Communicate with customers
- Disseminate information
- Provide updates to products/services (such as with new versions of computer software)

Private web sites, which might be anything from a company's employee-only intranet to a newspaper's business-to-business extranet, require accounts and passwords to gain access. This restricted access often indicates the goals for the site are much different than those for public web sites. A few examples of goals for private web sites might be the following:

- Facilitate employee communication, especially between different departments and offices
- Enable employees to self-maintain human resources information, such as health benefits and contact information
- Educate
- Archive business documentation
- Enable resellers to access purchasing and inventory information easily
- Communicate with resellers/business partners/contractors
- Track employee billable time, vacation time, and so forth

Identifying overall site goals, in order of precedence, is important. So, in the case of a web site for a summer camp, the main goals for the site might be as follows:

- Increase public awareness of the organization and its services
- Sell the camp to potential campers (teenagers) and their parents

- Enable parents of campers to (virtually) participate in the camp experience
- Facilitate communication between the organization and campers, parents, alumni, and interested parties
- Recruit camp staff
- Enable interested parties to support the organization through online donations and potential other means
- Enable campers to sign up and purchase online
- Sell T-shirts, sweatshirts, hats, and other products branded by the organization

During such a brainstorming process, you might also identify business objectives that are more long-range or that cannot be met within the scope of the current project. This is an important step! It's great to capture those objectives and list them as goals for the next version of the site.

NOTE
Remember these goals when developing the pages of the site to avoid unnecessary content. If a page on your site doesn't meet one of the goals, it may confuse and/or turn away visitors and should probably be deleted.

What Functions Will the Target Audience Perform?

A big part of the Why question revolves around the target audience: Why will the target audience come to the site? What functions will they expect to perform at the site?

One of the best ways to evaluate the target audience is to create a user scenario for each of the main groups within that audience. Here's your chance to be creative by placing yourself in the shoes of the intended user. Give yourself a name, an age, and some likes and dislikes, and then write down how you might actually navigate through the proposed site, keeping in mind the tasks you'd likely perform.

Here's an example of a user scenario for the summer camp web site. In this scenario, my name is Corinna and I'm an 11-year-old girl researching summer camps on the Internet.

My mom just told me she and my dad agreed I could go to a sleep-away camp for the first time this summer. I'll be 12 in May (only two more months!) and I don't think I'll be homesick. My friend Moriah is coming over today and we're going to research summer camps on the Web. Kim's mom said she might be able to go, too, if she can help raise some of the money by babysitting and doing extra chores.

We have an awesome new MacBook computer and I get to use it a lot. We connect to the Internet through our cable company, and it's pretty fast. I'm going to start by searching on Google for summer camps.

I'm mostly looking for a camp where I can pick my own activities, not one that makes me play tennis all day or anything. I like to swim, take photos, listen to music, and hang out with my friends. I'd like a camp that lets me do these types of things. I also want to find one that has boys and girls, and that has lots of kids my age. I want to ask if Moriah and I can be in the same cabin, because I don't want to be all by myself! I also want to try and talk to some other kids who've been there, since they'll probably tell me all the camp secrets and whether or not it's a cool camp.

If I like some camps, my mom said I should ask for a brochure or DVD to be mailed to our house, so she can look at them and see which one looks best. I'm also going to bookmark the sites, so I can find them quickly next time.

So, in my scenario, I tried to think about how this girl might use the site. What is she looking for? What's important to her? How technically savvy is she? What are any limitations with regard to her web access? This scenario could certainly be expanded on, to include an actual visit to some camp web sites, for example. Let's consider how a scenario for Corinna's mom might be different:

My daughter, Corinna, will be 12 in May and has been begging us to go to sleep-away camp this summer. She's been to day camp before, but never to sleep-away camp, so I'm a bit nervous about how she'll do.

She and her friend Moriah spent some time today visiting camp web sites on our computer and she bookmarked some sites for me to look at. When I visit these sites, I'll be looking to see what type of activities the camp offers to determine if it's a good match for Corinna, She likes many water-related activities and I'd also like her to take a few camping trips, maybe go hiking or canoeing, like I did when I was a kid.

I'd like to hear from parents of other kids who've attended this camp because I think they'd be able to answer the types of questions I have best. I also want to make sure the camp is certified by the American Camping Association, so I'll probably visit their web site, too.

I definitely want to know about how the camp selects its counselors and how they deal with kids who are homesick or are away from home for the first time. In fact, if we live close to the facility, I think I'd like to visit before enrolling Corinna.

Writing user scenarios can be a great activity in which a whole team can participate, especially because it tends to foster a high amount of creativity and brainstorming.

Functions Performed

After you brainstorm about the target audience, you can use the knowledge to identify what functions each part of that audience might perform at your site. You might use a table to help you make your plans. Table 1-1 was created for the summer camp I've been discussing, but you could use it as a starting place for any site you're creating.

You can use all this information to determine the appropriate direction for the site. I like to break down each group into two major sectors: the "accidental tourists" and the "navy seals." Most sites have a little of both. Have you ever been surfing a certain site, and then wondered how you got there from here? This is the accidental tourist, a.k.a. the serendipitous visitor. At the other end of the spectrum is the student on a mission, looking for a specific piece of information for a homework assignment, who I call the navy seals.

User Group	Functions Performed	Ages	Gender
Potential campers	research camp contact alumni request additional information/ask questions	11–17	male/female
Parents of potential campers	research camp research organization's history, mission, and staff request additional information/ask questions contact parents of alumni	35–60	male/female
Potential employees	research jobs apply online request additional information/ask questions	18–25	male/female
Potential donors	research organization's history, mission, staff, and services request additional information/ask questions support organization	25–70	male/female
Parents/friends of current campers	view daily schedule see photos e-mail camper meet/correspond with staff	30–60	male/female
Alumni	correspond with friends access organization news support organization	12+	male/female

Table 1-1   Sample User Groups and Functions Performed

TIP

Does your site target mostly navy seals as visitors? These individuals prefer to use search engines, especially when trying to locate information quickly. Providing a good search engine on your site can greatly increase your repeat visitors. Visit **www.searchtools .com** for more tips on adding a search engine to your site.

What

After identifying the key stakeholders and the core objectives of the site, the discussion typically moves on to the type of content to be housed on the site's pages. Use caution when working with the content this early in the process, as you want to avoid getting too specific in terms of which sentences go where.

I like to focus on the higher level content categories, to make sure everything has a place. For example, instead of ironing out the exact paragraphs to be listed on each page, identify each type of content located there. To formalize the possible, I like using a table to answer these key questions:

- What is the content area?
- What is its purpose?
- Where will it come from?
- Who is responsible for it?

Table 1-2 shows how I might record the answers to such questions.

Content Area	Features/Purpose	Current Location (if available)	Is Content in Current Location Usable?	Owner
Home page	Introduce customers to company Provide links to other content Give company news Show stock ticker (interactive)	www.mysite.com	Needs overhaul	John
Company information	Provide history of company, to gain respect and credibility with customers List contact information Link to audio recording from last year's annual meeting	company.htm	Needs updating	Mary

Table 1-2   Sample Content Area Details

It's important to align each content area with the site goals. If a page or section of content doesn't meet at least one of the goals, it may confuse or turn away visitors and should be removed. I discuss more about structuring the content in future chapters, but for now you should be asking the client about the type of content to be included.

Where

The "Where" question involves where the site will be located and how users will access it. During development, the site may be housed on your own personal computer, but it can't stay there when the site goes "live." All public web sites must be transferred or uploaded to a host computer with 24-hour access to the Internet. Businesses pay monthly fees to companies who *host* (or store) web pages, so they have 24/7 availability to web surfers.

If the project is to create a brand new site, the client likely will not yet have obtained hosting for the site. But if the project involves working on an existing site, the client may prefer that you continue using the contracted hosting. In any case, you need to find out the hosting requirements at the start of the project so you can plan accordingly with regard to development technologies.

You might wonder why it matters where the site is hosted. For basic sites using HTML and CSS (cascading style sheets) only, the host locale won't matter. However, sites using content management systems or blogs may require a particular type of hosting (such as Linux or Windows). Knowing the hosting requirements and/or restrictions up front will enable you to develop a site that will run successfully in the intended hosting environment.

When

Ah…the dreaded scheduling question. You knew this was coming, right? At the start of any web project, all participants need to be in agreement about when the site will go live. In other words, when will it be finished enough to be accessible to the target audience?

Notice I said finished *enough*.

Web projects are notorious for being a continuous cycle of work. Because web pages are never "set in stone" like printed advertisements or annual reports, companies can often fall into the cycle of continually editing the content.

Web developers need to be prepared for this never-ending cycle by stating up front what constitutes a finished project. In the end, this comes back to establishing solid goals for the site, and then developing a site that satisfies those goals in a measurable way.

How

Finally, when beginning a web project, you undoubtedly need to answer the question of how the site will be built. While not purely a design question, this really moves into the underlying structure that will create the site. This section is important because of how much the technology choices can affect the design and even impose limitations on it.

What Standards/Technologies Will Be Used?

HTML is the most basic of all web technologies and, arguably, the easiest to learn and master. The acronym stands for Hypertext Markup Language, which, for the purposes of our discussion, is a language of sorts that tells a web browser how to display content and link to related information.

The vast majority of web pages you view on the Internet use HTML in some way, shape, or form. You can easily recognize HTML code by its *tags*, (formally called *entities*), which are instructions to the browser. Because HTML was originally designed to mark up text and its structure (that is, titles, headings, lists, and so forth), as opposed to dictate page layout, newer technologies—which are better at handling page layout, as well as conveying the meaning of the page content—have appeared on the landscape. Specifically, CSS is used in conjunction with HTML to structure and format web pages.

So what can HTML do? HTML provides a way to tell a web browser how to display pieces of information. For example, you use a certain HTML tag to indicate where paragraphs start and finish. Most tags are quite easy to learn and remember, because the tag itself has some reference to its function. Given that bit of information, could you imagine what the paragraph tag might look like? Take a look:

```
<p>This is a paragraph of text.</p>
```

All tags use brackets to separate them from the other text on the page. Also, most tags have starting and ending variations. In the case of my paragraph example, you can see how the **<p>** tag tells the browser this is the beginning of the paragraph, and the **</p>** tells it this is the end of the paragraph. (All ending tags are really just the starting tags with the addition of a forward slash.)

HTML serves as a way to structure the page, to tell the browser which pieces of content are paragraphs, which are lists, and so on. Then, we use CSS to tell the browser how to style each section. So if we use the paragraph tag to specify a section of text as a paragraph, we might then add a style declaration to cause that paragraph to have certain font and color characteristics.

We'll look a whole lot more at exactly how this happens in later chapters of the book.

HTML History

In its earliest years, HTML quickly went through much iteration, which led to a lack of standardization across the Internet. The *World Wide Web Consortium* (W3C—**www .w3.org**) stepped in and began publishing a list of recommendations, called *standards*, for HTML and other web languages. As of this writing, the last official standard for HTML was HTML 4.01.

In an attempt to move the standards away from the old-style HTML and closer to a more flexible language, *Extensible Markup Language (XML)*, the W3C rewrote the standard in 2000. The resulting set of standards, called *Extensible Hypertext Markup Language (XHTML)*, provided a way for HTML to handle alternative devices, such as cell phones and handheld computers.

NOTE

You might have heard of CSS as a component of HTML and XML. CSS is used to separate the design from the function of the page. For example, HTML is used to specify items in a list, while CSS is used to change the font, color, and spacing of those list items. We will use HTML and CSS extensively throughout the coding section of this book.

XHTML 1.0 offered many new features to make the lives of web developers easier, but it was poorly supported by web browsers at its launch in 2001. In the years immediately following, the W3C updated its recommendation to XHTML 2.0. However, the world didn't adopt XML as quickly or as warmly as the W3C had anticipated, and the organization ended up abandoning the separate XHTML route.

So in 2008, the W3C released a working draft of the future of hypertext markup: HTML 5. This is very much a "work in progress," which will likely take several years to finalize and be adopted. In the meantime, you can check the status of HTML 5 on the W3C's web site: **www.w3c.org/TR/html5**.

Beyond HTML

When web content needs to do more than is available with basic HTML, an additional technology may be required. During the past 20 years, plenty of options have emerged, most of which fall into two basic categories.

Server-side Scripting   This type of web technology involves a script that is stored and executed on the web server. After the script is "run" (activated), the results generate dynamic and customized web pages. Server-side technologies require that specific software to be installed on the server. Therefore, some technologies are available only on certain operating systems (for example, ASP, or Active Server Pages, is a Windows-based server-side technology).

Suppose you want to offer your web site in both English and Spanish, but you don't want the added hassles of maintaining two separate versions of the site. You could store all the text content for the site in a database or plain text files, and then reference the database or text files within your HTML code using a server-side script.

You might have an option on your home page that allows users to choose whether to view the site in English or Spanish. Once the user selects a language, the script then builds the pages on demand, importing the English or Spanish text segments from the database/text file, as needed.

The biggest benefit of using server-side technologies in this instance is that you need to maintain only one page of code for each page on your web site. In addition, because the text content of the site is separated from the code and contained in either a database or plain text files, it can be easily edited and maintained by anyone, regardless of his or her level of HTML or scripting knowledge.

Using a normal, or static, approach of straight HTML, you'd have to maintain two separate pages of code for each page of content: one containing Spanish content and one containing English content.

NOTE

Another great application of server-side scripting involves processing a web form.

You might have heard of some of the more popular server-side scripting choices:

- ASP/ASP.net (.asp or .aspx)
- ColdFusion (.cfm)
- Java (.jsp)
- Perl (.pl)
- PHP (.php)
- Ruby (.rb)
- SMX (.smx)

Client-side Scripting   The alternative to server-side scripting is client-side scripting. Most client-side scripts are located within the HTML file (but may also be included in an external file that is then referenced from inside the HTML). Because client-side scripts are visible within a web page's source code, you can learn this type of scripting simply by viewing the HTML source in your browser.

Client-side scripts do not interact with the server and therefore do not require any additional software to be installed on the server. For this reason, they are popular among developers who don't have access to install software on the web server.

Client-side scripting is often used to do things like changing images when the user moves the mouse over them (also called a *rollover* or a *mouseover*), or to make certain fields required on web forms. You could also use a client-side script to customize the look and size of the browser window, or to move certain elements on a page and animate or "script" others. Still another common use of this type of script is to add the current date and time to a web page.

JavaScript is the most popular and widely used client-side scripting language. Other options include AJAX (asynchronous JavaScript and XML), JScript, and VBScript.

NOTE

If you're just getting into web development, you might wonder how anyone could learn all of these technologies. The good news is you don't have to! Most developers choose to focus on a few technologies that complement each other. This means you might have one team who primarily uses Microsoft technologies such as ASP and SQL (Structured Query Language). Alternatively, another group is proficient with PHP and JavaScript.

What Development Tools Will Be Used?

The software used to develop the site depends on a variety of factors, most important of which is the web technologies used. For example, if you are building a site purely in HTML, you can use something as simple as NotePad or TextEdit (free text editors that can be downloaded and installed in minutes). Other web tools can handle HTML in addition to other technologies.

To help you identify the tool for you, I've outlined a few of the most popular in Table 1-3. This is by no means an exhaustive list of valid web editors. It is merely meant to help get you started by pointing out the key benefits of each.

NOTE

WYSIWYG editors don't require knowledge of HTML. Instead of looking only at the HTML of your pages, you have the ability to view a "preview" of how the page will look in a browser. This way, you can simply drag-and-drop pieces of your layout as you see fit.

Flash

You might have noticed one glaring omission from the preceding two sections on web technologies. Flash warrants its own section for several reasons, not the least of which is that it includes *both* client-side and server-side scripting options.

Tool	Average Price (US)	Key Features
Amaya www.w3.org/Amaya/	Free	Open-source software project hosted by W3C Windows/Mac/Linux WYSIWYG visual editor (but no browser preview) Spell-checking
BBEdit www.barebones.com	$30 – $125	Also offers a free, scaled-down version called TextWrangler Mac only Browser preview FTP upload Multiuser editing Text-based editor capable of handling many popular programming languages, including C, C++, CSS, Java, JavaScript, JSP, Perl, PHP, Ruby, HTML, SQL, and XML
CoffeeCup www.coffeecup.com	$49	Windows only WYSIWYG visual editor FTP upload Spell-checking Templates
Dreamweaver www.adobe.com/products/dreamweaver	$399	Windows/Mac WYSIWYG visual editor with browser preview FTP upload Spell-checking Templates Server-side scripting Multiuser editing
Expression Web www.microsoft.com/expression Note: Expression Web replaced Microsoft's Front Page.	$299	Windows only WYSIWYG visual editor with browser preview FTP upload Spell-checking Templates Server-side scripting Multiuser editing
Visual Web Developer www.microsoft.com/express/vwd	Free	Windows only WYSIWYG visual editor with browser preview FTP upload Spell-checking Templates Server-side scripting Multiuser editing

Table 1-3 Common Tools Used to Edit HTML

Tool	Average Price (US)	Key Features
NoteTab www.notetab.com	Free/$29.95	Free and pro versions available Windows only Text-based HTML editor The Pro version is highly customizable and includes features such as spell-checker and templates

Table 1-3   Common Tools Used to Edit HTML *(continued)*

Adobe Flash (previously called Macromedia Flash) is a software application capable of developing beautifully animated, feature-rich, self-contained web sites. Flash files can contain graphics, animation, text, and interactivity. Web browsers must have a Flash player installed in order to view Flash files, but thankfully the player is free and widely distributed. (One notable exception are mobile, web-enabled devices, many of which are not capable of displaying Flash files.)

Flash's scripting technology is called ActionScript. You can use ActionScript on the server-side or the client-side, depending on what you're trying to do. This makes Flash a highly customizable, flexible solution that is hugely popular with web developers.

You have probably seen a lot of Flash on entertainment and marketing sites, because it provides a lot of eye candy. However, it is not recommended as a site-wide solution for e-commerce sites or web applications, because it can cause the site to be difficult to maintain and inaccessible for some portions of the target audience.

Summary

At the start of any web project are many questions. In fact, asking the right questions is key to starting off on the right foot. This chapter discussed many of the necessary questions for typical web development projects. In Chapter 2, we move on to answering those questions (in the form of a proposal to your client) and formalizing the design process.

Chapter 2

Formulating the Answers

Key Skills & Concepts

- Identify the appropriate documentation for your web project.

- Describe a typical web development proposal.

- Understand the technical aspects of the target audience as they relate to the web project.

- Explain the purpose and use of a site map.

A sking the right questions is only half the battle. To plan and prepare for a successful web site, you need to be able to formulate the best answers to those questions. At this point in the process, formulating the best answers typically involves a lot of research and networking to identify the most efficient and effective team and technologies.

This chapter helps you along that path by clarifying the documentation used throughout the process and assisting in some of the research and networking portions.

Documentation

One of the toughest aspects of the development process for many people, including me, is documentation. While employed by other web firms, I learned the ropes regarding development methodologies and proper documentation. However, after going freelance, I questioned the need for "all that paperwork" within my own business. Boy, was I wrong.

Every project needs a certain amount of documentation, regardless of the size or scale of the endeavor. *Documentation* can be defined simply as the recording (somehow) of the problem(s), the proposed solution(s), the steps taken to reach the solution(s), and the results. Some of the more common types of documentation for web projects include the following. (Note that many other types of documentation might exist, according to the needs of the project, and certainly some projects may not require all of these.)

- **Request for Proposal (RFP)** States problem/need, as explained by the client (as discussed in Chapter 1). This document is created by the client and given to the potential designer(s).

- **Proposal/ Statement of Work (SOW)** Evaluates problem/need before a project is started. States proposed solution (at a high level) or a way to meet the need(s), as well as estimated costs and timeline, as explained by designer(s)/developer(s). Also may be called a *Requirements Definition* and/or *Needs Assessment*, and is usually considered a contract because the client signs-off on it. This document is created by the designer/developer and presented to the potential client.

- **Design and Architecture Specification**   Details exact course of action to be taken during the project's development phase, including exact project schedule, scope, and cost. Requires client sign-off prior to developing the document. Also may be called a *Thick Spec* and/or *Technical Specification*, and may be referred to as another contract. An addendum may be included to record changes made to this document during the development process. This type of document is used primarily for more complex design solutions and may also include other items. such as wireframes, a site map, and a navigation approach. In most situations, this document is created during the first phase of a project, after a contract has been signed.

- **Mockups/Comps**   These deliverables are created after a contract is in place. They provide visual descriptions or pictures of how the project will be implemented. (These may be part of the Design and Architecture Specification, or they may be completed and delivered separately.) Mockups must be extremely detailed because the clients will probably need to sign-off on them to give you authority to produce the final pages. You should develop mockups or comps for each major section/aspect of the site.

- **Usability Report**   Specifies steps taken to test the usability and functionality of the site, as well as the results found and any changes made. Also may be referred to as the *Testing Report* and/or *Quality Assurance Analysis.*

- **Maintenance Plan**   Outlines the process by which the site can be maintained; should include sections for each part or aspect of the site (for example, a Style Guide for updating the front end and a Technical Maintenance Guide for the back end).

- **Acceptance Letter**   Delivers final product to the client; requires sign-off to signal completion of the terms of the contract.

NOTE

I provide electronic samples of each of these types of documents on my web site (**www .wendywillard.com**). Feel free to download and use them to help document your web development projects.

After you have reviewed the RFP and/or met with the client to discuss his needs, you need to formulate your response. In most cases, clients expect some sort of proposal from you that outlines how you plan to meet those needs. The rest of this chapter outlines aspects of web development you should discuss in your proposal, but first I want to mention briefly the stages of development your proposal should address.

Development Lifecycles

Many pieces of documentation are edited throughout different parts of the typical development lifecycle. For example, although the Statement of Work is probably defined during the planning phase of the project, if changes occur during later stages of development, addendums will be added as needed.

While the actual names of each stage might vary according to the project, the vast majority of web development projects use a lifecycle similar to the following:

1. **Planning and analysis**   The project is scoped out and defined. The contracts are written, reviewed, and signed.

2. **Design**   The structure of the project is designed, as specified in the documentation. Storyboards, wireframes, and/or mockups are created for the various aspects of the project and presented to the client for approval.

3. **Development**   The project is built and tested, according to the specifications approved in the first two phases. Images, multimedia, code, and so on, are developed and tested.

4. **Transfer and maintenance**   The project is uploaded to the final web server and tested. Ownership is then transferred to the client or another team for maintenance.

The four stages listed here are only the beginning. Each stage may have many ministages within it, and some stages may overlap others. This entire process is an iterative one that continues as the site grows and evolves. In fact, you could say the project lifecycle doesn't really end at all, until the project is either removed from the Web or changed into something entirely different. I discuss these phases more specifically as we move through them throughout the course of this book.

The Proposal

The first piece of documentation typically used to communicate with a client is the proposal. As a response to a client's RFP or informal request, this document varies according to the project at hand. However, most will have the following key components:

- **Purpose**   Your restatement of the client's business needs, to make it clear you understand what you are being asked to do

- **Scope/SOW**   Details about the work to be completed, including a list of all "pages" to be built and features to be included (this may also include a site map)

- **Conditions/assumptions**   Any conditions and/or assumptions you made while developing the proposal that may impact the cost and/or schedule if changed

- **Hosting**   Instructions about how and where the site will be hosted

- **Cost**

- **Schedule**

- **Biographies**   Statements about the experience of all key players on the development team, as related to the project

Throughout this chapter, keep in mind that the purpose of the proposal is two-fold: you want to win the work with the client, and you also want to define the project you have agreed to complete.

Purpose

The first thing you should do in a proposal for a web project is state your interpretation of the purpose of the project. You want to make sure you and the client are in agreement with regard to why this site is being built. This section doesn't need to be lengthy, but just long enough to assure the client that you understand the business need and any goals that should be met with the project.

Scope/Statement of Work

After stating the purpose of the site development project, take some time to explain how you intend to meet those business needs. This section of the proposal could be anywhere from a few paragraphs to a few pages, depending on the extent of the project.

For my web design projects, I also use this portion of the proposal to explain my process, as it related to the scope of work. Table 2-1 shows a basic example of how you might explain your process and verify the scope of work for a client.

Step	Purpose
I. Design requirements gathering	Consultant will work with client to refine the design of the style needed for the graphics and web site, starting with the requirements stated in the notes. Client will provide at least three sample URLs of sites the client likes (at least one must be a competitor), and three the client dislikes (with regard to design style). Client will provide all text and photographic content for the site via e-mail, CD/DVD, or flash drive. Client will provide any known demographic information about the target audience. Consultant will review text and photographic content and refine it for web presentation. Sign-off is represented by mutual agreement expressed via fax, e-mail, or ground mail.
II. Web template design	Consultant will finalize the site map. Consultant will deliver three unique design concepts for the client's home page, each with a suggested layout and color theme to follow through the entire site. After client has selected the preferred concept, consultant/client move through two rounds of edits to finalize the concept.
III. Coding & development	After the design concept has been determined and client approved, consultant produces standards-compliant, screen-based XHTML and CSS for the final pages. Three rounds of edits will occur after templates are complete. A total of no more than ten pages will be created. Proposed outline is as follows: Home Page Company Info Services Portfolio Contact Us The final pages will be uploaded to the client's hosting server and run through one more round of testing before launch.
IV. Project management	Project management costs cover client/consultant communication, e-mail, timesheets, billing, and scheduling.

Table 2-1 Sample Statement of Work Structure and Language

Conditions/Assumptions

Use this portion of the proposal to identify any assumptions you are making about the project, its goals, and its target audience. You might cover the following topics in this section, as applicable to your particular project:

- Method of file transfer between you and client

- Status of text and graphical copy upon your receipt (For example, is it final?)

- Amount and method of weekly communication between you and client (via phone? In person? 30 minutes? 4 hours?)

- Testing circumstances (For example, for which browsers and operating systems will the site be built? What is the target screen resolution?)

- Guarantees

- Consequences of lapses in schedule

- Copyright ownership

- Handling typos and edits after a site goes live

Unfortunately, this is one section of your proposals that may need to grow with your experience. As you spend more time in the industry, you will undoubtedly encounter new issues that might have been avoided with some good old-fashioned preparation. Use those experiences to build a better working relationship with future clients by spelling out all conditions up front, to avoid confusion about who is responsible for what, and when.

Testing Circumstances

An important consideration for any project is this: for what end user is the site being built? Chapter 1 discussed the target audience from a business standpoint, but at this point I want to focus more on the technical aspects of the target audience. Ultimately, you will want to test your site according the target audience, which means you will try to look at it and work with it the same way the audience might. All web site users bring their own baggage, whether it's a slow Internet connection or a small monitor. While you can't control most of that baggage, you can plan accordingly by asking a few questions. For example, will the majority of the site's users be visiting from home or from work?

When the first edition of this book was written, work users were much more likely to have high-speed Internet connections than users at home. But by the end of 2009, the percentage of home users with high-speed (broadband) connections grew to at least 60 percent, versus just 7 percent with dial-up telephone modems. In the last ten years, the landscape for web design has changed dramatically, as users have obtained faster connection speeds.

So why is it important to know whether users are connecting from home or work if their connection speed will likely be the same? Additional differences between the two types of connections might include the following:

- Work users are less likely to have plug-ins and third-party software installed, particularly within government and large commercial corporations where computer users are blocked from installing anything.

- Work users are less likely to have access to social media such as Facebook, YouTube, and Twitter.

- Work users are less likely to be able to view images or attachments within e-mail.

Target Platforms   Today a more important condition of usage is likely whether your target audience is connecting from a traditional computer (desktop or laptop) or a mobile, handheld device with Internet access (such as a cell phone, game console, or MP3 player). By April 2009, a Pew Internet research report found that 33 percent of Americans access the Internet on mobile devices.

If you are part of that 33 percent, you know how differently web sites display on mobile devices versus computer screens. Compare Figures 2-1 and 2-2 to see how Target's web site looks in a traditional desktop setting versus on an iPhone screen.

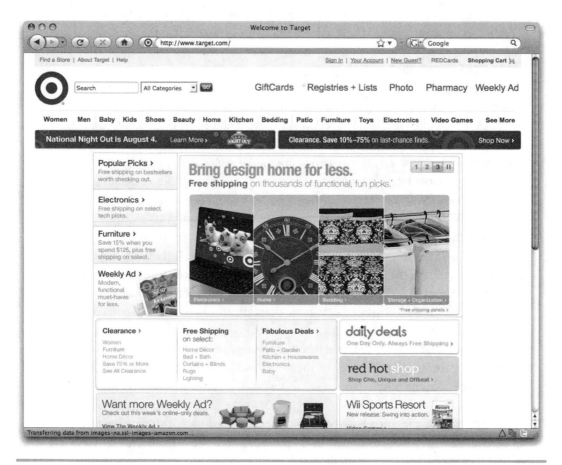

Figure 2-1   Target.com standard site viewed from a desktop computer

Figure 2-2   Target.com standard site when viewed from an iPhone

While Apple does a good job of allowing you to zoom in on various parts of a web page, you can't see all of it at once, which makes for somewhat cumbersome web surfing.

Thankfully, the folks at Target have designed a custom site for mobile device users. Figure 2-3 shows the default page that is displayed when you visit www.target.com using a mobile device. (The developers have included a script on the server to sniff out mobile users and display the appropriate site.) Notice how you can view the entire page at once without zooming or squinting.

Figure 2-3 Target.com custom mobile site viewed from an iPhone

If your project's target audience includes a lot of mobile users, you'd be wise to create a mobile-friendly version of your site. Because of the additional time and effort involved in creating such versions, you should make sure to build that time into your overall project schedule and budget within the initial proposal and contract.

In summary, this type of information is important because of certain differences between these operating systems that might affect the design of your site. Table 2-2 outlines the most common such differences.

Target Screen Area/Resolution   While many people are familiar with different monitor sizes (such as 15, 17, and 21 inch models), fewer recognize that they must also contend with multiple screen areas. *Screen area* refers to how much actual viewing space is available on the monitor, regardless of the monitor's physical size. To see these different

Aspects Affected	Description of General Differences
Font sizes	Text displayed on a Macintosh appears smaller than its counterpart on Windows-based PCs. Browsers' latest versions help combat this problem by offering Mac users the option of displaying type at PC sizes.
Colors	Various platforms and monitors display color differently. Because some colors may not be available on all platforms, carefully consider which colors to use in designing your web pages (for more detail see Chapter 3).
Available real estate	Different computer systems use different on-screen layouts for elements such as menus and folders. These differences mean that a varying amount of space is left over for the browser and, consequently, your web page. This space, also called *screen real estate,* is discussed in more detail later in the book.
Form-field elements	Some organizations' web sites ask you to fill out forms to communicate with them. Each platform has its own way of displaying form items. For example, a default text box is typically much larger on a Windows-based PC than on a Macintosh. And filling out forms on a mobile device is completely different.
Browsers/plug-ins	Software manufacturers work not only on new versions of their browsers and plug-ins, but also on different renditions for each operating system. Some software may not be available for certain platforms. For example, as of this writing, Flash is not available on the iPhone.

Table 2-2   Common Display Differences Among Popular Browsers

sizes in action, use the following steps, depending on your operating system. Table 2-3 lists some typical screen areas for the most common monitor sizes.

For Windows-based PC users, the steps depend on the version of Windows you're running. In Vista and most new systems, right-click the computer's desktop and select Personalize from the context menu. Then, choose Display Settings from the options. In NT and older systems, right-click the computer's desktop and select Properties from the menu. Then, choose the Settings tab at the top of the window. In either case, the resulting window shows information about your monitor settings that can be changed.

For Macintosh users, locate your System Preferences (either by using the Apple menu at the upper-left of your desktop or by accessing them in your hard drive file list.) Then, find the control panel called Displays. Here you can also find information about your monitor settings, such as the number of colors available and the screen area, also called *resolution.*

Monitor Size	Typical Screen Area
14–15 inches	640 × 480 800 × 600
17 inches	800 × 600 1024 × 768
21 inches	1024 × 768 1152 × 870 1280 × 960 or 1280 × 1024
Laptops	Varies widely; typically 1024 × 768 or 1280 × 960
Handheld devices	Varies widely, from 150 × 150, to 320 × 240 or 320 × 480 (iPhone)

Table 2-3   Typical Screen Areas for Common Monitor Sizes

The screen area is an important consideration when you're dealing with how much content you can realistically fit on a single web page. Unlike pages printed on paper, where everyone sees a design at the same size (perhaps 8.5 × 11 inches), the designed web page will vary in size according to the screen area of its viewer.

In the early days of the Web, designers focused on the lowest common denominator (640 × 480), especially when it came to screen area. This meant the most important page content was designed to fit within a space about 600 × 300 dpi (dots, or pixels, per inch), so the user didn't have to scroll to see it. The extra 40 pixels in width and 180 pixels in height is taken up by the *browser chrome* (its menus, buttons, scroll bars, and so forth) and the operating system (such as the Start menu on Windows and the Apple menu on Macs).

Now, however, because so many different monitor sizes and screen areas are being used, your best solution is to create what's commonly referred to as *liquid pages*, which grow and shrink in size according to the available screen area on the visitor's monitor. (This topic is discussed in much more detail in later chapters.)

When they're not using liquid pages, many designers choose to target an 1024 × 768 screen area, making sure the most important information is viewable without scrolling in a 800 × 600 screen area. And, of course, if you're designing a private web site, you likely know exactly what screen size your users have and can target their specific screen area.

Target Browsers   Finally, not only are browsers sometimes unavailable from one platform to another, but they also may look and behave differently when they *are* available on multiple platforms. For example, Microsoft is up to at least version 8 of Internet Explorer (IE) for the PC, but the company never got past version 5.0 of the same product for the Mac. As such, the features within the browsers, as well as support for various technologies, vary between the two versions.

The most popular browser is indeed IE; as of this writing, some estimates give IE upward of 65 percent of the market share. One explanation is that IE comes preinstalled with Windows and few seek out alternative browsers. Apple's preinstalled browser with the Mac OS is Safari.

Most of the other popular browsers are part of a breed called "Mozilla-based" browsers. This name comes from the fact that each browser is based on a framework named Mozilla, which has its roots in the old Netscape browser. The most popular Mozilla-based browser is Firefox, which is available for both Windows and Mac operating systems.

TIP

To keep current on statistics about browser use, visit **http://en.wikipedia.org/wiki/ Usage_share_of_web_browsers**.

Browsers are updated regularly, changing to address new aspects of HTML or emerging technologies. Some people continue to use older versions of their browsers, however. This means that at any given time, two to three active versions of one browser may be in use, with several different versions of other browsers being employed by the general public.

What if there were several versions of televisions, each of which displayed TV programs differently? If this were true, your favorite television show might look differently every time you watched it on someone else's television. This would not only be frustrating to you as a viewer, but also to the show's creator.

Web developers must deal with this kind of frustration every day. Because of the differences among browsers and the large number of computer types, the look and feel of a web page can vary greatly. This means web developers must keep up-to-date on the latest features of the new browsers, but we must also know how to create pages that are backward-compatible for the older browsers many people may still be using.

As with the rest of these conditions of use, the key is to identify the most common types of browsers used among your target audience. Then you can design for and test on those browsers. Because browser support of HTML tags, CSS properties, JavaScript functions, and other things is integral to the development process, I discuss the differences between the most popular browsers in many places throughout the book.

TIP

Check out Adobe BrowserLab at **http://browserlab.adobe.com** for a great new way to test your pages for cross-browser continuity. With Dreamweaver CS4 integration, Adobe has provided web designers with a fabulous cross-browser testing solution.

Ask the Expert

Q: Where can I find some statistical information about typical web users who might visit a particular site?

A: You can check several places. First, if you're redesigning a site, be sure to ask the current system administrator for copies of any existing site logs. The majority of host companies run software on their web servers that track information about web site traffic. For example, by looking at the site logs, you can often find information, such as the following:

- Number of unique visitors in any given hour/day/week/month
- Number of times each page on the site was accessed
- How long the average visitor stayed on the site
- What page each visitor was on *before* visiting your site (also called the *referring page*)
- A breakdown of all the browsers used to access the site
- A listing of all the domains used by visitors to the site (for example, if you use AOL as your service provider to access the Internet, you register on the site logs as coming from aol.com)
- Information about the visitor's screen size and number of colors
- A breakdown of all the operating systems used to access the site
- A listing of how many users had any necessary plug-ins
- Information about whether additional functionality, such as JavaScript, is enabled within the user's browser

As you can see, a large amount of important information can be gleaned from the typical site log. A few of the most popular tools for tracking this information are WebTrends (**www.webtrends.com**), SuperStats (**www.superstats.com**), and VisiStat (**www.visistat.com**).

In addition, many sites also provide this same sort of statistical information about other web sites, in case you don't already have logs for your site. Check out **www.internetnews.com/stats/** to see an example.

Hosting

One of the most basic answers you must provide in your proposal is where the site will be housed, or hosted. This means you probably can't just keep the files on your own computer or on a computer at your client's office. Some clients have already arranged for hosting before they start looking for a designer. If that's the case, you need only to gather information about the hosting environment from the client.

But others may look to you for advice in this regard. In that case, many different options are available for those who want to publish a site on the Internet. For the purposes of this chapter, I group these options into two categories: personal site hosting and business site hosting.

Personal Site Hosting

When you want to publish a personal web site (for you or a client) and you aren't concerned about having a custom domain name (such as wendywillard.com), a wide range of free options is available. For example, all the following sites offer free web space for personal sites to anyone who asks for it. If you (or your client) currently have an e-mail account with any of these companies, you're already halfway there.

- Homestead (**www.homestead.com**)
- Google Sites (**http://sites.google.com**)
- Tripod (**www.tripod.com**)

Because these sites are largely targeting beginners, they make uploading and maintaining your web pages a breeze. Most use web-based tools to help you create a site, so you don't need to purchase or install any additional software.

Blogs

The preceding list of suggestions for personal web sites include companies that provide space on their servers for anyone wanting to upload web pages (although some do offer the option to install additional features, such as blogs). But what about those who are looking to "journal" online and don't want to bother creating custom web pages for that purpose? Many sites offer free blogs, where you can journal, vent, gossip, or simply share to your heart's content—with little to no HTML knowledge required.

As a bonus, if you can handle coding some HTML (which you can do, since you're reading this), you'll be able to tailor your blog to meet your specific needs. The following two sites are the most popular free blogging tools online. Both offer tutorials to help you get started, as well as tons of templates for customizing the look of your blog.

- Google's Blogger (**www.blogger.com**)
- WordPress (**http://wordpress.com**)

While all of these sites offer free hosting to anyone who requests it, remember to check first with your current *Internet service provider (ISP)*. ISPs frequently throw in some free web space with all accounts. If none of these free options suits your project's purposes or if you need to register a custom domain, move on to the next section about business site hosting.

TIP

Before you sign up with any ISP, be sure to check the terms of service to verify your site fits within the confines of the ISP's requirements. For example, the majority of ISPs prohibit sites distributing pornography or illegal copies of computer software. In addition, free ISPs usually limit the amount of space and/or bandwidth you can use. Finally, if you change ISPs, you'll need to locate a new host. I mention these only to point out that restrictions do exist and you'd be wise to review all terms and details carefully to avoid incurring unexpected fees.

Business Site Hosting

On the business side, your options vary from onsite, to colocated, to offsite. In the case of *onsite hosting,* the company purchases a server, its software, and a dedicated Internet connection capable of serving the site to web users 24 hours a day, 365 days a year. For small businesses, this isn't a viable option because it requires expensive start-up costs and on-staff information technology (IT) talent.

For businesses that already own the appropriate equipment and have an experienced webmaster but don't want to spend the money for an expensive, dedicated Internet connection, *colocation* is an option. In this case, you use your own equipment and personnel but rent space and a high-speed Internet connection from a host company. Your equipment is housed in that space and can be reached any time of day by your personnel, thereby enabling you to maintain a higher level of control over your site as desired.

For the majority of small to mid-size businesses, *offsite hosting* is the most cost-effective and popular solution. Hosting can be on either a *shared* or a *dedicated* server. While a shared server can be significantly less expensive than one dedicated to your needs, it may not be possible in all situations. For example, if your site runs custom web applications, requires a high level of security, or needs a large amount of space, a dedicated server is preferred.

Many service levels, and therefore, many price levels, exist within shared offsite hosting. For this reason, be wary of comparing apples to oranges. When you are considering two or more hosting providers, look closely at the fine print to be sure they offer similar services before making a final decision solely on price.

The following are some questions to ask when you look for business hosting:

- How much space on the server is included? How much extra does it cost if I go over that space?

- How much traffic can the site generate over a month? What are some average traffic rates for some similar sites you host? How much extra does it cost if the site generates more traffic than allowed?

- Is multimedia streaming supported? If so, how much traffic is supported for any given event and at what point will the system overload? What are procedures for dealing with excess traffic?

- How many e-mail accounts are included with this account?

- Can you handle a custom domain name(s) (as opposed to www.hostcompany.com/mybusiness)? Will you help me register the domain? (If you haven't already registered one.) Will you charge extra for multiple domain names pointing to one web site? If so, how much more?

- What kind of access will developers have to the web site? For example, is FTP (File Transfer Protocol) access available for uploading files?

- What kind of support do you offer? (For example, if you need help adding password protection to your site, will the hosting company help you?) What hours are your support staff available?

- Can a developer load additional applications (database tools, e-commerce tools, and so forth) onto the server? What requirements or restrictions do you have regarding those? Are additional costs involved?

- What additional services do you offer? (For example, can you also host an online store, and, if so, how much would it cost in addition to the current fees?)

- How many Internet connections do you have? (The more connections a host has, the better chance a site has of staying "live" if one connection goes down.)

- How often do you perform backups? How easy is it to gain access to a backup if needed?

- What are the start-up costs? What are the monthly costs? Are there any guarantees?

- Do you offer a service to measure statistics for a site, such as how many people have visited? If so, can you provide details?

- Can you provide references?

Many services online let you compare different web site host companies. To get started, you might try these:

- HostSearch (**www.hostsearch.com**)
- CNET Web Hosting (**reviews.cnet.com/web-hosting**)

Or try searching in Yahoo! using the phrase *web site host* to see lists of hosting companies.

If you don't already have a relationship with a hosting company, finding one may seem like a daunting task. Searching online shows you that thousands of hosting companies are trying to woo you. In the end, you'll probably get the best ideas about which hosting provider to use by asking friends or business associates. In that vein, here are a few of my suggestions:

- Site5 (**www.site5.com/**)
- DreamHost (**www.dreamhost.com/**)
- BlueHost (**www.bluehost.com/**)
- Hostway (**www.hostway.com/**)

NOTE
While I have used some of these hosts, I encourage you to do your own thorough research to make sure a particular host suits the needs of your project.

Select Possible Domain Names for a Site

If you're working on a project for a business, you will most likely be considering domain names. Even if a client has an existing web site and domain name, it might be worthwhile to research additional options that may be more recognizable or more easily searchable.

Many people underestimate the power of a guessable and memorable domain name. Consider a company called Acme Landscaping Incorporated. While it may seem logical to its business owners to purchase the domain name *alinc.com,* this is probably not the first thing a potential customer would guess.

TIP
You could research and register a domain in probably thousands of places online. A few options include PCNames (**www.pcnames.com**), Network Solutions (**www. networksolutions.com**), and Go Daddy (**www.godaddy.com**).

The name *acmelandscaping.com* would be my first guess, but if that domain were already taken, I might try *acmelandscapers.com, acmelawns.com*, or even something like *beautifullawns.com.* If more than one of those were available, you might even register a couple. Purchasing multiple domain names is an inexpensive way to bring in some additional customers and build your brand identity online. Whenever appropriate, you might also purchase the same domain name ending with different extensions, such as *beautifullawns.com* and *beautifullawns.net.*

Ask the Expert

Q: What are the valid characters for a domain name, and how long can a domain name be?

A: According to Network Solutions (**www.networksolutions.com**), you can use letters and numbers in a domain name. You can also use hyphens, although they may not appear at the beginning or end of your web address. Spaces or other characters such as question marks and exclamation marks are never allowed.

Your complete domain name (including the extension—such as .com, .edu, .net, .org, .biz, .tv, or .info) can be up to 67 characters long. Remember, "www" isn't included in the domain name you register, so you needn't count those characters. Having said that, shorter is better—after all, most of us have trouble remembering ten-digit phone numbers (555-555-5555)!

Cost

After you've clarified the project purpose and identified the specific scope of work to be completed, it's time to spell out the associated costs. Web design and development costs vary widely, according to the geographic region, the experience level of the development team, and the scope of the project.

If you're just getting started in the industry, I recommend connecting with a local networking group to find out how others in your area are pricing similar projects. Depending on your background and skill set, you might be interested in seeking out a local chapter of one of these national organizations with web design members:

- American Institute of Graphic Artists (AIGA) (**www.aiga.org**)
- Graphic Artists Guild (**www.graphicartistsguild.org**)
- HTML Writers Guild (**www.hwg.org**)
- National Association of Photoshop Professionals (NAPP) (**www.photoshopuser.com**)
- Webgrrls International (**www.webgrrls.com**)

In addition, check out these social networking communities for web developers and designers:

- Adobe Developer Connection (**www.adobe.com/devnet/**)
- CreativeBits (**www.creativebits.org**)

- Design:Related (**www.designrelated.com**)
- DeviantART (**www.deviantart.com**)
- Graphic Design Network (**http://graphicdesignnetwork.ning.com**)
- Microsoft Developer Network (**http://msdn.microsoft.com/**)
- SitePoint (**www.sitepoint.com**)

Schedule

Another key component of the proposal is the schedule. This section of the proposal should outline the deliverables and the associated due dates. Be sure to include any dependencies for all deliverables. For example, if you specify that your initial design mockup is due on a certain date, also list anything the client must provide to you before you can start working on the mockup.

In addition to due dates and dependencies, confirm the consequences of missed due dates.

Biographies

Finally, be sure to include brief biographies of all key team members. This usually involves relevant experience, skills, and similar projects. If you are using a subcontractor or another third-party, allow space to introduce them as well.

Site Map

At this early stage of the project (you probably haven't even won the work yet…), try not to solve too many of the client's business problems. Instead, focus on answering the client's questions and needs at a high level, so you can win his confidence that you will answer them more thoroughly throughout the course of the project.

With that said, a general site map can be an appropriate starting point. Such a document outlines each page or section of the site, as well as the basic relationships between them. This is likely your first step in a very important web development process, often referred to as the *information architecture* (IA).

Information Architecture

First, I need to say that there is no perfect way of organizing content, at least not one that works for everyone. Tons of different options are available, and your task is to select the one that best fits your particular project needs.

So how do you get started? Most people begin by arranging content according to one of two thoughts:

- How other similar web sites arrange content
- How the content is arranged "in real life" (in other words: a business might set up its online store using the layout of the physical store, with the products organized by "aisles")

Unfortunately, these aren't always the best ways to start organizing content. A better way is to let the users' needs drive the organization and flow of the content. For example, a college web site might be built around its different audiences: students, parents, alumni, and so on. All content would then be placed according to who needs to access it, and prioritized around the site goals.

Multitudes of organizational models are available to help you in this process. Let's look at a few of the most common.

IA Model: All-in-One

The most basic model for organizing content is to include everything right on the home page. Obviously, this doesn't work for large or complex sites, but it can be surprisingly successful for smaller sites.

IA Model: Flat

With a flat information architecture, all pages on the site are at the same level in the structure. This means every page is accessible from every other one. Basic small business web sites are frequently built this way, with pages titled "About Us," "Contact Us," "Our Services," and "Home."

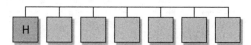

IA Model: Index

Similar to a flat model, an index model has one additional feature: a table of contents. On some web sites, this page is actually called "Site Map." In other cases, a list of content areas is included on another page as a resource for quick linking.

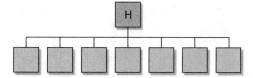

IA Model: Hub-and-Spoke

A hub-and-spoke pattern (sometimes referred to as a "daisy" pattern because the content areas look like petals on a flower) works well for sites with distinct user groups or particularly linear workflows. One example might be an online training site, where you return to your "desk" after watching a class lecture or taking a test.

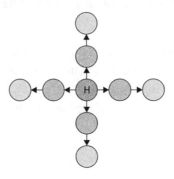

IA Model: Strict Hierarchy

Have you ever visited a site with distinct sections, in which you couldn't access a different section without first going back to the home page? This type of model might be considered a strict hierarchy. A good example of this type of structure is a web site for a global business, where you must select your country before accessing the site content. Users who select Mexico, for example, will not be able to access Canadian content without first switching to the Canadian section of the site.

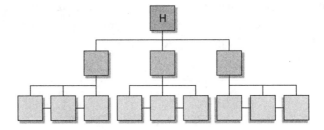

IA Model: Multidimension Hierarchy

A multidimension hierarchy is similar to a strict hierarchy, with one key difference: In this case, it is possible to access content from a different section without first returning to the home or gateway page. A great example of this type of structure might be a large online bookstore that lets you view books by title, author, subject, or even keyword. The content can be reached by any of these methods.

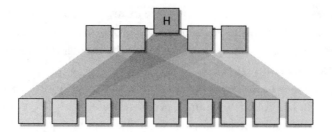

IA Model: Search

While a lot of web sites have search features, some rely on their search features to get users to the content they want as fast as possible. For example, the best way to get around a large auction site like eBay is to search. While the site does have a hierarchical structure as well, the search tool acts like an elevator to get users quickly to the content they want.

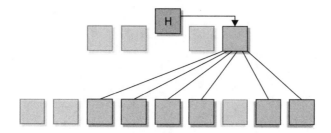

NOTE

A great resource for learning more about web development is Web Design from Scratch (**www.webdesignfromscratch.com**), which is run by a web design agency in London called Scratchmedia. The information architecture classification system I used here was based on Scratchmedia's research and included with their permission.

Content Organization

Now that you have a few ideas about how information might be structured, your next step is to gather all the types of content for the site. This can be a simple handwritten list or a detailed spreadsheet. Ultimately, all the content for the site should then fit under each of the topic areas in the site structure. You might include several subcategories in each topic area. In addition, always consider the user in this process. To reiterate, the recommended site content isn't necessarily what the client already has (or thinks she should have) but instead what the user expects to find or needs to find for a successful experience.

Sometimes it helps to look at a few more examples. Consider a store that sells office supplies, whose two main site goals are to sell products and to retain employees. A very rudimentary site map, following the strict hierarchy model, might start off with a structure similar to that shown in Figure 2-4.

Drilling down even further in the structure, the "shop for office supplies" section from Figure 2-4 might be broken down into several subcategories, according to the different types of products available, as shown in Table 2-4.

In the case of the summer camp web site mentioned in Chapter 1, I identified the key functions we might expect users to perform on the site. Those could become the main sections of the site. Table 2-5 shows these main sections, as well as the list of content that might be housed in each one.

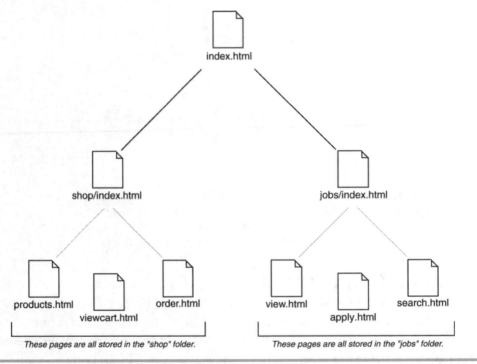

Figure 2-4   A tree diagram showing a portion of the structure for a sample office supply site

Category Name	Folder Name
Paper	shop/paper/
Pens	shop/pens/
Software	shop/software/
Furniture	shop/furniture/
Furniture > Desks	shop/furniture/desks/
Furniture > Chairs	shop/furniture/chairs/
Furniture > Bookcases	shop/furniture/bookcases/

Table 2-4 Organizing Content

TIP

For the beginning stages of this exercise, the list of content needn't refer to actual web pages but, instead, to the type of content you expect to place within those sections. After you finish organizing the content, you can finalize each section by deciding how much content can reasonably be placed on a single page.

Section	Content
Home	Links to all the main sections, photo(s), news (especially camp dates and availability)
Camp	Information about the prices, dates, and availability (again), activities (daily and evening), cabin life, meals, trips, staff enrollment form ways to contact us photos from last summer schedule and photos from current summer jobs available (requirements, salaries, how to apply) testimonials from alumni
Mission	Information about history and background of the organization and its founders ways to support us ways to contact us
Communication	Ways to contact us ways to contact alumni (bulletin boards/chat?) ways to contact kids at camp
Store	Camp-branded clothing for sale link to enrollment form

Table 2-5 Moving Site Goals into a Site Structure

TIP

Remember to place content within your structure according to how the users will look for it, not only how the client's business already organizes it. Also, avoid matching the company's organizational structure unless that is what really makes sense for the user.

While documenting the relationships between each page of the site, be sure to consider how a user might navigate between them. You can use a variety of brainstorming and documentation techniques to accomplish this task. For example, you might start with simple hand drawings, such as those shown in Figure 2-5. Or you could work with a team of people to organize sticky-notes on a white board. Still others create technical drawings using programs such as Microsoft Visio (see Figure 2-6) or even Adobe Illustrator or Microsoft PowerPoint.

TIP

If working in a program such as Visio seems too "official" in the beginning stages of a project, stick with paper and pencil until you have the details finalized. Tossing away a piece of paper and starting over is often easier, which means you probably won't commit to a faulty navigation structure too soon in the process.

You might create many, many diagrams and charts like these over the course of a single project. You can document this type of information in many different ways, so feel free to experiment until you find the method that works best for you. Ultimately, your objective is to do the following:

- Determine the most appropriate information architecture model
- Organize the site's content around that model
- Ensure that all site goals are met
- Enable users to access the content easily and quickly

Figure 2-5   This hand-drawn storyboard shows how a user might navigate through a portion of the camp section for the summer camp web site

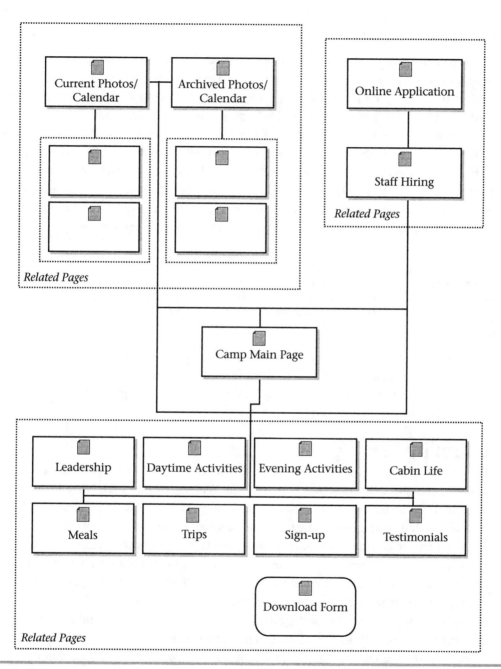

Figure 2-6 Products such as Microsoft Visio make creating technical diagrams like this one a breeze

Measuring Success

The final topic I want to cover in this chapter is the concept of measuring success. Whenever you start any web project, you must have methods in place to measure the success of the end product. Such measurements provide a way to determine when the site goals have been met and therefore when the project has been completed.

The success of web site projects can be measured in a variety of different ways, some of which are more visible and easily accessible than others. For example, earlier in this chapter I mentioned that a large amount of statistical information can be gleaned from the typical site log. This includes demographics of particular site visitors, as well as how long each page is viewed and the path used to navigate through the site. These stats are easily accessible and can sometimes be helpful in measuring the success of a site.

TIP

You don't have to use tracking software that is loaded on your site's server. Many developers prefer to use a third-party solution such as Google Analytics for measuring web traffic and site effectiveness. Visit **www.google.com/analytics** for more information.

Other ways of measuring success are not as easily accessible but may provide more concrete answers in terms of how well a site is meeting its goals. One such tool is called *usability testing*. In fact, usability testing is often employed throughout the entire web design process to gauge the success of each stage.

Usability Testing

The purpose of usability testing is to observe how members of the target audience use a web site, to figure out what needs improvement. When performing usability testing on a web site, I like to give participants several tasks to perform on the site, and then watch to see how much time and how many steps are required to complete those tasks.

As errors occur or mistakes happen along the way, I get to witness them firsthand and record the steps necessary to reproduce them. After the tasks are completed, any remaining time can be used to ask how the participant felt about the process and whether she might recommend the site to someone else.

I have even performed usability testing on web site mockups, by printing sample screens of a site and asking participants to point and "click" the printouts to show where they might go next. This can be a great and quick way to identify navigation systems that aren't working, before a lot of time and energy is spent actually building the back-end systems to support them.

I bring this up during the proposal point of the web process so you can decide whether to include usability testing in your overall plan and schedule. You can find out a lot more about usability testing online by visiting any of the following web sites:

- Usability.gov (**www.usability.gov**)
- User Interface Engineering (**www.uie.com**)
- Human Factors International (**www.humanfactors.com**)
- uiAccess.com (**www.uiaccess.com**)

Summary

Chapter 1 introduced you to plenty of questions to ask about any new web projects. This chapter spent time discussing how to formulate your answers to those questions in the form of a web project proposal. Your next step is to submit the proposal to your client for approval. After gaining approval and signing a contract, you can begin work on the meat of the site. The following chapters move throughout the process to help you work through the design of a typical web site project.

Part II

Designing

Chapter 3

Anticipating Web-Specific Design Issues

Key Skills & Concepts

- Determine the best design tools for your needs.

- Identify design considerations that are specific to web design.

Chapters 1 and 2 outlined how to identify a client's needs and then respond to those needs. After a contract is in place and all the "business" business is set, it's time to get to the good stuff! (If you're reading this book, you likely agree with me that designing is the good stuff.)

To make sure we're all on the same page at this stage of the game, let's go over a few web design basics and set some ground rules. We'll start with the tools of the trade.

Deciding Which Design Tools to Use

If you walk down the software aisles of your local computer store, you might be surprised by the sheer volume of graphics-related software available. You can buy clip art and photography, fonts, scanning utilities, animation titles, photo-editing programs, desktop publishing applications, drawing tools, and so forth.

NOTE

You'll hear the term *layers* used a lot in graphics software discussions. Using layers in a graphics program is similar to making a bed. You place sheets, blankets, and pillows over the mattress, but you can change any of those items freely if you decide you dislike one. The same is true with layers—you can paint on a layer, and then delete it later if you don't like it. Layers offer much flexibility in graphics programs.

For the purposes of this discussion, I focus on software titles that offer you the best tools for creating web graphics. Two main categories of software titles exist: vector and bitmap.

Bitmap applications, also called *raster* applications, create graphics using tiny dots known as *bits*. Bitmap images are more difficult to resize because you must change each individual dot, but these image types have been around longer and enjoy more support from file formats. GIFs and JPEGs are bitmap images.

Vector applications, also called *object-oriented* applications, are based on mathematically calculated lines and curves that can be easily changed and updated. Images created with vectors tend to be smaller in file size and, for that reason, are increasing in popularity on the Internet.

The programs discussed here are by no means the only products available for creating web graphics. Given the scope of this book, I thought it best to limit the discussion to the most popular programs. If none of these tools suits your needs, try searching in Yahoo! (**www.yahoo.com**) or CNET's download center (**www.downloads.com**) for "web graphics," and perhaps you'll find one more suitable for your purposes.

Adobe Photoshop

Adobe is the world leader in graphics and imaging software. It offers such renowned titles as Photoshop and Illustrator, which have been used in the printing and design industry for years.

Photoshop (**www.adobe.com/photoshop**) is a bitmap program, best known for image manipulation, using layers to allow for virtually limitless flexibility in design. In fact, if you've recently bought a new scanner, you might have acquired a scaled-back version of Photoshop with it. Illustrator, on the other hand, is a vector tool, more suited for freehand drawing and illustration. Both products can save and open web file formats.

In many design circles, Photoshop is *the* product to use. For the typical home user, the price for the full version is a bit steep, but for the professional, it's likely worth the business expense. If you're familiar with Adobe's products and enjoy them, I recommend sticking with Photoshop. Likewise, if you're interested in creating web graphics as well as editing images for printed publications, Photoshop is your best bet.

If you don't fall into either of those categories, you might be interested in Photoshop Elements (the scaled-back, but still fabulous, version), which costs a lot less than the full version. While this version doesn't have all the high-powered image-editing tools used by the professionals, it's more than capable of handling the needs of someone just starting, and it even has a few bells and whistles that the full version doesn't offer. Photoshop Elements, available for both the Mac and the PC, is a superb gateway graphics program for the typical home or novice user.

TIP

If you are a student or are employed by an academic institution, remember to check into academic pricing for software, since Adobe offers significant academic discounts. Also, consider Adobe's bundles. By purchasing multiple products together, you can usually save on the individual prices.

Adobe Fireworks

Fireworks (**www.adobe.com/fireworks**) is a web-specific tool used for creating web graphics. I use the term *web-specific* because, unlike many other graphics software titles, Fireworks was created specifically for the Web.

Fireworks offers such features as web animation, file optimization, image slicing, rollover creation, and web previewing. It also seamlessly integrates with Adobe Dreamweaver, a top-rated WYSIWYG tool for web authoring and page layout, making the two software titles a highly regarded and powerful web development suite.

Fireworks has a particularly strong following among web designers who never got hooked on Adobe's products, because up until 2006 Fireworks was owned by Adobe's fiercest competitor, Macromedia. (Adobe purchased Macromedia in 2006.) Although the Fireworks learning curve is a bit steeper than that of the other options discussed at the end of this section, it's midrange price allows it to remain a viable alternative for cost-conscious users.

NOTE

Fireworks also integrates well with Flash, which is worth mentioning, even though it doesn't directly compete with any of the other products listed here. Flash is a vector application specifically designed for creating animations and interactive presentations on the Web.

Other Options

Although Photoshop and Fireworks are by far the most popular web graphics applications, several other options are available that might be more appropriate for you. Corel fans enjoy Paint Shop Pro (**www.corel.com/paintshoppro**), which offers much for a low price. Features include animation, direct digital camera support, layers, filters, watermarks, special effects, and advanced text tools such as allowing text to be typed along a curve or custom path.

Another option for the cost-conscious user is GIMP, which is short for GNU Image Manipulation Program. The best part about GIMP is that it's free! GIMP is freely distributed from **www.gimp.org**, for the Mac, Windows, and UNIX platforms. Its features include photo retouching, image composition, and image authoring. GIMP is a perfect place to start if you're just getting started with web design and don't want to spend a lot of money. And, who knows, you may even decide you don't need anything else.

Screen Design Considerations

Consider a printed magazine. Regardless of where the magazine is purchased, the images displayed inside look the same in every copy. In fact, only those who are color-blind or vision-impaired will encounter differences in printed graphics. This isn't the case with web graphics, because each person viewing a web site is doing so with a different set of experiences, affected by his or her computer, browser, monitor, lighting, and modem, to name a few.

When designing for the web (as opposed to a non-screen–based medium), several issues directly affect the outcome and must be considered:

- Platforms
- Code
- Browsers
- Color
- Bandwidth
- Fonts

Platforms

A person's web experience is affected by his or her web *platform*, or the type of device being used to access the Web. While obvious differences exist between computers and mobile phones, both are used to view web pages. Furthermore, many differences exist between the types of computers used—for example, consider the differences among handheld computers, laptop computers, and desktop computers.

And among those different types of computers, Windows, Macintosh, UNIX, Linux, and many other operating systems are running. Many computers even enable you to surf the Web from your television. Undoubtedly, many more such devices are yet to come.

The most important thing to consider about platforms is that the one you're using probably won't be the only one your site's visitors will use. Here are a few general things to consider when you're designing for more than one platform:

- Graphics generally look darker on most PCs running Windows than they do on a Mac, but Windows gamma (or brightness) can vary widely. A graphic that appears fine on one Windows PC screen might look much darker on another Windows screen with different settings.

- Software (such as browsers, plug-ins, and ActiveX controls) available for your platform might not be available for other platforms.

- The size and settings of the viewing device (be it a 17-inch monitor, a 27-inch TV, or a 2-inch handheld screen) used by your visitors will alter the appearance of your graphics.

The moral of this section is that you need to be aware of these differences and plan accordingly. In addition, test your web designs on a variety on platforms to be sure you are achieving the results you want.

Screen Size

Many designers choose to begin designing the look and feel of a web page within a design program such as those mentioned in this chapter, while others starts with pencil sketches on paper. In either case, one of your first steps should be to identify the most appropriate size at which to design the page.

In Chapter 2, I talked about identifying the most common screen area used among your site's target audience. This meant considering sizes such as 800 × 600 and 1024 × 768. Unfortunately, making that decision isn't the final step in the process, because the browser itself, as well as the operating system, also take up some space on the screen.

You need to consider several things when you look at the usable part of the screen area, including the operating system and the browser itself. The amount of space used by the operating system depends on which operating system is in use and how the user has it customized.

For example, suppose the user is running Windows XP at a screen resolution of 1024 × 768, with the taskbar across the bottom of the screen. If he expands (maximizes) the web browser to fill the remaining space, the screen might look like Figure 3-1. Compare

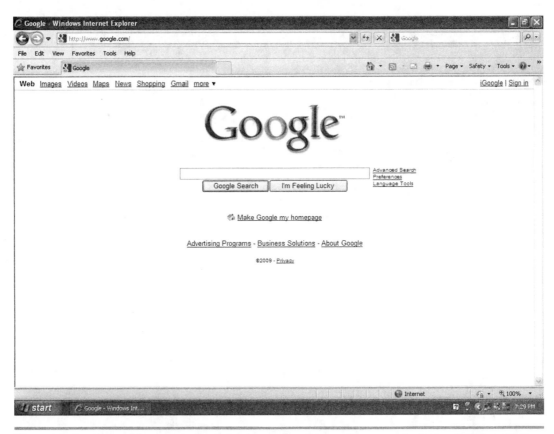

Figure 3-1 Viewable area when the browser window is expanded at a 1024 × 768 screen resolution, in Windows XP.

that to Figure 3-2, which shows the default view for maximized browsers in Windows Vista, also running at 1024 × 768. In both cases, the amount of space available for the actual web page is roughly 1000 × 600 pixels.

When you start designing your web pages, you need to decide how much space will be available for your target audience. As of this writing, the top choice of many designers is to target the 1024 × 768 resolution, while making sure the pages still perform well in other resolutions. After taking into account the browser edges, scrollbar, and operating system menus, you probably want to make sure the most important information is in the top 1000 (wide) by 600 (tall) pixels of the page.

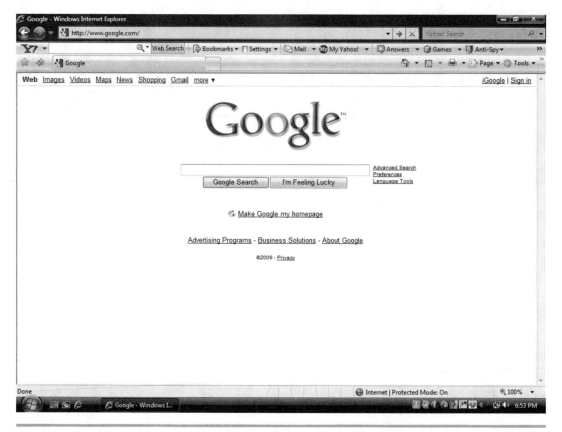

Figure 3-2   Viewable area when the browser window is expanded at a 1024 × 768 screen resolution, in Windows Vista.

Users can customize their desktop and/or shrink the browser window to change the available screen area dramatically. For example, if you click and hold on the taskbar in Windows, you can drag it from horizontal view to vertical view, reducing the average usable web space by about 60 pixels horizontally. Likewise, if you shrink the browser window while viewing web pages targeting 1000 pixels of horizontal space, you'll end up with a horizontal scroll bar, as shown in Figure 3-3.

I tell you this not to cause frustration, but to help you get used to the fact that web pages live in a fluid environment that changes with each user. As a web designer, you need to focus on making your pages accessible to the widest possible audience, even if some members of that audience see the page a bit differently from others.

Figure 3-3   Shrinking the browser window will force a horizontal scroll bar to appear if the web page is designed for larger window sizes.

How to Deal with Inconsistent Screen Areas

So, how do you manage this? Of course it's impossible for a single design to look perfect under all these circumstances, but, with proper testing, you can ensure that, at the very least, all the content is accessible. In the best-case scenario, your content is visible without needing a horizontal scroll bar. Why? Because most people just don't bother to scroll horizontally when viewing web pages (although scrolling vertically is considered common), and you therefore risk no one seeing any content located outside the default page view.

The most common ways of dealing with this inconsistent screen area are outlined in the next few paragraphs.

Design for one specific screen area and forget about everyone else.   Um… hopefully not! It used to be that all designers did this, back when everyone used monitors capable of displaying only 640 × 480 screen resolution. The problem with doing this now is that with so many different types and sizes of screens accessing the Web, you need to at least consider more than just one.

Design for one specific screen area, but optimize the site to function well on a variety of screen sizes.   Even if you target one specific screen size, you should always test the site on different screens to see how the designs translate. With a good bit of testing (and maybe some slight revising), you can make sure your site's content is visible on the vast majority of screens used by your target audience.

When you design for one specific screen size, you typically create graphics and content areas of a fixed width. This means that regardless of the user's monitor setup, she will always see the page at the same width. Consider Figures 3-4 and 3-5 to see what I mean.

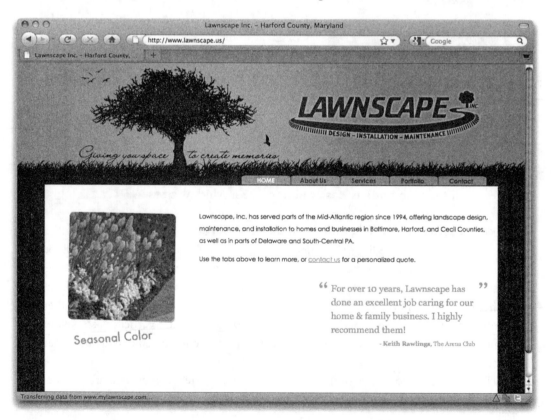

Figure 3-4   This site was built for 1024 × 768 screens and therefore fills the screen (without forcing a horizontal scroll bar) when viewed at that resolution.

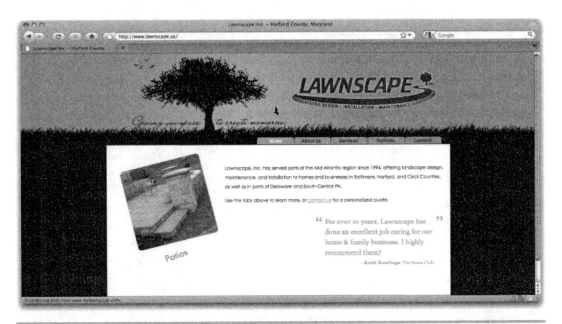

Figure 3-5 When viewed on a larger resolution, with the browser window extended, the design doesn't get any larger. Instead, it is centered on the screen.

Create liquid pages that grow and shrink according to the available screen area.   If possible, a great way to handle the varying screen sizes is to design what is commonly referred to as "liquid pages." These pages grow and shrink as the browser window is extended and condensed. Sites built with liquid pages always seem to fill the browser window (magically, of course), and empty space never appears around a design as shown in Figure 3-5.

Compare Figures 3-6 and 3-7 to see how liquid pages grow according to the size of the browser window. If you visit **www.amazon.com** in your own browser, you can experiment with the browser window size to see this in action. You'll notice a limit to the shrinking. Most sites with liquid pages do have a minimum width set in the code, to make sure the page elements do not move around on the page and "break" the layout. For example, the Amazon site will not shrink below 1000 pixels. If you do reduce the size of your browser window below 1000 pixels wide, you will end up with a horizontal scroll bar.

NOTE

If your site is particularly text heavy, you may want to avoid liquid pages, because these pages can grow so large that the lines of body copy become too long to be readable. If you decide to move forward with liquid pages for a text-heavy site, consider using the `max-width` property in your code to set a maximum width for each column. (This is discussed more in Chapter 9.)

Figure 3-6 This page is built for 1000 pixels of horizontal space, but it is capable of growing according to the browser's window size.

Detect the user's screen area and serve a different version of the page according to that user's needs. Another way to deal with the inconsistent screen area is to build separate versions of your page (usually through custom style sheets, which I'll get to a bit later). You can then use a technology like JavaScript to detect the user's screen area when he enters the site and display the correct style sheet for his screen area.

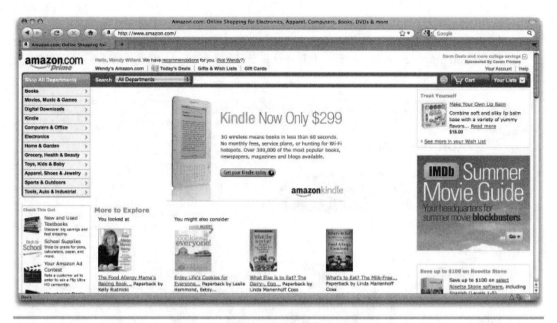

Figure 3-7 When expanded beyond 1000 pixels in width, the page elements grow to fill the available space.

This method can be time-intensive, because you must create and test multiple versions of your code. However, it can be particularly effective for sites designed for a particular screen area that don't fare well when viewed in alternative situations.

In the end, you (as the designer) need to decide up front how you will handle the width of the page so you can design an appropriate layout.

Code

The most basic method of coding web pages is HTML. If you've used any HTML, you might have already noticed the code has some restrictions and limitations that can affect the way graphics are used on a page. For example, all graphics in a web page must be contained in a rectangular "box," even if that box isn't readily apparent to viewers. Any text flowing around a graphic must either follow the rectangular shape of the box or be contained within the graphic.

Without understanding these limitations, you'll find it hard to create web graphics that will work in an HTML page. This is especially true because graphics editors enable you to mix text and graphics. A layout like this one is entirely possible in a graphics editor:

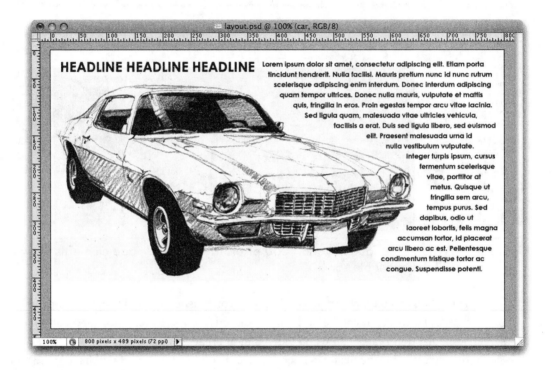

While this layout is easy to achieve in a print layout, it is more complicated in a web design. Those with HTML experience recognize that this layout isn't possible using standard HTML, unless the text itself is contained within that graphic (which isn't usually the best method of applying body text to a web page, but more on that later). A more suitable layout using the same text and graphic might be the following:

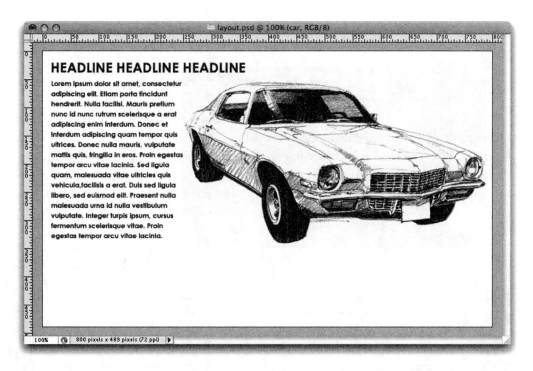

Whenever you create your own web graphics, it's important to remember the limitations and possibilities of HTML presented in this book. As your skills (or those of your team) increase, you will find creative ways to achieve more complex layouts.

Browsers

While the most popular browser might be Internet Explorer, many other browsers are in use by web surfers. Firefox in particular has gained significant ground in recent years. Web sites such as CNET's **www.browsers.com** list lots of other browsers, such as Safari, Google Chrome, Opera, NetCaptor, NetPositive, Lynx, iCab, and NeoPlanet. All told, **www.browsers.com** lists more than 200 different versions of browsers, the vast majority of which are free to download.

What does this mean to you as a web developer? That depends. As I mentioned, knowing your audience affects more than just your marketing plan. It affects which browsers you build the site for and why. Because it's ultimately the browser creator's decision on which tags to support, you might find that some browsers display your pages much differently from others.

In fact, some of the alternative browsers are text-only browsers, created for systems incapable of displaying graphics. Anyone using these browsers won't be able to see the graphics you include on your web pages. Because of this, remember that if the most important information on your site is shown in graphics, alternative text-only versions should also be made available. Figure 3-8 shows a page viewed without the graphics.

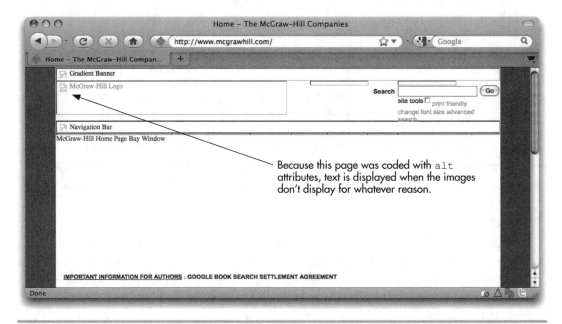

Figure 3-8 When this page is viewed with graphics turned off, empty spaces appear where the graphics should be. Whenever alternative text is included using the **alt** attribute, users will have an idea of what the graphic displayed.

Remember the following when you're designing web graphics for different browsers:

- **Use standard HTML tags**   As you learn HTML, you'll sometimes encounter tags that aren't supported by all browsers. While in some cases using these proprietary tags might be considered acceptable, you shouldn't do so if you are trying to reach the widest possible audience. Try to stick with standard HTML tags recognized by the World Wide Web Consortium, or W3C (**www.w3.org**), and you'll be better positioned to reach the most people.

- **Provide alternatives**   Whether this means coding your pages with the `alt` attributes for those who can't view images or including different ways of accessing the information, providing alternative means of navigating and viewing your site is important. This is especially true for anyone accessing your page from web-enabled phones and personal digital assistants (PDAs).

- **Test, test, test**   Don't settle for viewing your pages in only Internet Explorer on your personal computer. Go to your neighbor's house or your office computer and view the pages there. You'll undoubtedly find differences you may or may not appreciate.

NOTE

Don't forget web-enabled mobile phones! While the iPhone uses Apple's Safari browser, other phones use their own (phone-only) browsers. If your site expects frequent visitors using mobile phones, make sure to test your graphics from web-enabled phones. (And if it means you need to talk your boss into getting you a new phone—for "testing" purposes—why not?)

For additional resources on browser differences, visit either of the following web sites:

- **www.browsers.com**   CNET downloads

- **http://dir.yahoo.com/Computers_and_Internet/Software/Internet/World_Wide_Web/Browsers/**   Yahoo! Directory

Color

A big consideration for those developing web graphics is color. While graphics created for the printed page look relatively the same to all who view them, web graphics may look vastly different from one computer to the next.

NOTE

All color used in screen-based designs is created with the RGB (red, green, blue) color palette, as opposed to the print-standard CMYK (cyan, magenta, yellow, black) palette.

This variation in color can be caused by differences in system color palettes, as well as lighting and gamma issues related to the user's monitor. In fact, only 216 colors will display uniformly across all Mac and Windows systems (but even these colors can be affected by lighting and gamma issues). Those 216 colors are commonly referred to as "web-safe" colors.

TIP

Refer to www.visibone.com/color/chart_847.gif for a visual representation of a web-safe color chart, complete with RGB and HTML values for each color.

In the past, web designers were leery of using anything but web-safe colors, fearing their choices wouldn't be available on every user's operating system. When colors weren't available, the browser sometimes displayed those areas of the page with completely different colors. This often caused web pages to look awful on some systems (even though they were beautiful on others). But as computer systems and monitors have gotten better, the risk that web users will not be able to see a particular color on a web page has decreased. Because of this, most web designers now ignore the web-safe palette altogether, in favor of whatever color looks best.

However, if you find you do need to render a specific color to look *exactly* the same on as many systems as possible, consider using a web-safe color. You can create a web-safe color in any graphics editor by altering the red, green, and blue values to those shown on this chart: **www.visibone.com/color/chart_847.gif**. To make things easier, you can also load premade web-safe color swatches into most graphics editors. These color swatches are often called *CLUTS,* short for *color lookup tables.* You can find several different CLUTS for use in many graphics programs on VisiBone's web site at **www.visibone.com/swatches**.

Bandwidth

Another big difference between graphics created for the Web and those created for virtually any other medium is bandwidth. The term *bandwidth* refers to the speed at which web users access the Internet. Users who log on to the Internet from computers using telephone modem connections offer access at speeds of 28.8 to 56 Kbps (kilobits per second), while cable and DSL (digital subscriber line) users' speeds increase significantly to an average of 2 to 3 Mbps (megabits per second) (2000–3000 Kbps). Because people visiting your web site will probably be doing so with many different access speeds, you must design your graphics accordingly.

The biggest issue related to bandwidth is file size. The larger the size of your graphics files on your web pages, the longer they'll take to download onto a user's screen. Whenever I ask my friends or family how long they're willing to wait for pages to download on the Internet, they usually give their answer in seconds as opposed to minutes. It's true that most of us are quick to click that mouse button and zoom off to a new web site if the current one takes more than a few seconds to download. This means the graphics files used on your web pages need to be quite small.

Determining File Size

So exactly how small is *small*? Let's use a 56 Kbps modem connection as our example. A 56 Kbps modem will download about 7000 keystrokes of information per second. That translates to about 2.5 single-spaced typewritten pages of text, or about 6–7 kilobytes (K) of web content per second.

As you know, web pages consist of text and images. To estimate the size of a web page, you have to add together the sizes of the text (the HTML file) and the images (the GIFs and JPEGs). Using the preceding approximation, a page totaling 30K in content might take 5 seconds to download on a 56 Kbps modem. Table 3-1 shows the best download speeds per second for the most common connection types.

If you're creating web pages for the general public, a good rule of thumb is to limit your main content pages to around 100K in total size. HTML files usually weigh in at about 1–3K, so that leaves just under 100K for other content such as graphics. This guideline can often restrict you to using the most important and necessary graphics on a page. There will always be exceptions to this, particularly for pages with a designer's portfolio or a video archive.

Connection Type	Average Download per Second
T1/T3 network	40,000 Kbps+
FIOS	5,000–30,000 Kbps
Cable/DSL/Mobile 3G (stationary)	2,000–5,000 Kbps
Mobile 3G (moving)	350 Kbps
56 Kbps modem	6–7 Kbps

Table 3-1 Average Download Speeds for Popular Connection Types

NOTE

To put things into perspective, consider that a floppy disk (remember those?) holds 1.4MB, or about 1400K, of data. A CD typically holds 700MB, or 7000K, of data.

You can determine the actual file size of an image in several ways. Many graphics editors display the file size and approximate download speed right within the program. For example, Figure 3-9 shows how the size of a web graphic is displayed within Photoshop's Save For Web feature. (If you do the math yourself, you will see that Adobe is giving you the worst-case scenario for each download speed.)

TIP

Internet Explorer 7 users can right-click a graphic to view its size.

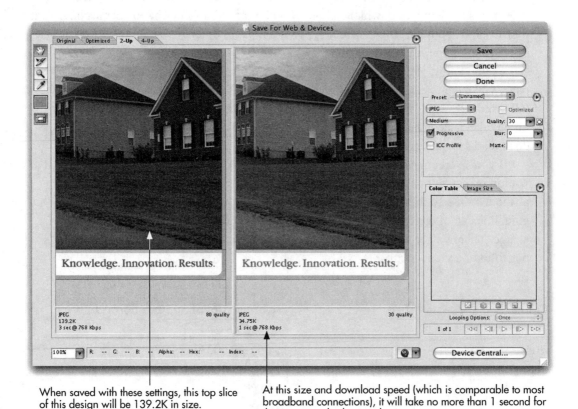

When saved with these settings, this top slice of this design will be 139.2K in size.

At this size and download speed (which is comparable to most broadband connections), it will take no more than 1 second for this image to display in a browser.

Figure 3-9 In Photoshop's Save For Web feature, you can see the file's size and approximate download time.

With all this talk about best download speeds, I must warn you that many things might cause a connection to be slower at any given time. Just as detours can happen when you drive somewhere, detours can also occur in the route taken from your computer to the one housing a particular web site. So while you can use the numbers in Table 3-1 to give you an idea of how fast your page *might* download, remember that it could be significantly slower for some users.

And, as home and office access speeds move higher, we must not forget the mobile phone user! Use of web-enabled mobile phones has increased significantly in recent years, meaning more people are logging on to the Web from out in the middle of nowhere (can you hear me now?) with less than ideal connection speeds. While most web sites can't cater to such visitors with their primary home pages, large companies now commonly offer mobile users custom versions of their sites. Refer to Chapter 7 for tips on adding a "mobile-friendly" external style sheet to your site.

Ways to Reduce Image File Sizes

You can reduce the file sizes of your images in two ways:

- Reduce the actual height and width.
- Compress the image.

When you reduce the height or width of an image, you make it smaller in physical size and in file size. This can be accomplished by shrinking the entire image or by cropping it to show only a portion of the original.

TIP
Another way to reduce your overall page size is to remove images altogether. In some cases, you may find that a text solution works just as well, if not better.

If a file needs to remain at its original size, you might try compressing it instead. *File compression* refers to the way in which data is stored or packed. Just as different people can stuff more or less clothing into a single suitcase, different compression types can pack more or less data into a file.

Specific compression methods—GIFs, JPEGs, and PNGs—work best for web graphics. Chapter 5 discusses these file formats, and their compression methods, in further detail.

Fonts

Typography on the Web can be a bit of a tricky issue. The biggest obstacles typically encountered when mocking up text for a web page layout are font faces and sizes. In addition, you must also consider the styling of that text and how it's going to be translated into the final web page.

Text in a web page is typically created by one of two basic methods: HTML or images. When you visit a web site like **www.craigslist.org**, you see a page filled with HTML text. Compare that to a site like **www.apple.com**, which frequently uses image-based text. For example, consider Figure 3-10. Can you identify which text is HTML and which text is image-based?

Visit **www.apple.com/itunes** to see this page in your own browser. You can move your mouse around the screen to help answer my question. HTML text can be selected and highlighted, while text contained within an image cannot. If you right-click (CONTROL-click on a Mac) image-based text, you typically are presented with the option of viewing the image by itself to see exactly what it contains.

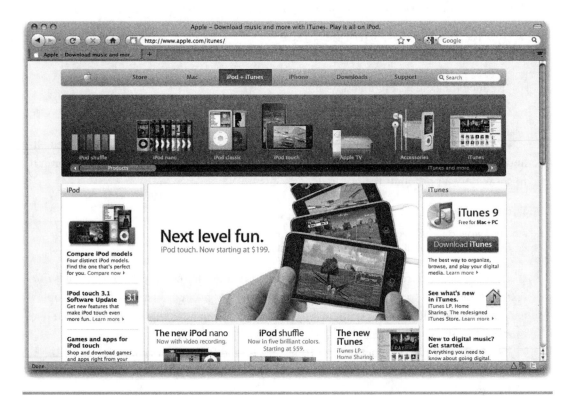

Figure 3-10 Can you identify which text was created with HTML and which is contained within an image?

When you create designs for web pages, you need to be aware of how the text will ultimately be added to the page. HTML text is limited to certain fonts, simply because the font must be installed and running on the user's system to be viewable on your pages on their screen. This means you can't specify that all of a site's body copy should be displayed in the Melanie font, because it's highly unlikely many people in your target audience will already have that font loaded on their systems.

Wondering which fonts you *can* use for any text that will be rendered by the browser? Table 3-2 lists the most popular fonts currently available.

Font Name	Example Text	Availability
Arial	ABCdefg 123456 !?@	At least 99% of Windows and Mac systems
Times New Roman	ABCdefg 123456 !?@	At least 98% of Windows and Mac systems
Verdana	ABCdefg 123456 !?@	At least 98% of Windows and Mac systems
Courier	ABCdefg 123456 !?@	At least 97% of Windows and Mac systems
Arial Black	**ABCdefg 123456 !?@**	At least 97% of Windows and Mac systems
Comic Sans MS	ABCdefg 123456 !?@	At least 96% of Windows and Mac systems
Courier New	ABCdefg 123456 !?@	At least 96% of Windows and Mac systems
Trebuchet MS	ABCdefg 123456 !?@	At least 96% of Windows and Mac systems
Georgia	ABCdefg 123456 !?@	At least 95% of Windows and Mac systems
Impact	**ABCdefg 123456 !?@**	At least 95% of Windows and 84% of Mac systems
Helvetica	ABCdefg 123456 !?@	At least 88% of Windows and 99% of Mac systems
Tahoma	ABCdefg 123456 !?@	At least 88% of Windows and 55% of Mac systems
Times	ABCdefg 123456 !?@	At least 87% of Windows and 99% of Mac systems
Arial Narrow	ABCdefg 123456 !?@	At least 84% of Windows and Mac systems
Century Gothic	ABCdefg 123456 !?@	At least 80% of Windows and 60% of Mac systems

Table 3-2   Popular and Widely Supported Web Fonts

Ask the Expert

Q: If I want to use a font that is not listed in Table 3-2, what are my options?

A: Great question. Say, for example, you're working on a web site for someone whose logo contains a fairly unique font not normally found on most users' systems. You should definitely include the logo as an image, to ensure that it displays consistently across the widest possible audience. But you would never want to include *all* the text on a site in images because that text wouldn't be searchable or accessible by non–image-based browsers (such as those used by vision-impaired readers or some mobile phone browsers).

So does that mean you're limited only to the fonts listed in Table 3-2? For the bulk of the text on your site, yes. But you could use images for display text (such as titles and quotes) to add a little pizzazz to your pages. Image-based text does not require specific fonts to be loaded on an end user's system, because an image is essentially a "snapshot" of the text using the particular font. But images are harder to maintain and update because they must be edited with a graphics program and then reuploaded to the server.

Another option that is not yet widely used, but remains full of possibility, is a Flash-based font-replacement tool. Check out Mike Davidson's sIFR for one such tool that replaces plain browser text with text rendered in your typeface of choice, regardless of whether users have that font installed on their systems: **www.mikeindustries.com/blog/sifr**.

TIP

Having trouble trying to match a particular font you've seen before?
Try **http://new.myfonts.com/WhatTheFont** to help you figure out what font it is.

Even though you may be limited to certain fonts for HTML text, there's still plenty of room for creativity with fonts. Here are a few other places to go for fonts and font inspiration:

- **www.bvfonts.com**   BV Fonts
- **www.typophile.com**   Typophile
- **http://carsonified.com/blog/category/design/fonts**   Font archives at ThinkVitamin blog
- **www.youthedesigner.com/2009/06/10/18-fresh-font-designs**   YouTheDesigner Graphic Design Blog
- **www.dafont.com**   DaFont.com

Summary

This chapter outlined most of the unique aspects of web design, particularly those that impact your design decisions when working with screen-based media. The next chapter focuses more on the content of the page, as you move through the web design process.

Chapter 4

Laying the Groundwork for Good Design

Key Skills & Concepts

- Draw inspiration from successful and functional sites.

- Select an appropriate navigation scheme.

- Identify appropriate visual metaphors for your site's navigation.

- Create a useable layout for your site.

- Design appealing and complementary color schemes for your site.

- Find images.

- Create mockups of your site.

A s you move through the design process, you must keep in mind all the business knowledge you gathered at the start of the project. The idea is to translate your team's written solution to the client's needs into your visual designs, without letting your own personal design preferences (with regard to color and other factors) get in the way.

This chapter, like Chapter 3, gives you some guidelines to help keep you focused on managing the client needs with the user's best interest. It starts with some tips on finding inspiration, and then moves on to creating a navigation scheme and coordinating design metaphors.

Inspiration

Whenever I sit down to design a new site, I like to spend some time researching similar sites to see what the competition is up to. But that's not always very inspiring, so I visit a few other sites purely for some inspiration. Before I discuss navigation and design metaphors, here are a few all-encompassing sites you might consider for inspiration:

- Design organizations and magazines
  - **www.veer.com**
  - **www.smashingmagazine.com/category/showcase/**
  - **http://thedesignmag.com/category/inspiration**

- Design collections
    - **http://patterntap.com**
    - **www.designmeltdown.com**
    - **www.webcreme.com**

Navigation

Selecting the navigation for your site is twofold. First you determine the navigation scheme—how the pages relate to each other. Then you choose the visual metaphor used to aid the user in making the jump from page to page.

Selecting a Navigation Scheme

Essentially, a navigation scheme determines which links go on each page of the site and how each page relates to others. How do you decide which scheme to use? First, you need to review the purpose and content of each type of page on the site, because these things should drive the navigation.

You can start by considering all the links your home page needs to include. Not every page on a site needs to be accessible from the home page, so you must figure out which ones must be included, and then of those, which are most important. You can usually divide the links into levels of navigation: primary, secondary, and tertiary or supporting.

Primary navigation is typically included on every page of the site. These are the most important links that must be accessible everywhere. Secondary navigation commonly houses the department-level navigation that is included only in certain sections of the site. Finally, tertiary or other supporting navigation levels might include miscellaneous pages that don't clearly fit into the department-level navigation, but aren't important enough (based on the page's purpose in the site) to include in the primary navigation.

The following illustration shows how this might play out on a page requiring three different levels of navigation:

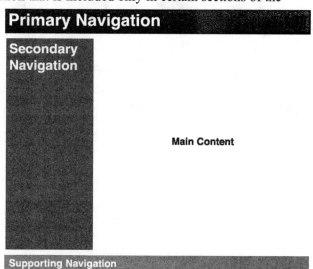

Complex web sites often include many levels of navigation on the same page. The trick is getting them all to work together to offer plenty of options to the user without being overwhelming. Let's look at two screen captures to see how this works. Figure 4-1 shows a page from Amazon.com.

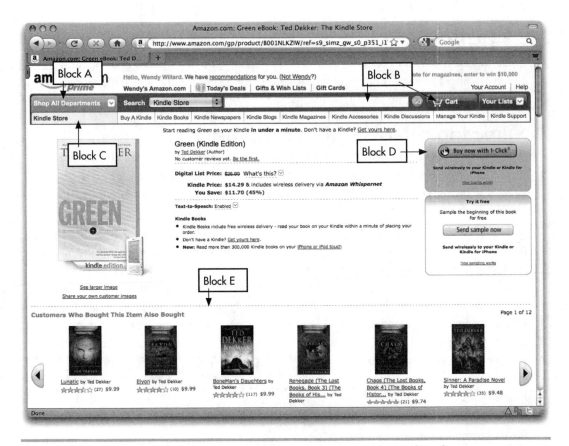

Figure 4-1 Amazon.com home page with navigation blocks outlined

I've outlined a few key areas of navigation, to make it easier to discuss:

- Block A links to all the departments on the site. This is the "hierarchical navigation block" that links to the site's structure (since this site is primarily organized by department). For this web site, the hierarchical navigation block acts as the primary method of navigation.

- Block B is what I call the "dynamic navigation block," because the resulting pages (search results, cart contents, and so on) are different for each visitor. On Amazon. com, dynamic navigation is a secondary navigation method.

- Block C is commonly referred to as "local navigation," in that those links are local to the particular section currently being browsed (in this case, the Kindle Store). Note that these links will not appear when another section of the site is being viewed. This e-commerce site depends on its local navigation as an important tertiary method of navigation.

- Block D shows shortcut navigation, which offers one-click access to essential functions of the site. For Amazon, the Buy Now button is perhaps the most important link available. Shortcut links are typically included in a variety of places on the site and don't live in just one department or section.

- Block E, reference or related navigation, is a different type of navigation that is custom to each page, as related content is pulled from a database behind the scenes. For the Amazon page, that's a display of items that other customers also bought after purchasing the book currently being viewed.

TIP

Reference and shortcut navigation are also typically sprinkled throughout the text content of a site. On the Amazon.com page, notice that users can click the author's name to see a list of his books (related navigation) or click a link to write a customer review (shortcut navigation).

Additional types of navigation blocks might include the following:

- **Header/footer navigation** This type of navigation typically houses less important, but still essential, links to content such as copyright and privacy information. In Figure 4-1, you can see a header navigation area in the upper-right corner of the screen that holds links to your account and help.

- **Breadcrumb navigation** Sites with deep local navigation often use "breadcrumb trails" to help orient users and provide easy access to pages along their path in the site.

Take a look at Figure 4-2 to see breadcrumb navigation in action near the top of the page. The main navigation includes links to all the top-level sections of the site. To get to the page shown, I clicked Get Involved. Next, I clicked a link on the Get Involved page called Activities & Volunteering.

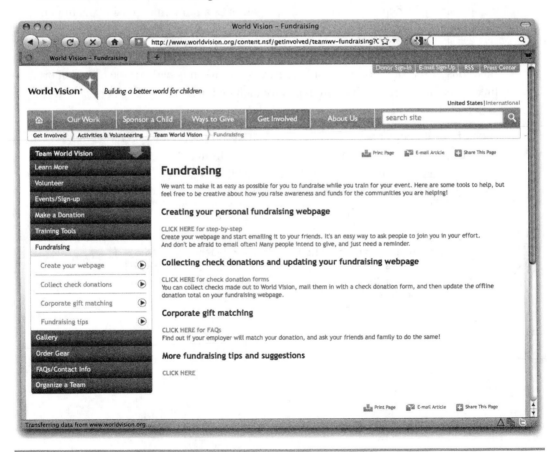

Figure 4-2 This site uses breadcrumb trails as an important method of navigation, as well as to orient the user.

The way this site is structured, I no longer have access to the Activities & Volunteering page in the primary (top navigation bar) or secondary (side bar) navigation. So the only way to access the Activities & Volunteering page is through the breadcrumb navigation displayed just under the primary navigation bar.

Indeed, you can see the shortest trip up the hierarchy to the home page, by reviewing the breadcrumb trail: Get Involved > Activities & Volunteering > Team World Vision > Fundraising. Each of those page names is clickable to allow easy access back up the trail.

Whew! We've just looked through a ton of different levels of navigation. Hopefully, the first site you create will be a bit less complex to allow you to get a handle on this whole navigation thing. Now, to help you continue building your web site, consider the visual representation of the various levels of navigation on your pages.

Choosing Visual Metaphors to Support the Navigation Scheme

Creative navigation *can* be a good thing, but it can also be bad for business. You see, web users understand how certain navigation metaphors work. Things such as underlined text links and tabs work well because everyone understands these as things you can click for more content. Visit **www.alexa.com/topsites** and take a look at the most popular web sites. You'll probably see a lot of the same types of visual navigation metaphors—stuff like this:

- Tabs
- Vertical navigation bars docked to the left side of the screen, with each link on a separate line
- Horizontal navigation bars docked to the top of the screen, with links separated by characters such as the pipe (|), dash (-), bullet (•), and forward slash (/)
- Graphical buttons
- Text directory of links
- Inline text links that appear within the content itself
- Form elements, such as drop-down menus and search boxes
- Collapsible and flyout menus, where clicking a closed section opens it and reveals additional links
- Tag clouds—check out **http://en.wikipedia.org/wiki/Tag_cloud** for a visual explanation of these
- Sliders, which are something like product navigation bar at the top of **www.apple.com/itunes**

TIP

Visit **http://patterntap.com/tap/collection/navigation** for a whole slew of creative navigation ideas.

However, just because lots of sites do something doesn't necessarily mean it's a good thing. For example, while visiting these sites, I noticed several places where text links weren't underlined. I've heard many designers say that if we all turned off the underlines, the web would *look* so much better. Whether or not that's true, *looks* aren't the point of the web.

Instead, web users have come to consider underlined text links as a convention that they can depend on to help them easily recognize what to click. Turning those underlines off not only undermines that convention, but also reduces the usability of the page, all to make the page look a little prettier. I encourage you not to fall into this trap.

Much research has been completed to study the usability of many of these visual navigation methods. Search for "usability of different navigation methods" in Google and you will see a large number of studies to review. In the end, your site's success can be made or ruined by the choice of navigation.

To ensure as much success as possible, I suggest you review all your options and come up with a few promising concepts for navigation to present to your client and potential users. See which method(s) works the best among a few key members of your target audience before committing yourself to one. Then you can move on to the rest of the design process with confidence.

NOTE

Refer to Chapter 12 for tips on conducting usability studies with members of your site's target audience.

Layout

Which comes first—the layout or the navigation? It's the same as the old chicken and egg debate. Ultimately, you want both elements to fit together seamlessly to create an appealing, user-friendly page for your client.

A good web layout addresses the user's needs, while fulfilling the site owner's goals. Obviously, this can be done in a wide variety of ways, so there is no one "right" way to lay out a web page. But here are a few guidelines for you to consider:

- Provide consistent navigation (as discussed in the preceding section).
- Keep content accessible and relevant.

- Orient the user (help the user recognize what page he's viewing within your site's structure), usually with a relevant page title.
- Maintain an appropriate content hierarchy.

Let's spend a few paragraphs discussing the last guideline.

Content Hierarchy

As has often been stated on the Web, content is king. Indeed, the most important thing you can give your users is reliable, relevant, up-to-date content. With this being the case, the content should be the first priority within the structure of the page, and it should always serve to achieve the business objectives for that page and the entire site.

I remember my graphic design instructors in art school repeating this over and over again: "What's the first thing you want viewers to notice on your page?" That should be the same question you ask yourself when you develop the content structure for web pages.

TIP
View similar web sites with fresh eyes and quickly record the first three things you see on the page. Do these match up with what you believe are the goals of the site?

Remember that, as the designer, you're in the driver's seat when it comes to prioritizing what users see on the page. While it might be tempting to make every element on the page animated, moving, glowing, or brightly colored, use these extras sparingly. Usability study after usability study shows viewers are drawn to the real meat of the site, much more than the glitz and glamour, and it's the content that keeps them coming back.

To accomplish a successful content hierarchy, assign prioritization levels to each of the elements of the page, and then make sure those priorities stick when the page is designed. You might find it useful to line up each page element with the site goal it supports. That way, if you've prioritized the site goals, prioritization of the page elements is a snap.

Returning to the camp web site from Chapter 2, let's look again at the list of goals I compiled:

1. Increase public awareness of the organization and its services.

2. Sell the camp to potential campers (teenagers) and their parents.

3. Enable parents of campers to (virtually) participate in the camp experience.

4. Enable campers to sign up and purchase online.

5. Recruit camp staff.

6. Enable interested parties to support the organization through online donations and potential other means.

7. Facilitate communication between the organization and campers, parents, alumni, and interested parties.

8. Sell T-shirts, sweatshirts, hats, and other products branded by the organization.

While having goals for the entire web site is important, it's equally important that you have goals for each of the web pages within the site. As mentioned, if a page doesn't support a goal for your site, it might be best to remove it entirely or reorganize it so it supports a goal.

To that end, ask yourself, How will the site-wide goals apply specifically to the design of the home page, for example? You might have to come up with another list of secondary goals to help you achieve the original goals. Here are a few ideas as to how those page-specific goals might look:

- Orient users to the web site and business.

- Help users find related information.

- Distribute informative, relevant, and reliable content.

- Facilitate communication. Enable users to interact (with the company, each other, and so forth).

- Encourage users to make a business decision (such as buying a product).

Mapping out how the page elements support the site goals can be quite helpful. For example, Table 4-1 shows how these three things—page elements, site goals, and page goals—work together to give you an overall picture of the purpose of a web page. Notice that priority levels for the site goals are included in parentheses after each goal; these help determine the most important aspects of the home page as you begin developing the layout.

TIP

Looking for layout inspiration? Check out these sites: **www.designflavr.com**, **www.csszengarden.com**, and **www.cssremix.com**.

Home Page Element	Corresponding Site Goal(s)	Corresponding Page Goal(s)
Logo/name of organization	Increase public awareness of the organization and its services (#1).	Orient users to the web site and business.
Tag line (short phrase with mission statement)	Increase public awareness of the organization and its services (#1).	Orient users to the web site and business.
Navigation to main content areas	All site goals might be listed here, because users navigate to each of the areas served by those goals; as such, this takes on a higher level of importance.	Orient users to the web site and business. Help users find related information.
One large (or two or three small) photo(s) representing the organization	Sell the camp to potential campers (teenagers) and their parents (#2). Increase public awareness of the organization and its services (#1).	Distribute informative, relevant, and reliable content.
Copyright notice and privacy policy	Doesn't really support a site goal but states required, though lower in importance, legal information.	Distribute informative, relevant, and reliable content.
Contact information	Facilitate communication among the organization and campers, parents, alumni, and interested parties (#7).	Facilitate communication. Enable users to interact (with the company, each other, and so forth).
Camp news/highlights	Sell the camp to potential campers (teenagers) and their parents (#2). Recruit camp staff (#5). Enable parents of campers to (virtually) participate in the camp experience (#3).	Distribute informative, relevant, and reliable content. Depending on the type of news: Encourage users to make a business decision (such as buying a product or service).
Sign-up now link	Enable campers to sign up and purchase online (#4).	Encourage users to make a business decision. Enable users to interact with the company.

Table 4-1   Mapping Site Goals

Wireframes

Depending on the size and scope of the project, your next step might be to create wireframes to refine a page's navigation and content. Wireframes establish a site's flow and functionality, not its colors or graphics. When you're considering the entire project's timeline, you should create wireframes before any detailed design mockups.

Suppose you were asked to create a single landing page for a client who is embarking on a new e-mail marketing campaign. The client wants two paragraphs of text, plus a form where users can register for the promotion. Sounds simple enough, right?

Creating a wireframe for this project would likely reveal new functionality and answer questions the client (or designer) hadn't even thought to ask. Here's a wireframe showing the basic content of the proposed landing page. Look at this illustration as if it were an actual web page. What might you try to click? What might happen when you click or edit certain aspects of the page?

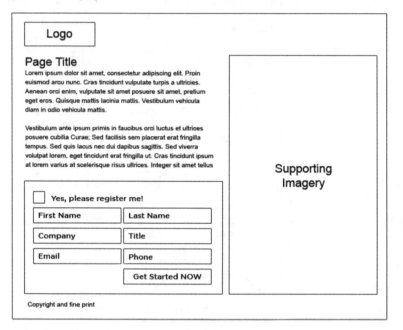

Here are a few things that came up when I presented a wireframe for a project very similar to this one:

- Many people expect the logo to be clickable. Upon asking the client about that, I found out the home page is under renovation through another design firm and they don't actually want to publicize the current site (good to know!). So the logo will not be linked.

- The check box in the form needs to be checked by default.

- What happens when you click the Get Started NOW button? Guess what? We need to create another page with additional information and a "thank you" to be presented to the visitor after this submit button is clicked.

- The client now realizes she doesn't want any empty forms sent through, so we need to add some form of validation to warn users who try to submit incomplete forms.

In the end, a simple addition to the flow chart (shown in the following illustration) clarified the functionality and flow in a way that satisfied both client and designer.

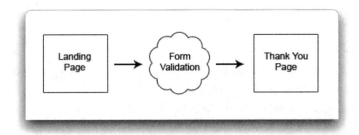

While this exercise gives you an idea of how a flow chart or wireframe might help a very small project, these documents can also be crucial to the success of large, complex projects. Figure 4-3 shows a more complex wireframe used to document a web application for PowerReviews customers. Notice the focus on functionality and usability.

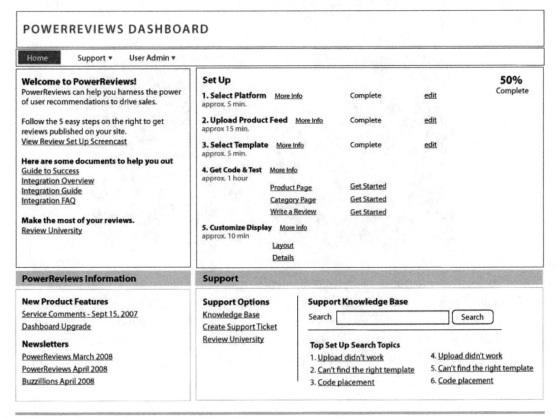

Figure 4-3 Wireframe for web application

You can find lots more examples of wireframes by searching for "wireframe example" in Google. Check out **www.gliffy.com/examples/wireframes** for a few samples to get you started.

Transitions

As you finalize your wireframes and continue work on the designs, don't forget about transitions. In web terminology, a transition occurs when the content changes. In other words, you are transitioning from one piece of content to another.

The most basic type of web transition is simple: the new content replaces the old content. Usually this means a new web page is displayed in place of the old one with little or no fanfare.

You've undoubtedly also experienced other types of web page transitions. For example, consider the mockup shown in the following illustration. The white "action box" in the center is displayed when the user clicks an alert button on the screen. Instead of the entire page changing, the main page is darkened and the white action box overlays the page with the necessary content.

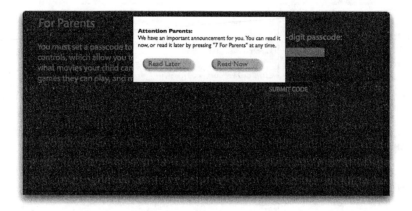

Another way to transition between content is to have the new content display as an inlay within the currently displayed page. So instead of replacing the page with a new one, the new content is added within a section of the existing page. If you have a Facebook account, you've seen this type of transition many times. For example, the next illustration shows a link to a YouTube video that I posted on Facebook.

Now here's what happens when someone clicks to view the video. Instead of the page switching to YouTube, the video becomes larger and plays right within the existing page.

Using custom transitions like these can be a great way to get content to your users faster and more successfully. I encourage you to be creative as you consider how users move between pieces of content, in an effort to get the information to the user in the most efficient and effective means possible.

Progress Check

It's time for a quick progress check. First, we talked about how projects typically get started, with the client posing a business problem (either formally with an RFP or informally) and you asking questions to clarify the need.

Next we saw the project progress as you learned how to formulate your response to the client's RFP, in the form of a project proposal. Proposals typically go through a couple of iterations until a contract and statement of work are finalized.

Your project may have many phases, but all projects require some sort of documentation to nail down the content and functionality of each page. Before you add color and other design details, you absolutely must remember how important it is for you to have the content and functionality approved by the client. This can be accomplished in various ways (such as spreadsheets, flow charts, or wireframes), as long as you present the information to the client in written form and get a signature of approval.

Color

Ahhh…color! I love color, be it on a web page, in my bedroom, or on a dinner plate. I suppose it's the "curse" of a designer. On the Web, just as in "the real world," color can make or break a design. These days, there aren't a whole lot of rules about color on the web (aside from those discussed in Chapter 3). Having said that, you should follow a few guidelines (if not rules).

Use the Right Amount of Color

In everything, moderation is best. Too much color causes the eye to dart around the screen searching for a place to rest, while not enough color can render the page boring and uninviting.

For example, consider Figure 4-4. When I took this screen capture, AirTran's home page consisted of three main colors: white, black, and blue. (The site may have changed since publication. Visit **www.airtran.com** to check it out in color.)

Without another accent color, nothing really "pops" when you view the page. You might even go so far as to say that all the content on the page feels equal in value, because the colors are so uniform.

Figure 4-4   This page could use a bit more color to help certain bits of content "pop."

Compare that to another page that also uses only three main colors (red, black, and white): ESPN's home page (Figure 4-5). (Visit **http://espn.go.com** to see the site in full color.) This site has a ton of content, which makes things pretty tricky for the designer. However, color is used rather well here to help move the user's eye around the busy page.

The gradation in the background of the ESPN site places prominence on the content at the top of the page, allowing the viewer to move from top to bottom smoothly. The light background in the Headlines section serves to bring a lot of contrast to that area of the screen, which in turn attracts the user's eye to the top stories.

Figure 4-5 Sample of a page that uses color to move the user's eye around the page

The large photo in the center of the screen focuses the eye and immediately grabs our attention. The headline below the photo is of equal important, given its stark contrast (white on black). Whenever you have a lot of photographic content, as the ESPN site does, it's wise to limit the amount of extraneous color used around the site. In this case, ESPN sticks with a single predominant color (red for the home page), which then lets the photographs really pop.

Use Adequate Contrast

Whatever colors you select, be sure the page offers enough contrast to allow any text to be readable. This is especially true when mixing hues with similar values. While it can be beautiful to mix a mid-tone blue with a mid-tone green, some people just won't see the difference.

So what creates contrast? Here are a few ideas:

- **Changes in hue**   Place a red box next to a yellow one, and you've achieved contrast because of the difference in hues.

- **Changes in value**   White text on a black background causes a distinct contrast because of the different values (shades) of the colors.

- **Changes in pattern**   A striped background next to a solid color background creates contrast because of the variation in pattern.

- **Changes in movement**   Good design moves your eyes around a page according to what's most important. Contrast in movement occurs when you design with the intention of gently moving the user's eye down the page, perhaps with a gradation of color, and then abruptly stop them with a different shape, filled with a different color.

Contrast can be good when it succeeds in helping you focus the user's attention; but it can be bad. Bad contrast typically happens when the designer loses focus on what's important—that is, creating a readable, user-centered site that fulfills its goals.

While we're talking about having a user-centered focus in color, let's touch on text backgrounds. While it is true many designers choose otherwise, white is the best color for text backgrounds. Let's face it: it is easier to read dark text on a light/white background than the opposite. While white text on dark/black backgrounds can be beautifully moving, this is not typically appropriate for large blocks of text. Therefore, I suggest sticking with light colored backgrounds for your main text areas.

TIP

To reiterate: Stick with white or light-colored backgrounds behind paragraphs of text whenever possible.

While large areas of text are easier read on light backgrounds, it can be quite beneficial to use dark backgrounds to add contrast and draw attention to smaller areas of text. We've already looked at one site that used contrast well, but here's another. Check out **www.jiffylube.com** to see Figure 4-6 in full color.

Figure 4-6 Sample of a page that uses contrast to draw attention

On its home page, Jiffy Lube uses light text on dark backgrounds to draw your eye to certain areas of the screen. The navigation bar jumps out because of the red gradation behind the text. Next, the photograph below the navigation area draws your eye because of its color and depth. Finally, the section headlines grab attention because of their contrast. These three areas serve to fulfill three major goals of the company's web site:

- Provide easy access to information about services.
- Educate viewers about promotions.
- Gain feedback from customers.

Accommodating Colorblind Users

Contrast is of particular interest to anyone who is colorblind. A few online tools will help you visualize what people who are colorblind see when viewing certain colors. Check out **www.newmanservices.com/colorblind/default.asp** to see one example. Or you can download a desktop-based tool to help you analyze the contrast of your designs: **www .stainlessvision.com/projects/colour-contrast-visualiser**.

TIP

To gauge whether your design has enough contrast, squint your eyes. Areas with little contrast blend together, while those with a lot of contrast still stand out. If your page passes the squint test, you can feel comfortable it has enough contrast.

If you're using a graphics editor such as Photoshop, one method of quickly checking the contrast of a design is to switch to the grayscale color mode temporarily. Viewing colors in grayscale can help identify problem areas. Another more low-tech method of spot-checking color contrast is to squint your eyes while looking at the design. Areas with little contrast tend to blur away when viewed with squinted eyes. While this may be OK for color meant only as a background texture, it's not appropriate for body copy or headlines.

Consider Color Meaning

I can't write a section about color without mentioning color meanings. While in art school, we studied why a live TV show has a "green room," and why McDonald's restaurants are typically red and yellow. Certain colors do evoke certain feelings and emotions. You can research the topic of color meaning online, but here is a quick glimpse as to what a few key colors help express in the United States (color meanings vary according to culture):

- **White**   Purity, innocence, cleanliness, goodness
- **Black**   Seriousness, negativity, death
- **Blue**   Stability, peace, trust, hope, youth, faith
- **Green**   Movement, nature, freshness, wealth, safety
- **Red**   Speed, action, courage, danger, power
- **Yellow**   Warmth, cheer, happiness, energy
- **Orange**   Fun, enthusiasm, attraction, stimulation
- **Purple**   Royalty, luxury, power, wisdom, romance

NOTE
Green is the most restful color for the human eye, which is why people paint rooms
meant to be relaxing green. Red, by contrast, has been shown to increase blood
pressure and heart rate, and it causes people to work (or eat) faster. It's probably
appropriate, then, that red is often used for error messages and warnings on the Web.

Create Harmonious Color Schemes

Rarely will you create a web design using a single color. But you will commonly be faced
with the task of finding multiple colors that work well together on the page. At the start of
any design project, I recommend spending quality time identifying an appropriate color
scheme (if one doesn't already exist that you're required to use).

I typically start by looking at the client's logo, branding, and any existing marketing
material whose style needs to be emulated on the web site. Then I play around with
various different colors in Photoshop until I'm happy with a certain theme. Next I save
the colors as a unique set of swatches in Photoshop, so I can easily access them any time.

TIP
Not sure how to save custom swatches in Photoshop? Check out this online tutorial:
www.photoshopessentials.com/basics/custom-swatches.

If you need some inspiration, you'll find a ton of online tools to help. Consider one of
the following to get you started:

- **www.colorschemedesigner.comr**
- **www.colourlovers.com**
- **http://kuler.adobe.com**
- **http://carsonified.com/blog/category/design/color/**

NOTE
If you like experimenting with color as much as I do, you might not want to visit any of
these sites when your schedule is tight. Consider yourself warned: these tools can be
addicting!

Here's a final word about color schemes: Avoid using the same colors for links
and other nonclickable aspects of the site. I suggest selecting one or two "clickable
colors" that are used only for linked elements. You can select link colors that are easily
identifiable and do not blend in with the rest of the page.

Use 3D Effects to Add Richness

As of this writing, many web designers are fond of using shadows and highlights to create three-dimensional effects. Apple familiarized one such effect, in which objects seem to be sitting on a glassy surface and projecting off the page. The following illustration shows what I mean:

Effects like this can be very effective when used appropriately and in moderation. In particular, 3D effects typically serve to achieve two things in web design.

- Add richness and depth
- Identify clickable objects

When elements appear to be three-dimensional, the user's eye is tricked into thinking the page is a multilayered environment. This draws attention and invites the user to read more and do more.

As with everything I've discussed in this chapter, moderation is key. If everything on the page appears to be three-dimensional, the effect loses the ability to grab the user's attention. Instead, a viewer might feel as though she is being screamed at (similar to using all capital letters in e-mail). But if one or two key elements appear 3D, it helps to focus the viewer's attention on those elements.

Navigation is one area where 3D effects are common. Because real-world buttons tend to be three-dimensional (such as buttons on a remote control), many designers add 3D effects to clickable web objects. This practice has become so commonplace that users frequently expect 3D shapes on web pages to be links.

You can also use 3D effects in navigation to indicate a user's path. Apple's navigation provides a great example. The following illustration shows how a link within the navigation bar appears to be "pressed" when the user is currently visiting that section of the site.

TIP

Be aware of your light source when you're adding shadows and highlights to multiple elements on a page. Avoid a shadow that falls to the right of one image, and to the left of another image, unless it is believable.

Finding Stock Media

The use of photography and illustration can often add a sense of professionalism to a business web site, but many businesses don't have the budget to hire photographers or artists to do private work. If you're in this predicament, have no fear. Plenty of stock companies offer royalty-free photography and illustrations that can be used for almost any purpose, except for resale.

You can purchase entire CDs of photographs or illustrations with a particular theme at your local computer or office supply store. These CDs range in cost from $20 to $500, depending on the quality of the work and the type of license you're given.

You can also search online and purchase the rights to use an individual photograph or illustration. The costs vary according to how you plan to use it. For example, if you want to purchase the rights to use a photo only on your web site, you can expect to pay a minimal fee of as low as a few dollars (especially on sites like **http://istockphoto.com**). If, however, you want to use the same image in all your printed publications, as well as in any digital presentations, the fees typically start around $100 and go up from there.

You might also check the software licenses that came with your favorite graphics or presentation program. For instance, registered owners of Microsoft Office have access to Microsoft's free image and clipart gallery at **http://office.microsoft.com/clipart**.

TIP

You can even find stock video and audio and many stock companies, making it inexpensive to add multimedia to web sites of any budget.

When using any stock imagery, be sure to read the terms of use and license agreement carefully. While you may find free stock images, they are often restricted to noncommercial use only. Here are a few more places where you might find suitable stock media:

- www.shutterstock.com
- www.gettyimages.com
- www.fotosearch.com
- http://sxc.hu
- http://punchstock.com
- www.photos.com
- www.clipart.com

Creating Design Mockups

So far, I've talked a lot about lots of things to consider when creating your web designs. Once you're ready to start actually designing the style of the page, refer to any notes you took to verify the target audience, business goals, and client branding, as well as any wireframes that have been approved. You want to have all of that at the forefront of your mind as you start designing.

If for some reason you don't already have wireframes or flow charts to help you plan the layout and navigation scheme of your pages, consider creating small thumbnail sketches before working in Photoshop (such as those shown in the following illustration). I find that even when I'm going to create electronic documents, paper and pencil are sometimes still be the best way to plan a page's structure.

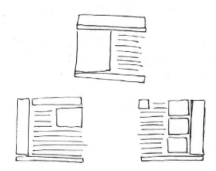

When creating small thumbnails like these, I try to focus on the blocks or chunks of information I'll be presenting, as opposed to the smaller aspects of each element. The idea is to create many of these block-level sketches to help envision how the page's focus might be divided. When you're doing this, keep those prioritization levels in mind, making sure the user's eye first moves to the most important elements.

When designing the page structure, think about how you look at a web page. You'll probably agree that you look in the center first, and then move your eyes around the page according to what jumps out at you. Other common first glances include the top-left portion of the screen (close to those back buttons!) and the right edge (near the scroll bar). Check out **www.useit.com/eyetracking** for some eye-tracking studies on where people look when viewing web pages.

After you've selected a sketch (or a few) to move forward with, you'll probably be ready to jump into whichever graphics tool you've selected. Remember to start off with a page size appropriate for your target audience, at 72 dpi (dots per inch).

Sharing Copies of Your Mockups

As you work on your mockups, you refine them until they've reached a point at which you feel comfortable seeking feedback from the client and/or other team members. Every team has its own method of managing mockups, from the very simple to the hugely complex.

As a freelancer, I typically create a page for each client on my personal web server, where I can store and track design mockups. Figure 4-7 shows an example of how I handled this for one client. The client could click the links to display each mockup within the browser to see how the final page will look surrounded by the browser chrome.

TIP

Always keep the final product in mind, because clients are probably looking at this page as if it were the final product before signing off or giving approval. Avoid showing clients mockups that don't accurately represent your idea of the final product.

Alternatively, you can use an online document or project management tool to share and manage not only your mockups but also any related client communication. Some popular packages include these:

- **www.basecamphq.com**   Basecamp
- **www.freelancesuite.com**   FreelanceSuite
- **http://projects.zoho.com**   Zoho Projects

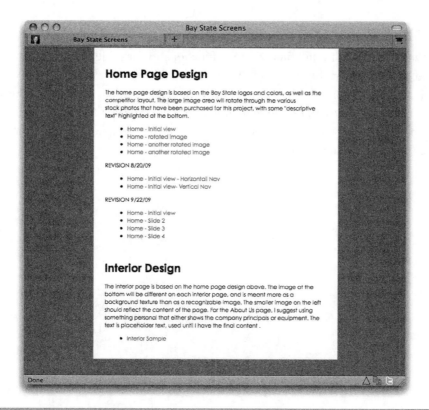

Figure 4-7   One way to share and manage copies of your mockups is through a simple page like this.

Finally, it might make sense to collaborate with clients and/or team members through a tool such as Google Docs (**docs.google.com**). One of my clients prefers to use this method of communication to track deliverables, tasks, and deadlines. We even use a shared spreadsheet for tasks. About nine team members have access to the spreadsheet, and we each can mark tasks as complete or add new to-dos. Best of all, it's free and requires no HTML coding for anyone involved.

Summary

This chapter moved through finalizing the functionality, navigation, and content of the site, and on to start the styling of that content. I hope Chapters 3 and 4 have given you plenty of concepts and ideas to help get your creative juices flowing. At this point, you probably want to spend some time in your preferred design tool working on your mockups. Whenever you're ready, continue on to the next chapter as we work to prepare your designs for production.

Chapter 5

Preparing for Production

Key Skills & Concepts

- Identify individual page elements for layout.
- Understand the differences among GIF, JPEG, and PNG files.
- Add interactivity to design files.
- Slice mockups for page production.

As you get ready to translate your designs into code, you still have a few key considerations to make. This chapter focuses on readying your pages for production by identifying individual page elements, adding interactivity (as needed), and slicing the designs. First, let's look at the different types of elements your pages might include.

Identifying Individual Page Elements for Layout

By now we've looked at the ideal sizes for web design, the best color mode, navigation schemes, and typography styles. I've told you it's usually beneficial to lay out a web page in a graphics program prior to coding the page. When doing so, you need to identify locations for all the aspects of the web page, whether each piece is ultimately going to be in the form of an image, a form field, multimedia such as Flash, or text rendered by the browser.

When you look at a typical web page, it might not be immediately discernable which parts are images and which aren't. Distinguishing between the two is important because they're treated differently when it comes to production.

To get a clearer picture of this, let's dissect a few screen captures from popular web sites. First, Figure 5-1 shows the ABC.com home page. At first glance, can you tell how this page was put together?

When you work with HTML (or most other types of coding), you designate various aspects of your page as images, text, form field elements, links, and so on. If you look at the page again with the images turned off in the browser (Figure 5-2), you can see which aspects of this page were saved by the designer as images. The words still visible are browser-based text, meaning they were typed into the web page code and not included in images.

Figure 5-1   ABC.com with images displayed

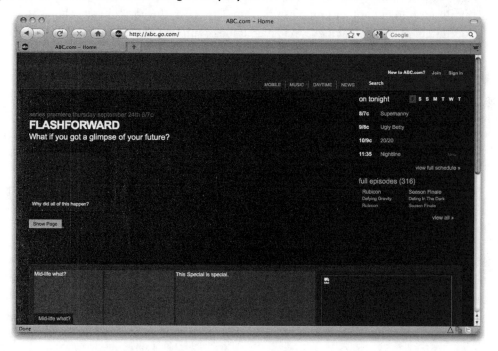

Figure 5-2   ABC.com with images disabled

TIP
To turn off the images in your browser, look under Firefox | Preferences | Content, or, in Internet Explorer, choose Tools | Internet Options | Advanced | Multimedia.

A few elements of this page may surprise you. First, while the tabs at the top contain text, they are actually images. When images are not displayed for any reason, those tabs are hidden. Even though the black space is still clickable, I doubt most users would know where to click for those three sections (Shows, Schedule, and Video).

Next, the Search box in the top-right corner appears to be a form field. It is indeed an editable form field, but the box itself has a background image that includes the little magnifying glass icon. Users can still enter search text even when the background image is not displayed, but they might not know where to type or how to click the search button.

These are the risks involved in using images for functional aspects of a page. With that said, you might wonder why someone would make something an image if it could easily be rendered by the browser instead. Several reasons exist:

- If text lies on top of, or is mixed with, a photograph or other graphic, it might need to be saved as an image along with that graphic. The reason is it can be difficult to consistently "layer" elements on a web page, even though it might be easy to do so in Photoshop or another graphics program. However, the abc.com site shows it is definitely possible to achieve the layered look with text placed on top of a photograph. (Consider the text listing tonight's shows on the right side of the screen, for example.)

- If you need text to be displayed with specific formatting, you may need to save it as an image. HTML text formatting is limited somewhat, mostly by the fonts available on the user's system (as discussed in Chapter 3.)

- If you want to display an element with a particular style not possible with HTML or CSS (cascading style sheets), you might need to save the style as an image and load it into the background of an element. An example of this is the Search box on the abc.com site. The outer glow and rounded edges are not possible with standard HTML and CSS, so the designer chose to include this style as a background image of the form element.

Let's take a look at another example to help identify how many web pages are put together. Figures 5-3 and 5-4 show the Macy's web site with and without images. The first thing you will probably notice when comparing these two screens is that the vast majority of the page is contained in three large images (the thin gray bar on the left side is one, the red bar across the top is another, and the large photo in the middle is the last).

Figure 5-3   Macys.com with images displayed

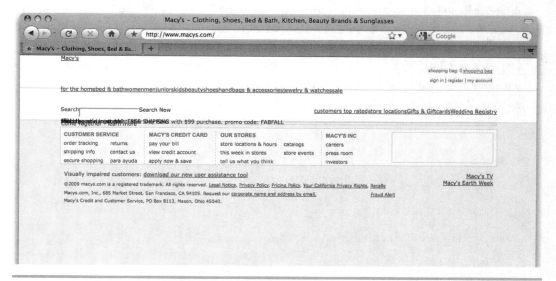

Figure 5-4   Macys.com with images disabled

Ask the Expert

Q: With the majority of users having broadband Internet connections, no one views web pages without images anymore. Why bother discussing the risks of using images on a web page?

A: While it is true that the majority of users have broadband Internet connections, there are new reasons to consider those viewing text-only web pages: mobile users. With the exception of the iPhone, many web-enabled mobile phones display web pages without images.

I do not advocate removing images from your web pages just because a few people access your pages with images turned off. Instead, I encourage you to be aware of how your page displays for those few users, and to make sure it does what might be referred to as "graceful degradation." In other words, you want to make sure the site doesn't break for those users, even if it is not as pretty.

This means you should always include alternate text (using the `alt` attribute, as discussed in later chapters) for your images, as well as create alternate versions of pages that become unusable without images.

You will also notice most of the shopping links are inaccessible without the images. Because the designer did not include height and width attributes to tell the browser how much space to allot to each image, the browser runs them all together. So even though the designer included alternate text that displays when the images don't, the lack of height and width attributes renders them unreadable (and therefore unusable).

A good addition to this site is the link for visually impaired customers. When the images don't display, this link is still accessible to provide visually impaired customers with an alternative view. Hopefully, Macy's will add an alternative view for mobile users as well (it was not available as of press time).

Contrast the Macy's site with Target's site (shown in Figures 5-5 and 5-6). Does it surprise you that the large image in the center displays even with images turned off? This image is part of a Flash animation, which means it displays as long as Flash is enabled in the browser (regardless of whether images are).

Notice how the structure of the Target page doesn't change when the images are turned off. This occurs because the designer has included the height and width of each image in the code. So the browser knows exactly how much space to save for each image, even if the image doesn't display.

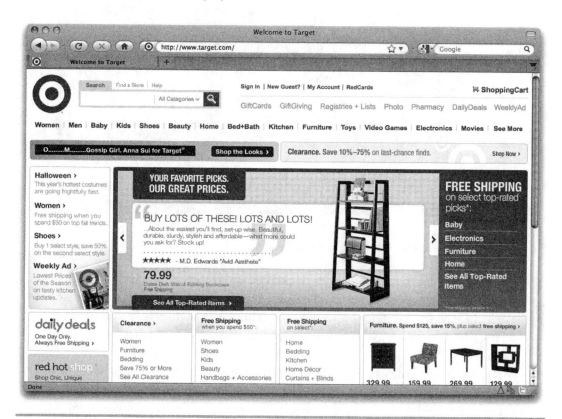

Figure 5-5   Target.com with images displayed

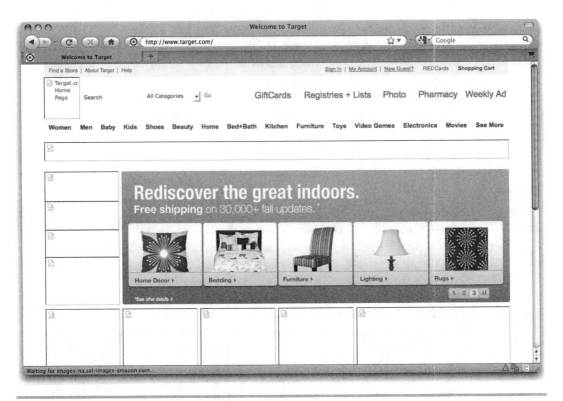

Figure 5-6　Target.com with images disabled

You might remember in an earlier chapter the screen capture (Figure 2-3 in Chapter 2) showing how the target.com site displays on a mobile phone. The target.com developers have included a special style sheet to customize how the site displays on tiny mobile screens. This is a great way to help your site "gracefully degrade" in less-than-optimal situations.

So how did these designers get from the complete mockups to the individual pieces and then to the final product? Keep reading. Now that you know a little about the types of elements you might have in your pages, let's focus for a few minutes on the three most popular image file formats.

Recognize Graphic File Formats for the Web

If you try to load a TIFF or PICT into your web page, users will see a broken image symbol. This occurs because graphics in web pages must be in a format understood by the web browser. The most popular graphics file formats recognized by web browsers are

GIF, JPEG, and PNG (Graphics Interchange Format, Joint Photographic Experts Group, and Portable Network Graphics).

Terminology

Before we dive into the actual file types, you need to learn a few terms that relate to web file formats.

Compression Methods

Web graphic file formats take your original image and compress it to make it smaller for web and e-mail delivery. Two basic types of compression methods are used for web graphics: lossy and lossless.

Lossy compression requires data to be removed—permanently—from the image to compress the file and make it smaller. Typically, areas with small details are lost as the level of lossy compression is increased. *Lossless* compression is the opposite of lossy, in that no data is lost when the file is compressed. In these cases, the actual data looks the same whether it's compressed or uncompressed.

Resolution

In an earlier chapter, you learned about monitor resolution, but in this case I'm referring specifically to file resolution. Whenever you create or edit a file in a graphics editor, you need to specify a file resolution (see Figure 5-7). The standard file resolution for web graphics is 72 *pixels per inch (ppi)*.

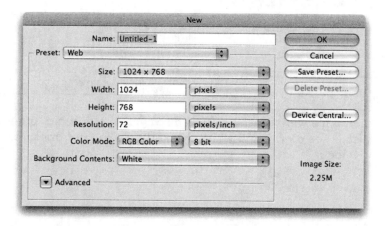

Figure 5-7   When working with web graphics, use a file resolution of 72 ppi.

NOTE
Don't be confused if you see *dpi* (dots per inch) used interchangeably with *ppi*. Technically speaking, dpi is more often linked to a printer's "dots per inch," while monitors are considered to have "pixels per inch."

Transparency

When you view an image and are able to *see through* parts of it, that image is said to have *transparency.* Some graphics editors show this transparency by displaying a gray and white checkerboard behind the image. Figure 5-8 shows an example of this in Photoshop.

When a web graphic contains transparency, the page's background color or background tile shows through in the transparent areas.

File types that support transparency fall into two categories: binary and variable. *Binary transparency* means any given pixel is either transparent or opaque. *Variable transparency,* also known as *alpha channel,* allows pixels to be partially transparent or partially opaque; therefore, it is capable of creating subtle gradations.

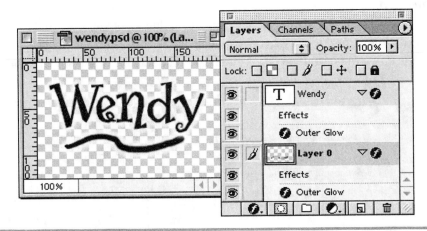

Figure 5-8 When a file with transparency is displayed in a graphics program, you typically see a gray and white checkerboard in the transparent areas of the image.

Certain file types don't support transparency. If the image shown in Figure 5-8 were to be saved in a file format not supporting transparency, the areas shown in a checkerboard would be filled in with a solid color.

Interlacing

Have you ever viewed a web page and noticed that a web graphic first appeared blocky or fuzzy before gradually coming into focus? *Interlacing* is a process by which the graphic is displayed at multiple levels of clarity, from blurry to clear.

Noninterlaced images must be fully loaded before the browser displays them on a page. If you have a large image on a page, users may see only blank space if the graphic takes a while to download. If it takes too long, users may leave your site.

NOTE

Some graphics programs use the term "progressive" when referring to JPEGs that use interlacing.

Because interlaced graphics appear more quickly, even if they appear fuzzy, users might be more willing to wait for the page to download fully. Ultimately, the choice in using interlaced or noninterlaced graphics depends on the size and style of the graphics on your page. I generally use interlacing for larger graphics that take up more space on the screen, as opposed to small buttons or icons that load quickly anyway. (Aside from download style, there is no other visible difference between interlaced and noninterlaced graphics.)

Animation

Some web file formats support animation as well as still images. These animation files contain two or more individual files called *animation frames.* The following illustration shows three frames of an animation. Notice that the position of the balloon changes from frame to frame.

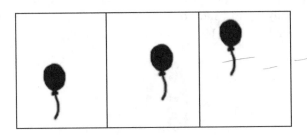

When the file is played back through the browser, viewers watch the various frames of the animation appear, one after the other. The rate at which the frames change can vary between a speedy filmstrip and a slowly blinking button. In the preceding example, the balloon appears to drift higher and higher with each frame.

The most common example of this type of animation—bitmap animation—is GIF animation. More robust animation tools use vectors instead of bitmaps. This means the animation is sent as a series of instructions instead of actual pixel renderings. The result is a much more fluid animation that downloads in a fraction of the time a similar bitmap animation would. Flash is the most common type of vector animation.

GIF

Originally designed for online use in the 1980s, GIF uses a compression method that is well suited to certain types of web graphics. This method, called *LZW compression,* is lossless and doesn't cause a loss of file data. However, several characteristics of GIFs restrict the type of files capable of being saved as GIFs. Table 5-1 lists these and other characteristics of the GIF file type.

NOTE

According to its creator, GIF is officially pronounced with a soft *g*. Because the word is an acronym, though, many people pronounce it with a hard *g*.

Because of these characteristics, the following types of images lend themselves to being saved as GIFs. Notice all of these are limited in colors.

- Text
- Line drawings
- Cartoons
- Flat-color graphics

TIP

The *g* in GIF gives you a hint about what types of images are best saved as GIFs: graphics (as opposed to photographs).

Characteristic	Description
Color mode	Restricted to no more than 256 exact colors (8-bit)
Compression method	Lossless
Animation	Supported
Transparency	Supported (binary only)
Interlacing	Supported

Table 5-1 GIF File Format Characteristics

Ask the Expert

Q: I noticed photographs aren't on this list. I've seen plenty of photographs used on web pages—can't they be saved as GIFs?

A: Images with photographic content shouldn't usually be saved as GIFs, unless they're part of an animation or require transparency. Other file types are more capable of compressing photographs. In fact, the JPEG file format was created specifically for photographs and shouldn't be used for other types of images such as flat-color graphics and text.

JPEG

The JPEG file format (pronounced *jay-peg*) was created by the Joint Photographic Experts Group, which sought to create a format more suitable for compressing photographic imagery. After reading Table 5-2, review Table 5-1 to compare JPEG's characteristics with those of GIFs.

One major difference between GIFs and JPEGs is that JPEGs don't contain an exact set of colors. When you save a photograph as a JPEG, you might consider all the colors in the file to be *recommended,* because the lossy compression might require some colors to be altered. In addition, all web JPEG files must be in the RGB (Red, Green, Blue) color mode, as opposed to the print standard—CMYK (Cyan, Magenta, Yellow, Black).

Characteristic	Description
Color mode	Displayed in 24-bit color, also called millions of colors. If the user's monitor isn't set to view 24-bit color, the file is displayed with as many colors as are available.
Compression method	Lossy
Animation	Not supported
Transparency	Not supported
Interlacing	Supported as progressive JPEGs

Table 5-2   JPEG File Format Characteristics

PNG

PNG, pronounced *ping,* is the newest and most flexible of these three graphics file formats. After looking at the list of characteristics for PNG in Table 5-3, you might think of PNG as being the best of both the GIF and JPEG formats.

TIP
The 32-bit color format is similar to 24-bit color because it also has millions of colors. However, 32-bit color also has a masking channel, which can be used for alpha transparency.

An additional benefit of PNG is its gamma correction. The PNG file format can correct for differences in how computers and monitors interpret color values.

One note of caution: While all these characteristics make PNG well suited for almost any type of web graphic, there is one drawback that has limited its use for some people— because it wasn't an original web file format, users of older browsers must download a plug-in to view web graphics saved in the PNG format. But as long as you test your use of PNG files thoroughly, and it performs to your satisfaction in all your target browsers, there's no reason you can't use this feature-packed format.

Choose the Best File Format for the Job

Now that you know a little about the different web graphics file formats, you're probably wondering how you might select the best format for the job. While I wish I could give you a foolproof method, the answer, ultimately, lies in your own testing.

Characteristic	Description
Color mode	Can be stored as 8-bit, 24-bit, or 32-bit
Compression method	Lossless
Animation	Not supported
Transparency	Supported (variable/alpha)
Interlacing	Supported (two-dimensional)

Table 5-3 PNG File Format Characteristics

Luckily, many of the popular graphics programs make this testing easy. For example, Photoshop and Fireworks enable you to compare how a single image might look when saved in any of these file formats. We'll look more closely at this feature in the next chapter, as we export images and HTML from Photoshop.

Adding Interactivity to Design Files

Interactivity has made the Web increasingly popular; it enables users to interact with the medium in ways previously impossible. On the Web, users can point-and-click their way around, forging new paths with each movement. Content is delivered specifically according to their likes and dislikes, as recorded by previous actions and inputs. Users are always contributing to the flow of information on the Internet. By contrast, traditional television and newspapers are primarily passive, in that users receive information and rarely contribute to it.

As you refine your mockups, keep the site's interactive elements in mind, working them into the designs wherever possible. While the possibilities are limited only by your imagination, following are a few of the most common types of interactivity you might consider in your mockups.

Rollovers

I'm sure you've encountered elements in web pages that change when your mouse interacts with them. We commonly refer to these elements as having *rollover effects*. A rollover can be as simple as a change of color, or more complex to include a new menu of options. For example, visit **www.anthemofhope.org/encouragement.html** in your web browser to see how a couple of these might play out. If you put your mouse over the Store link, you'll notice the background changes to give the appearance that the button has been pressed. But if you mouse over some of the other links in the top navigation bar, additional submenus appear.

To achieve rollover effects, the designer must create multiple sets of instructions in the HTML page, to tell the browser what to display when the mouse is in different positions on the page. If the images change upon interaction with the mouse, each version must be created and stored on the web server. (I'll go into more detail about how to create image-based rollovers in Chapter 10.)

What does this mean to you now? While designing your mockups, always consider whether any elements can have rollover effects. For those that do, create alternative versions of the mockup to show the desired effect. Compare Figures 5-9 and 5-10 to see how this was handled in a mockup for the Anthem of Hope site.

Figure 5-9 This shows a portion of the Anthem of Hope Donate page mockup, as it appears without any user interaction.

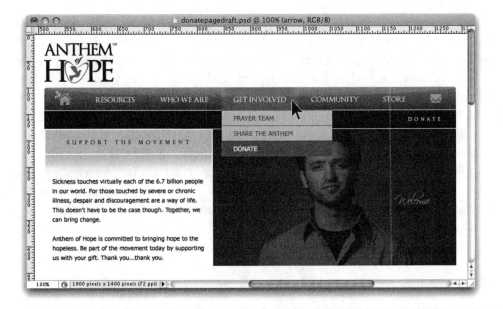

Figure 5-10 This shows the same screen and how it reacts to the user placing the mouse over the Get Involved button in the top navigation.

NOTE
For more comprehensive rollover effects, visit **www.istockphoto.com**. Then, search for "elephant." When the results are displayed, move your mouse over each photo and see what happens.

When the Anthem of Hope site was coded, the drop-down menus were built with text and code. In other words, even though they appear as images in the mockup, the final product is text. That's OK. At this point in the project process, you want to be able to show the client every design aspect of the final page. This way, you can gain approval while still in the mockup phase and avoid costly and time-consuming changes later in the project.

Form Elements

Likewise, if form elements will be included in the site, you want to add them to your mockups to gain client approval before the site goes to coding. You might initially think there isn't much to approve about form elements, but thanks to a little custom styling, you can actually achieve quite attractive and useful web forms.

I suggest you spend some time reviewing what is and isn't possible with regard to styling web forms. Table 5-4 outlines which common CSS styling options are possible with each type of form element.

Upon reviewing Table 5-4, you'll notice that text boxes and submit buttons are the only form elements that can be easily styled for a variety of browsers. Thankfully, these are the most common types of form elements used on web sites. Unfortunately for the rest of the form elements, they might look right in one browser, but they'll look completely different in most others.

In addition to the styling options shown in Table 5-4, you can also style the font (family, size, and color) for text displayed inside form elements. So when you create form elements within mockups, it's important to design them in a way that is possible to code. For check boxes and radio buttons (or other elements that can't be reliably styled across multiple browsers and platforms), I typically take a screen capture of the form element in an existing web site, and then place it in my mockup. This shows the client just how it will display when the page is coded.

TIP
Check boxes, radio buttons, and select menus are notorious for displaying differently depending on which browser and operating system is used. Know which browser and OS your client uses, so you can show form elements in your mockups as they will appear to the client.

Form Element	Add Background Color	Customize Borders	Alter Margins & Padding	Add Images
Text boxes (single-line)	Yes	Yes	Yes	Yes
Checkboxes	No	Yes	Yes	No*
Radio buttons	No	No	No	No*
Text areas (multiple-line text boxes)	Yes	Yes	Yes	Yes
Select (drop-down) menus	Sometimes	Sometimes	No	No*
Buttons (generic)	Yes	Yes	Yes	Yes
Submit buttons	Yes	Yes	Yes	Yes
File upload	Yes	No	No	No*

* There are ways to use your own custom images in place of these form elements, even if it's not possible with standard HTML and CSS. In most cases, you'll need some sort of client-side scripting (such as JavaScript) to accomplish this. For example, here's how one design firm used JavaScript to customize the radio buttons and checkboxes on a the Filament Group site: at www.filamentgroup.com, click the What We're Thinking link, and then look for the article entitled "Accessible, Custom Designed Checkbox and Radio Button Inputs Styled with CSS (and a dash of jQuery)."

Table 5-4 Styling form elements with CSS

The following illustration shows a form I included in a mockup for a recent project. You can see the styling decisions I made (and planned to translate into code), based on the way I designed the form elements in my mockup. (Notice the check box, which is actually a screen capture of a checked check box on a Mac using the Firefox browser, placed right into my mockup.)

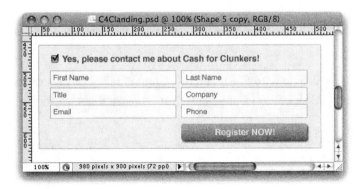

Now compare my mockup to the way the form appears in the actual coded web page. I was able to code the page so that it displayed just how it did in my mockup. This is the ideal situation for any designer—to move from mockup to coded page with no visible changes.

Animation

You can accomplish animation on the web in a variety of ways, but the most popular method is through Flash. Adobe Flash is a tool designed specifically to deliver animation and interactivity to web site visitors. Its vector format makes the process much more painless for visitors, because its file sizes are significantly smaller than many other similar formats. In addition, its streaming capabilities enable the files to be viewed while they're downloading, which is good because users can get to the actual content faster.

TIP
The term "Flash" can be used to refer to the Flash application (software), as well as the file format.

So what can you do with Flash? Plenty. Common uses of Flash include advertisements, navigation systems, movie previews/trailers, cartoons, training programs, and product demonstrations. In fact, many people build entire web sites in Flash. Those people typically are Flash developers, in that they have become highly skilled in working with the Flash software.

TIP

If you're new to web design, I suggest first becoming familiar with the basic web design process as I outline it (using a graphics program such as Photoshop and then coding with HTML). Once you become proficient with this process, you might move on to developing web content with Flash. I talk about this a bit more in the next chapter, when discussing page production.

GIF Animation

GIF animation is a much more basic form of web animation than Flash. While this makes GIF animation easy for even the beginning designer to develop, it also removes most of the interactivity.

As mentioned previously, an animated GIF is really just like a flipbook animation—in which multiple drawings are shown in succession quickly, to give the appearance of movement. To create a GIF animation, you need to design a series of images to serve as the individual frames of the animation. These frames can be created in any graphics program with web capabilities. Or you can use a custom GIF animation tool online, such as **www.picasion.com** or **www.gifup.com**.

Before Flash became popular, GIF animation was the only form of animation possible on the Web. However, as of this writing, GIF animation is used very infrequently. I mention it here just to keep you informed about different options.

Slicing the Designs

Now that you know a little about the major web file formats and how the individual page elements translate from design to coding, let's put your knowledge to a test by identifying how to slice a mockup. Figure 5-11 shows a mockup that is approved and ready for production. At this point, my next step is to slice the pieces that need to be saved as GIFs, JPEGs, or PNGs for the final coded page.

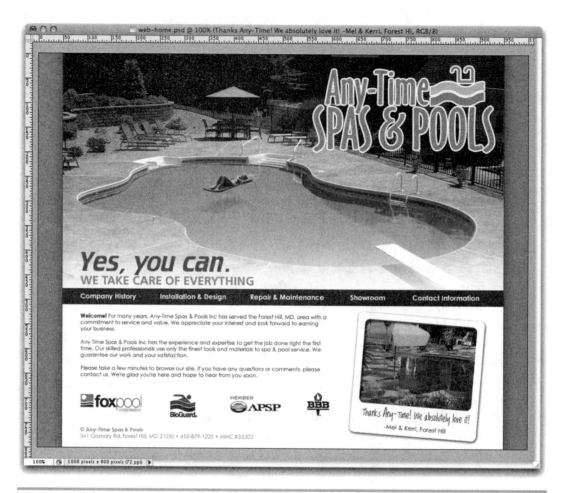

Figure 5-11 The approved mockup, ready to be sliced for production

When I designed this mockup, I tried to remember everything I knew about HTML, to make sure I wasn't designing something that would be impossible to implement. I kept all the individual elements on separate layers within Photoshop, to make things easy to change and move around later. If you're curious about how I used my layers, the next illustration shows a screen capture of my Photoshop Layers palette for this mockup.

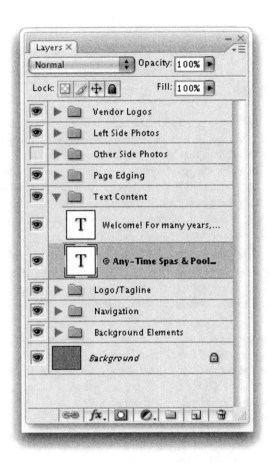

TIP

Group your layers together in file folders to avoid scrolling a long list of layers to find the one you need.

One thing that helps tremendously in planning the HTML layout of a page is the use of guides in Photoshop.

Ask the Expert

Q: Wait! I don't know HTML yet. How am I supposed to know what to remember when I design my mockup?

A: Well, I suppose this is where I tackle the unbeatable chicken-and-the-egg thing. In the web industry, the most successful web designers have a good handle on HTML before they ever design a page mockup. But that's why you're reading this book, right? I'm not saying you have to know it on an expert level, but you definitely should know what you can and can't accomplish in HTML to avoid designing pages that don't translate into code very well.

To help you along that path, you'll pick up some HTML starting in Chapter 7, if you don't already know it. Until then, consider the following list of dos and don'ts to make sure you're on the right track:

- *Remember that every image on your web page is, ultimately, saved in a rectangular box.* For example, you can't save a triangular-shaped GIF. All GIFs, JPEGs, and PNGs must have four sides and must be rectangles. You can use transparency to make things look like they aren't rectangular, but, in reality, everything is contained within some sort of box.

- *Because everything is contained in those boxes, you might need to break up some elements across several boxes to achieve a desired result.* These pieces likely are going to be put back together with HTML tables or CSS positioning. (I discuss these in later chapters.) Think of a table as a tic-tac-toe game, in which each element on the page is placed in a different square of the game. When you draw guides on your mockup, you're drawing the edges of those game squares.

- *Text is best.* Whenever you can achieve a desired result with straight HTML text, do it.

One final note—because teaching you HTML in full is beyond the scope of this book, I recommend you consider another resource, such as my book, *HTML: A Beginner's Guide* (McGraw-Hill), to learn it.

Q: Now that you mention it, I don't have graphic design experience either. How am I supposed to know what colors work together and stuff like that?

A: A web purist might say that color and graphic design principles have no place in a web design book, given that the primary purpose of the web is to disseminate information, not to make it pretty. Of course, every story has two sides, and I think a need exists for color and graphic design principles on the Web, in addition to the always-important information on architecture and navigation design.

Again, for me to teach you graphic design thoroughly in this book is impossible. I'd like to propose this: If you use the Web, you already know a bit about these concepts. Ask yourself, what works on the web sites I use most? You might find a particular layout helps you navigation a certain site, or perhaps a certain style lettering makes a headline easier to read than another.

Web design is all about making things work for the end user, so if you use the Web enough, you learn quickly what works and what doesn't. I think that's a pretty good place to start acquiring your "graphic design experience."

PS: If you want to go a more traditional route, you could always consider signing up for a graphic design or typography design course at a local university. Self-study options include the following:

- *Visual Literacy: A Conceptual Approach to Graphic Problem Solving* by Judith Wilde and Richard Wilde (Watson-Guptill Publishing, 2000)
- *The Non-Designer's Design Book* by Robin Williams (Peachpit Press, 2008)
- *Idea Index: Graphic Effects and Typography Treatments* by Jim Krause (North Light Books, 2000)
- *Envisioning Information* by Edward R. Tufte (Graphics Press, 1990)
- *Designing Visual Interfaces: Communication Oriented Techniques* by Kevin Mullet (Prentice Hall PTR/ Sun Microsystems Press, 1994)

Using Guides

Most graphics programs enable you to draw guides across an image. These guides can help you identify where each individual image begins and ends. For example, the following illustration shows how I drew some of my guides for the mockup shown in Figure 5-11.

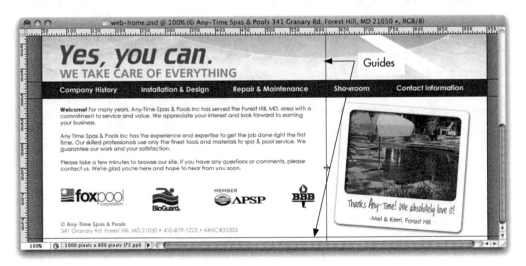

NOTE

Some programs call them guidelines, while others simply refer to them as guides.

When I drew these guides, I was attempting to determine how I'd break up this file into little GIFs and JPEGs. In addition, I was starting to lay the foundation for the final structure of the page that would be achieved with the code.

Identifying Slices

Wondering why we use slices at all? The answer lies in the fact that we're not saving the entire mockup as one big image and serving that up for the site's audience. On the contrary, some aspects of our mockups will be served as images and others will be created by the browser. Slicing enables us to save only the portion(s) of the mockup that need to be served as images, leaving other elements of the page to be created by the browser.

For example, in the case of my pool company mockup shown in Figure 5-11, I needed to save only a few elements as images, such as the large pool photo at the top (with the logo and tagline), the smaller pool image below the navigation, the vendor logos below the text, and the page shadows on either side of the background. Everything else was created by the browser (using color and text).

The specific steps necessary to create slices depend on which graphics editor is used. In Photoshop and Fireworks, the steps are essentially the same: you use the Slice tool to create slices. After selecting this tool from the tool palette, you draw boxes around each of the elements to define slice borders. Figure 5-12 shows the completed mockup, sliced and ready for production.

Notice how I keep mentioning that everything on a web page must fit into a "grid"? You can see this happening in Figure 5-12. I drew only eight slices on this page, but Photoshop displays at least eleven. The application basically fills in the gaps around my slices (which it refers to as "user-slices") with its own slices. We'll discuss those more in the next chapter, when we play around with exporting HTML and images from Photoshop.

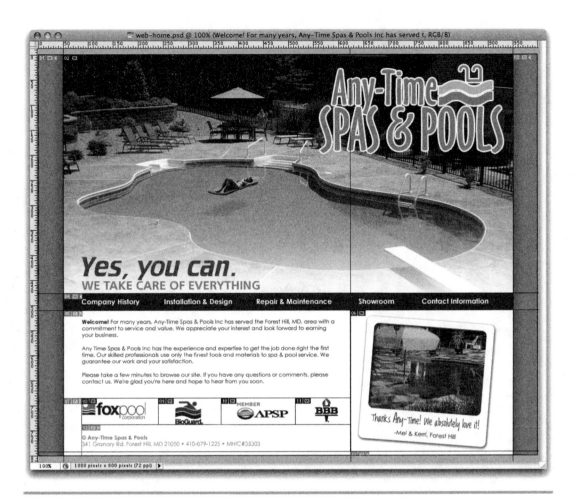

Figure 5-12   The mockup is sliced and ready for production

Summary

If you're moving through a your own web project while learning with this book, you should have finalized your page mockups by now. In a real-world project, all mockups must be approved by the client before you move the project into production. This helps prevent costly and time-consuming changes from being requested later in the project. Having said that, always keep layered copies of your mockups available, should the need arise for changes later.

The next chapter moves those mockups into production, where the individual images are saved and prepared for code. I'll also talk about moving mockups to Flash and saving HTML right out of your design application.

Chapter 6

Producing the Design

Key Skills & Concepts

- Save images from design applications
- Export whole designs
- Save HTML from design applications
- Use Flash
- Transfer Photoshop files to Flash

This chapter focuses on web design production, which may or may not be your job. In large teams, a designer may develop the mockups and work with them until they are approved before passing them off to someone else (perhaps another designer or developer) to save the individual pieces and start building the page in code. But for smaller teams, every aspect of the designs, from concept to completion, falls to the designer. Even if you aren't the person who will ultimately slice and produce your designs, it's important that you understand what's involved so you can successfully prepare your designs.

Saving Images from Design Applications

In Chapter 5, I discussed how each element of a web page must be saved (or created) independently for inclusion in the HTML file. When you move from mockup to code, this means you typically end up with several supporting files, along with your main HTML file.

The images, in particular, for a single HTML file can be quite numerous, depending on the layout of the page. Luckily, most web graphics applications make it easy to save multiple images at once. The next few sections outline how to save images in the most common web file formats: GIF, JPEG, and PNG. Then, we look at how to select the best file format for the job.

Save a GIF

When you save a file as a GIF in a graphics program, you have the option of saving your image with or without dithering. GIF color palettes have only a limited number of colors, and the fewer colors present, the smaller the file size. When you want to reduce the number of colors in the palette, the program must know what to do with the areas in your image that contain the colors you're removing.

TIP

Remember the *g* in GIF gives you a hint about what types of images are best saved as GIFs: graphics (as opposed to photographs).

If you tell the program to use dithering (you can specify any amount of dithering between 0 and 100%), it may use multiple colors in a checkerboard pattern in those areas to give the appearance of the color you removed. If no dithering is used, the removed colors are replaced with another solid color (see Figure 6-1). Dithering can be useful in providing the appearance of gradations or subtle color shifts—but be forewarned that it adds to the file size.

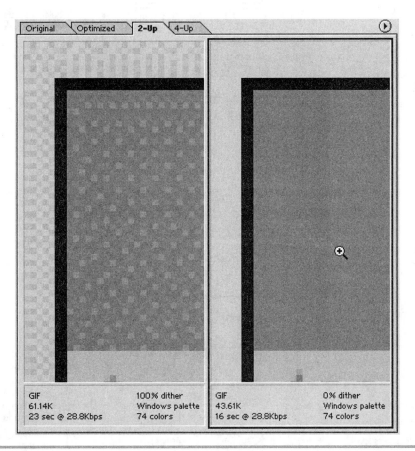

Figure 6-1   In this example, the graphic on the left is dithered, while the graphic on the right is not. The checkerboard pattern is a typical effect of dithering.

TIP

Few images actually need all 256 colors available in a GIF color palette. Try reducing the number of colors all the way down to 8 or 16, and work your way back up as high as you need to go to make the image look acceptable. This assures that you reach the minimum colors more easily than if you try to work from the most colors on down. Remember, the fewer colors in the palette, the smaller the file size.

The following two illustrations show the GIF settings typical in Photoshop and Fireworks, respectively.

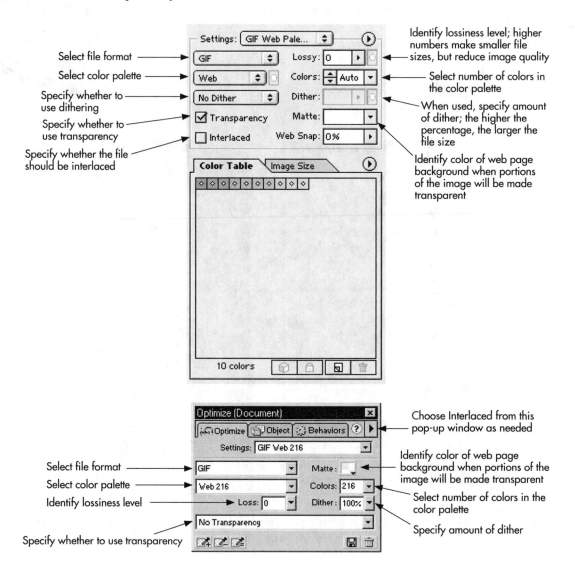

Save a JPEG

When you save an image as a JPEG, you choose between several different quality levels. The highest quality JPEG has the least amount of compression and, therefore, the least amount of data removed. The lowest quality JPEG has the most data removed and often looks blotchy, blurry, and rough. I usually save JPEG images with a medium quality. Your decision will be based on the lowest quality you can use without compromising the integrity of the file: the lower the quality level, the lower the file size.

JPEGs are most commonly used for images of a photographic nature and those that feature color gradations. The following two illustrations show the typical JPEG options when saving from Photoshop and Fireworks, respectively.

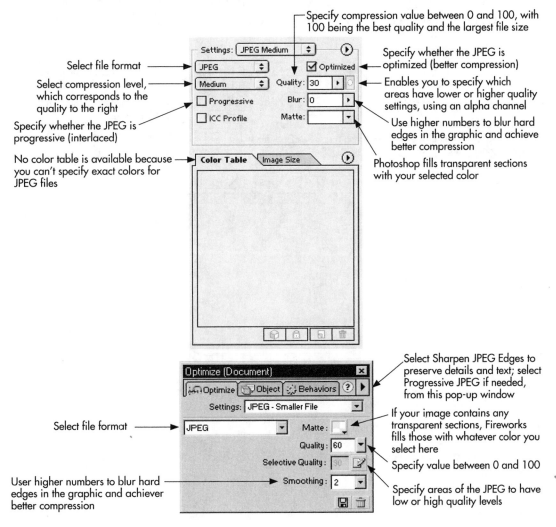

Specify compression value between 0 and 100, with 100 being the best quality and the largest file size

Select file format

Select compression level, which corresponds to the quality to the right

Specify whether the JPEG is progressive (interlaced)

No color table is available because you can't specify exact colors for JPEG files

Specify whether the JPEG is optimized (better compression)

Enables you to specify which areas have lower or higher quality settings, using an alpha channel

Use higher numbers to blur hard edges in the graphic and achieve better compression

Photoshop fills transparent sections with your selected color

Select Sharpen JPEG Edges to preserve details and text; select Progressive JPEG if needed, from this pop-up window

If your image contains any transparent sections, Fireworks fills those with whatever color you select here

Specify value between 0 and 100

Select file format

User higher numbers to blur hard edges in the graphic and achiever better compression

Specify areas of the JPEG to have low or high quality levels

TIP

Don't bother forcing your JPEGs into specific color palettes. Not only will they look terrible, but because you can't specify exact colors in the JPEG file format, the colors you specified will quickly change.

Save a PNG

When saving a file as a PNG, you must first choose how many colors to include in its palette. Saving as a PNG-8 uses an exact palette of 256 colors or less. Transparency and dithering are available in the PNG-8 setting. PNG-24 and PNG-32 offer 24-bit (millions) and 32-bit (millions, plus an alpha channel) color modes, respectively.

The following two illustrations show the typical PNG options available when saving PNGs in Photoshop and Fireworks, respectively.

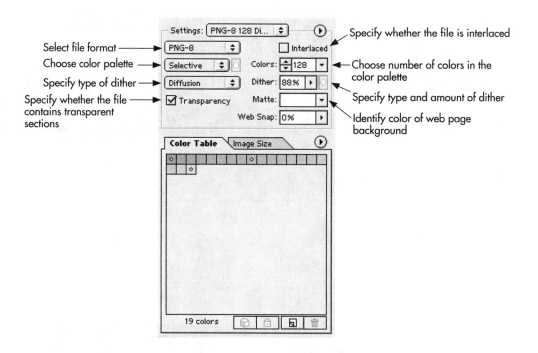

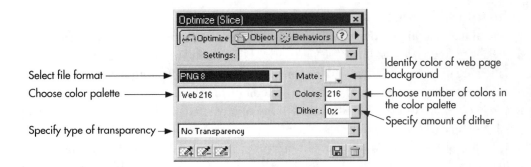

Select file format

Choose color palette

Specify type of transparency

Identify color of web page background

Choose number of colors in the color palette

Specify amount of dither

Ask the Expert

Q: What's the difference between 24- and 32-bit color?

A: Both 32-bit color and 24-bit color use millions of colors. However, 32-bit color includes an additional alpha channel, which can be used for transparency.

Q: What's an alpha channel?

A: An alpha channel is essentially a place within the file where you can store extra information about it. For example, in this case of 32-bit PNGs, you can specify that certain portions of an image should be made transparent and save those instructions as part of the image's alpha channel. Then, when another program capable of interpreting alpha channels reads the file, it displays only the portions of the file that aren't transparent.

Choosing the Best File Format

So now that you know a bit more about saving each type of image, how do you select which format to use for each particular case? Choosing the best file format is like shopping—you are looking for the file format that looks the best, but costs the least. In this case, the cost comes in download time for web page visitors.

Textbook Comparison

One of the first things you should think about is browser support. Wikipedia has a great resource to do just that. I've summarized the results (as of this printing) in the following discussion. Refer to **http://en.wikipedia.org/wiki/Comparison_of_web_browsers#Image_format_support** for the complete report.

As you can see by Table 6-1, the majority of the popular browsers completely support all the popular image file formats. The most notable exception is that Internet Explorer (which is also used by AOL) does not support progressive JPEGs or PNGs with gamma or color correction. Also, Internet Explorer 7 was the first version of IE to support alpha transparency in PNG files.

Browser support aside, Table 6-2 compares the top three image file formats in terms of color, compression method, animation, transparency, and interlacing.

Visual Comparison

The most important comparison you'll make is in how an image looks using each of the top three file formats. Thankfully, any graphics program geared toward web design will let you visually compare how each format affects your file. In fact, most programs offer a way to compare all three file formats at once.

Consider Figure 6-2, which shows a photograph using GIF, JPEG, and PNG formats at 100% size. This comparison is made possible by Photoshop's Save for Web feature,

Browser	JPEG	GIF	PNG
AOL Explorer	Partial+	Yes	Partial*
Google Chrome	Yes	Yes	Yes
Internet Explorer	Partial+	Yes	Partial*
Firefox	Yes	Yes	Yes
Safari	Yes	Yes	Yes
Opera	Yes	Yes	Yes

+ Does not support progressive display of progressive JPEGs

* Does not support display of gamma correction or color correction in PNG files; versions prior to IE7 do not support alpha transparency by default

Table 6-1 Summary of Image Format Support Among Popular Browsers

File Format	Color Mode	Compression Method	Animation	Transparency	Interlacing
JPEG	24-bit	Lossy	Not supported	Not supported	Supported as progressive JPEG
GIF	8-bit	Lossless	Supported	Supported (binary only)	Supported
PNG	8-bit, 24-bit, or 32-bit	Lossless	Not supported	Supported (variable/alpha)	Supported (two-dimensional)

Table 6-2   Comparison of Top Three Image File Formats

using the 4-up option. At 100, there is very little difference visually, although the JPEG definitely offers a bit of size savings. Even though we're talking about a 1-second difference, each second adds up. If you have 10 images on a page, and each takes 2 seconds to download as opposed to 1, you end up with a 10-second difference. Sit in front of your computer and count to 10 to see just how long 10 seconds is in web speed.

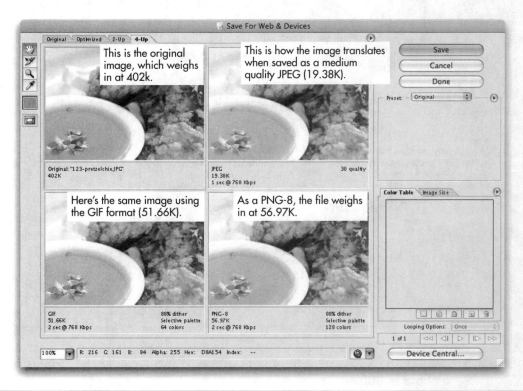

Figure 6-2   Photoshop's Save for Web comparing the GIF, JPEG, and PNG formats for a photo

You won't really see what's happening with the different file formats until you zoom in. Figure 6-3 shows the same image, zoomed in to 300%. Here you can see the pixilation and dithering that occurs with file compression. By zooming in, you can better understand what's happening to the file when it's saved in each of the file formats.

Even though some clarity is lost, the JPEG is clearly the best option for this photograph. Even at a relatively low setting (30%), the JPEG still looks good at 100%, and saves download time over both the GIF and PNG formats.

Let's try the Save for Web comparison again, only this time with a logo instead of a photograph (see Figure 6-4). In this case, I tried a 30% quality JPEG, a GIF with no dithering, and an 8-bit PNG. The GIF and PNG files are each about 3K in size, which is smaller than the JPEG option. However, even if the JPEG were closer in file size to the

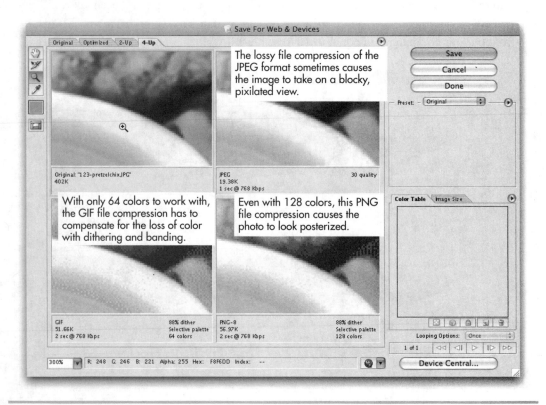

Figure 6-3 Photoshop's Save for Web comparing the GIF, JPEG, and PNG formats for a photo at 300%

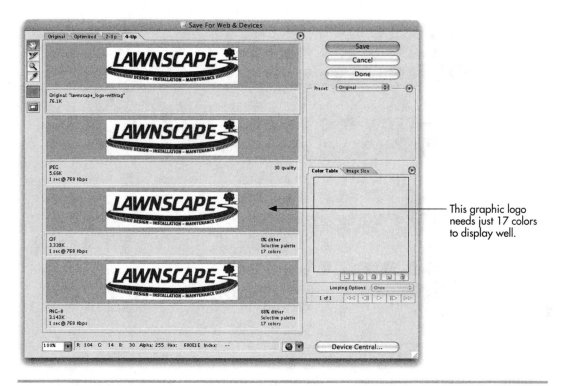

This graphic logo needs just 17 colors to display well.

Figure 6-4   Photoshop's Save for Web comparing GIF, JPEG, and PNG formats for a logo

GIF and PNG options, its quality is quite poor. The loss of clarity and focus is even more evident when we zoom in (Figure 6-5).

In this case, the GIF is probably the best option for two reasons. First, it offers the widest possible viewing audience. Second, it displays the logo without any loss of quality. Even though the PNG is slightly smaller in file size, it does not offer any increase in visual clarity. And given that there are some older browsers incapable of displaying PNG files, I would opt to use the GIF.

TIP

If the graphics program you're using doesn't allow you to compare and preview file types, save several different versions of the same file and preview each one in a browser. Compare their file size (download speed) and appearance to determine which file type and settings are the best.

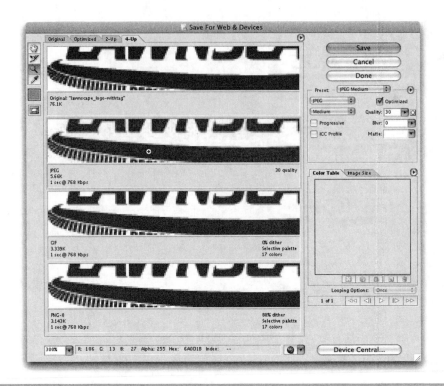

Figure 6-5 Photoshop's Save for Web comparing GIF, JPEG, and PNG formats for a logo at 300%

Exporting Whole Designs

Now that you know the basic steps involved in comparing and saving GIF, JPEG, and PNG files, it's time to put that knowledge to work on your own designs. In the last chapter, I discussed the concept of separating each element in your design into a unique piece to be saved as an image or re-created by HTML. I suggested that you use your favorite graphics editor to slice each element in preparation for production.

The time has now come for that production to be completed. Thankfully, web-focused design apps such as Photoshop and Fireworks make it easy to export all your images at once. In fact, after you have sliced your design, only a few steps remain to finish producing those images.

Naming Slices

To get started, you need to name each slice. In Chapter 5, I talked about using the Slice tool to draw boxes around each individual element that needs to be saved out of your graphics program. After you have created those slices, it's time to name them in preparation for export. Here are the basic steps to do that in the two most popular web graphics programs:

- In Fireworks, you can do this in two different places. You can select the slice and name it in the Property Inspector (as shown in the following illustration), or you can add the name after clicking the web layer in the Layers panel. (If you don't see the Property Inspector, choose Window | Properties.)

Enter the name of your slice here.

- In Photoshop, you use the Slice Selection tool to double-click the slice and access the Slice Options dialog box.

Regardless of which program you use, it's important that you come up with an appropriate naming convention for your site's assets (supporting files) before you start naming. Here are a few guidelines to consider:

- *Use descriptive filenames that might increase your site's search traffic.* For example, suppose each news article on the site displays a photograph of the article's author. You might name each photo something like "article1-photo." While that works great to help you identify which photo goes where, it doesn't actually tell you much about the contents of the photo. An alternative might be "joesmith-photo." Not only does this identify the image as being a photo of Joe Smith, but it allows anyone searching for "joe smith photo" to find the image.

- *Avoid numbering slices unless they will be used on a page that will never need to be updated.* It's very tempting to name images with schemes such as "home-01," "home-02.jpg," and so on. The main problem with this type of convention comes in the site maintenance. Suppose you need to add an image in between 02 and 03. Do you use 02b? It can get real confusing, real fast.

- *Use dashes instead of underscores.* Underscores have been a common way to separate words in filenames, because spaces aren't allowed. A better choice is the dash, because it is more easily recognized when the filename is linked (and underlines by default).

Auto Naming

Your web graphics program may include the option to automatically name each slice for you. For example, the following illustration shows the Output Settings in Photoshop. At the bottom of the window, notice the Default Slice Naming section. The first option selected is doc. name, followed by hyphen, and slice no. (01, 02, 03, ...). The resulting slice name is shown at the bottom of the dialog as MyFile-01.

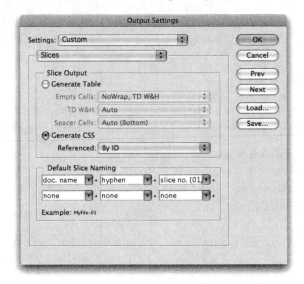

If you are producing a design with lots of individual slices, this can be a nice way to streamline the slice-naming process. However, it works best if you customize the naming options to suit your particular needs, and don't use the default settings. Why? As I mentioned previously, it can be difficult to maintain a site where all the images are named similarly, as with MyFile-01.jpg, MyFile-02.jpg, and so on. You'd have to open each slice just to figure out what it included, and then accurately rename it after making any changes. Having been through similar situations, I can tell you it's much easier to maintain a site where each image is named according to its contents.

Exporting Slices

After you've named all your slices, your next step is to optimize them. This means you select the desired file format (GIF, JPEG, or PNG) and the appropriate settings (number of colors, dithering, and so on), as discussed in the beginning of this chapter. When all your slices are named and optimized, your final step is to allow the graphics program to do its part and save each file. You can export all the slices at once or individually if you prefer. Depending on which graphics program you're using, the steps vary slightly.

Fireworks

In Fireworks, if you want to export a single slice, simply right-click that slice and choose Export Selected Slice…, as shown in Figure 6-6. Or, if you are ready to export all the slices in your file, choose File | Export.

Figure 6-6   Export options in Fireworks

Then, specify where you want to save the slice before clicking the Export button, as shown in this illustration:

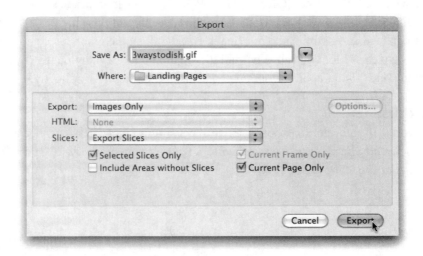

Photoshop

Exploring slices in Photoshop is a tad bit more cumbersome than with Fireworks. (Probably because Firework's main purpose is web design, whereas Photoshop is also used for other types of design.) The only way to access the Export options is to choose File | Save for Web & Devices.

Then, if you want to export a single slice, select that slice with the Slice Select tool (making sure you've already named and optimized it) and click the Save button. The last step is specifying where the slice should be saved. In addition, you can tell Photoshop whether to output All Slices, All User Slices, or Selected Slice (as shown in Figure 6-7).

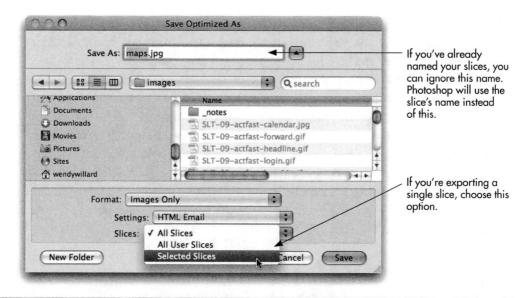

Figure 6-7   Save Optimized As dialog box in Photoshop

Exporting HTML

You may have noticed a couple of other options available when saving slices out of Photoshop and Fireworks. Both programs will also write HTML to display the slices according to your mockup's layout.

But wait…. This doesn't mean you are off the hook when it comes to learning HTML! On the contrary, if you plan to use a graphics program to write your HTML, it's quite important for you to understand HTML. The reason is that these programs write code according to the strict rules contained within them. If your layout doesn't fit into those rules, you will likely end up with buggy, inefficient code.

That doesn't mean you should never use code written by graphics programs either. Instead, I often suggest that beginners use this code to get started. I encourage you to see how the program wrote its code and determine what is working and what isn't. Don't feel bound to the outputted code, but consider it one possible way to code your design.

Photoshop

Already in this chapter you've read about exporting slices. You may have noticed that there are both "Image" and "No Image" slices possible in Photoshop.

When you want Photoshop to export the corresponding HTML for a design, you need to specify the type of slice for every square pixel on the page. Because much of your page will likely be browser-generated text, here's where the "No Image" slices come into play.

Consider Figure 6-8. This is a mockup for an HTML e-mail (which is really just a web page that is sent via e-mail to customers). To get to this point, I have already chosen File | Save for Web, and then double-clicked slice 07 with the Slice Select tool to display the Slice Options. From the Slice Type drop-down menu, I selected No Image, to let Photoshop know this slice contains text to be created by HTML, as opposed to a graphic that needs to be saved as a GIF, JPEG, or PNG.

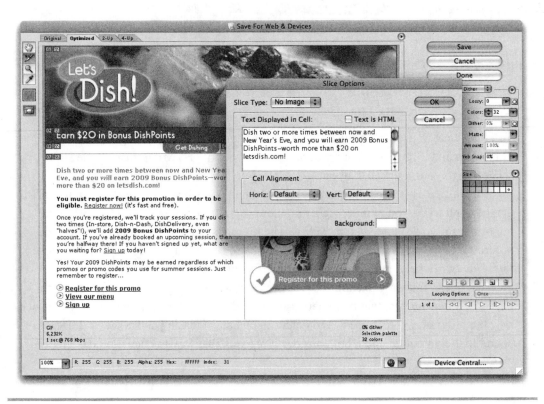

Figure 6-8 Mockup for an HTML e-mail

There's a spot in the Slice Options to enter the text to be created by HTML. You can type plain text, as well as HTML code, in the space provided. Options for cell alignment and background colors are also available.

After you've specified whether each slice contains images or text/HTML, double-click each slice with the Slice Select tool to confirm that you've given each one a unique name and appropriate optimization settings. If this is your first time exporting HTML from Photoshop, I suggest you take a look at your Output Settings before clicking the Save button. To do so, choose Edit Output Settings from the Optimize pop-up menu (to the right of the Preset menu), as shown in the following illustration.

HTML Settings   The Output Settings are the real driving force behind how Photoshop writes your HTML code. Choose XHTML from the Settings menu to get started. The first set of options to display relate to the type of code written. Here is where you can specify things like Always Add Alt Attribute (which makes sure your slices have associated comments to display in case the images don't) and Close All Tags (which prevents Photoshop from leaving HTML tags open, a practice that is no longer acceptable with the current version of HTML). Because XHTML is the currently approved standard, you don't need to change any of these options.

NOTE

If you don't yet understand how HTML works, a lot of this will be Greek to you. That's OK. At this point, I just want you to know how to access these options, so you can customize them as needed later.

Switch to the Slices option set to see a few things you may need to alter. The default method of Slice Output is Generate Table. This means Photoshop will use table tags to re-create the layout you've designed. The other choice is to Generate CSS, where the content is positioned using a style sheet instead of tables.

Slice Settings: Tables vs. CSS   So, you're probably wondering what is the difference, right? When HTML was first put into practice, the pages being developed were quite simple. At that point, "tables" were used to re-create tabular data, which is typically housed in spreadsheets. But then, web designers came on the scene and started using tables to lay out more complex web pages, placing different aspects of the page into each table cell, and then hiding the table edges (borders) to make the design appear seamless.

Eventually, the powers that be got together and came up with a better solution for laying out web pages: positioning with cascading style sheets (CSS). Thankfully, all modern browsers now support CSS for positioning, which is great news for web designers. Here are a few reasons why:

- CSS positioning requires less code than table-based page layouts.
- CSS offers more flexibility in terms of page layout, including the ability to layer elements on top of each other, and even to hide elements temporarily.
- CSS layouts are easier to maintain than table-based pages.

Having said all that, CSS positioning is not supported by most e-mail readers, as of press time. This means you can't use CSS reliably to lay out web pages that will be viewed in an e-mail program. To compensate, most designers rely on table-based layouts for any pages created for e-mail.

NOTE
More tips for creating e-mail–friendly web pages are included in Chapter 11.

In the case of the layout shown in Figure 6-8, I chose Generate Table for my Slice Output method, because this layout was destined to be viewed in e-mail programs. If this had been a page to be viewed in a web browser, I would have selected the CSS option.

Background Settings   The Background output settings give you the opportunity to specify the background of your page. This could be an image or a solid color to be displayed behind the rest of the content.

If you choose to display an image in the background, you need to remember a couple of things about background images:

- By default, all background images repeat horizontally and vertically across the page (this is also referred to as *tiling*).
- You can include only one image in the page background, although you can use additional images in the background of other elements (such as in the background of a table cell).

- Text in the foreground must be readable on top of the background. If you're using dark colors in your foreground, make sure the text on your page is much lighter. Likewise, try to avoid high-contrast backgrounds because they make it extremely difficult to read any text placed on top of them.

- Background images should be small in file size to avoid a long download time. Take advantage of the fact that the browser repeats a background image and cut your image down as much as possible.

NOTE
This particular setting is only for the page background, not for backgrounds applied to individual elements of the page. In the next section of this book, you'll learn more about coding those different page elements, and also about adding backgrounds to them.

Saving Files   The Saving Files output settings refer to file naming and location. I've already covered some good tips for file naming, and there's not much else to discuss in this section. However, I do want to draw your attention to the Put Images in Folder checkbox near the bottom of the window (shown in the following illustration):

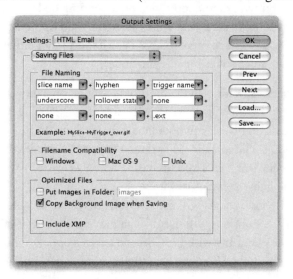

By default, Photoshop wants to put all images in a separate folder (titled "images") within whichever folder you specify as your output location. So if you've already selected an images folder as your file's final resting spot, you'll want to be sure and uncheck this option. (Otherwise, you'll end up with two images folders, one inside the other.)

Summary   After you've adjusted the settings as needed, your final step is to click the Save button in the Save for Web window, specify the location in which to save your files, and let Photoshop do the rest of the work. After the export is complete, you'll find one

HTML file and all the supporting images stored in your specified location. You can then edit that HTML page in whichever HTML tool you see fit. We'll talk about the details of HTML in the next section of the book.

Fireworks

Fireworks can also export a variety of different web formats. In fact, because it was created specifically for web development, it has a leg up on Photoshop in this arena. In fact, in version CS4, Adobe added a new "CSS and Images" export option. This enables designers to export all the HTML, CSS, and associated image files right from Fireworks, thereby speeding up the entire coding process in certain circumstances. (More on that shortly.)

TIP

Haven't upgraded to Fireworks CS4 yet? No problem, visit **www.adobe.com/devnet/ fireworks/articles/smart_css.html** to download a plug-in for CS3 that gives you the CSS and Images export option.

When you want Fireworks to export the corresponding code for a design, the first thing you should do is make sure your slices are set up and optimized appropriately. After your mockup's slices have been prepared, you can export them either as images only or as a page layout file (complete with images and code).

Page Layout: Tables vs. CSS   In the preceding section on exporting from Photoshop, I compared exporting page layouts using HTML tables vs. CSS. The same discussion applies here. The difference is in how Fireworks labels the options. In Firework's Export select menu, you have options that include "HTML and Images," "Images Only," "Dreamweaver Library," "CSS Layers" (or "CSS and Images"), and "Director." (These options vary slightly between the latest versions of Fireworks.)

Choosing HTML and Images will cause Fireworks to write table-based layout code, whereas any of the CSS options will use divs and layers instead of tables. For more information about the exporting with the CSS and Images option out of Fireworks CS4, visit **www.adobe.com/devnet/fireworks/articles/export_css_images.html**.

NOTE

"Divs" and "layers" are code-speak for two CSS-based structuring methods. You'll learn more about each of these in Chapter 8.

Ultimately, you need to base your decision on a few key concepts:

- Where will the page be viewed (e-mail, desktop browser, mobile browser, and so on)?

- If the page will fit into an existing site, which layout method is used throughout the rest of site (HTML tables, CSS positioning, Flash, and so on)?

- How comfortable are you editing the code that will be exported? It's rare that code written by a tool will not need to be touched-up by a human. You need to be prepared to troubleshoot and maintain any code Fireworks writes.

If you decide to export using HTML tables, you'll want to double-check a couple of settings in the Export Options. (The options are available by clicking the Options button in the Export window.)

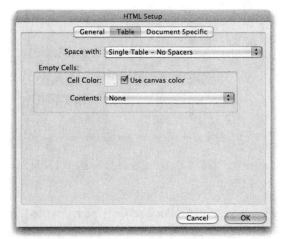

Just as with Photoshop, you can specify what method Fireworks uses to maintain your layouts with tables. You can specify to maintain the spacing with a single table, nested tables, spacer images, or some combination of those three.

If you decide to export using CSS, a few related settings are in the Export Options. First, you must identify the source of your CSS divs and layers, as shown in the following illustration. This is where Fireworks wants to know how to divide your mockup. If you've

already sliced the images the way you want them laid out, choose Fireworks Slices from the Source list. If you haven't sliced the images, you could instead have Fireworks create content areas based on either the frames or layers stored within the Fireworks document.

Exporting to Dreamweaver Fireworks and Dreamweaver are tightly integrated. As such, Fireworks can export your images and code specifically for Dreamweaver, to make for a seamless transfer. To do so, choose File | Export and select Export HTML File from the HTML select menu. Then click the Options button to the right to display a window similar to this one:

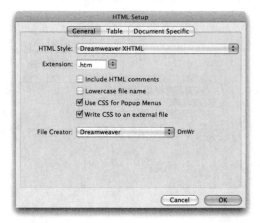

Make sure Dreamweaver XHTML is selected as the HTML Style, and that Dreamweaver is the File Creator.

Naming Files I haven't yet covered one settings panel in the Export Options. Click the Document Specific button to access settings primarily related to the default naming of slices. When you look at these settings (shown in the following illustration), you'll probably see some similarities to how Photoshop handles default slice naming.

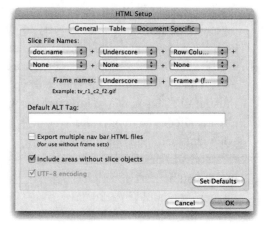

Use the select menus to identify your preferred method of naming slices. This naming convention will be used only when you don't otherwise specify a name for a particular slice. You can then adjust the remaining settings as needed. For the bulk of your work, you'll likely be able to use the default settings.

Advanced Settings   The Export Options I've discussed are used for most basic export methods. However, you should know that Fireworks is also capable of much more advanced exporting. For example, you can control exactly how Fireworks codes individual aspects of your mockups, and even create HTML form elements within Fireworks. Adobe has some great online resources available to walk you through this process, step-by-step. Visit **www.adobe.com/devnet/fireworks/articles/fireworks_web_design_css.html** to get started.

Summary   After you've adjusted the settings as needed, your final step is to click the Export button in the Export window, and let Fireworks do the rest of the work. After the export is complete, you'll find any code files and all the supporting images stored in your specified location. You can then edit the code files in whichever development tool you see fit. We'll talk about the details of HTML in the next section of the book.

Using Flash

If you've visited any entertainment-related web sites, you've likely encountered Flash. Adobe Flash is a tool designed specifically to deliver animation, interactivity, and dynamic content to web site visitors. Its vector format makes the process much more painless for visitors because its file sizes are significantly smaller than many other, similar formats. In addition, its streaming capabilities enable the files to be viewed while they're downloading, which is good because users can get to the actual content faster.

TIP
If you right-click (or CONTROL-click) content you suspect might be Flash, you can find out whether you're hunch is correct. Look for the option About Adobe Flash Player in the list of right-click-options for Flash files to learn more.

The Flash file format, recognized by its .swf file extension, has quickly become the most popular multimedia file format. Flash files can even be created from other applications (that is, you don't have to use the Adobe Flash software to create Flash files). For this reason, the term "Flash" can be used to refer to the actual Flash application, as well as the file format.

Ask the Expert

Q: What is streaming?

A: In its simplest terms, streaming means instant play. Typically, web files must be downloaded before being viewed. When a file is streamed, however, it's displayed or played while being downloaded, giving users instant access to its content.

Q: That sounds like a good thing. Why wouldn't you use streaming for everything?

A: First, not all file formats support streaming. Those that do often require special software on the web server to monitor and maintain the stream of information. Streaming can be taxing for a web server, particularly if more people attempt to access a file simultaneously than the web server is set up to handle. This occurs because streamed files maintain contact with the web server, while nonstreamed files require a connection only to the web server during the initial download.

Also, streaming isn't the perfect solution in many cases because of bandwidth limitations. Common problems with busy streamed files include jumpiness, loss of audio, and video freeze-ups. For more information about streaming audio and video on the web, check out **http://en.wikipedia.org/wiki/Streaming_media**.

So what can you do with Flash? Plenty. Common uses of Flash include advertisements, navigation systems, games, movie previews/trailers, cartoons, training programs, and product demonstrations.

If Flash can do all these wonderful things, shouldn't you be creating your own web site with it? Good question. The answer ultimately comes from the site's goals. If your site's primary purpose is to entertain, any drawbacks to using Flash will likely be outweighed by its inherent ability to create entertaining content.

Speaking of drawbacks, the most important one relates to the fact that Flash files require a plug-in to be viewed in the browser. This means users must have a Flash plug-in installed on their computer to view your Flash content.

NOTE
As of this writing, no Flash plug-in is available for the iPhone. This means that any Flash content included in your site will be unavailable to users accessing the site with an iPhone.

Another potential drawback involves file size. While it is true that Flash files tend to be smaller than those saved in some other file formats, Flash files still usually end up being larger than static images. This means you want to make sure other (non-Flash) content is available to users if your Flash content takes longer to download.

Even with those possible drawbacks, many web sites use Flash quite successfully. Here are a few places you can find examples of inspiring Flash design:

- **http://naldzgraphics.net/inspirations/45-excellent-examples-of-flash-websites-design/**

- **www.dailyseoblog.com/2009/10/15-examples-of-stylish-website-designs-using-flash-elements-effectively/**

- **www.smashingmagazine.com/2009/06/07/50-beautiful-flash-websites/**

Transferring to Flash

If you're designing content that will be produced in the Flash software, you'll need to change the way you "output" your designs. In the past, designers had to export individual pieces from graphics applications that were then imported into the Flash application.

But when Adobe acquired Flash a few years back, it sought to integrate fully all of its design applications. The result is that starting with version CS3, Flash is capable of importing complete Photoshop files. This means you simply save your layered Photoshop file in its native format (.psd) in preparation for production in Flash.

TIP
You can also import complete Illustrator (.ai) files starting with version CS3. And print designers are rejoicing that they can send InDesign (.indd) files directly to Flash, beginning with version CS4.

Then, after you (or your team member) has opened Flash and created a new document, she need only choose File | Import | Import to Stage to get things started. Figure 6-9 shows the result of selecting a .psd to import to stage. The Flash Import dialog box displays a variety of layer-specific options to help you import each layer exactly in the manner necessary.

Here are a couple of tips to remember when importing layered files into Flash:

1. Select the Editable Text option for all text layers you might need to edit using the Flash text tool.

2. For text you don't need to edit in Flash, choose the Vector Outlines option to reduce the file size by throwing out unnecessary fonts. These shapes will still be editable with the Flash pen tool.

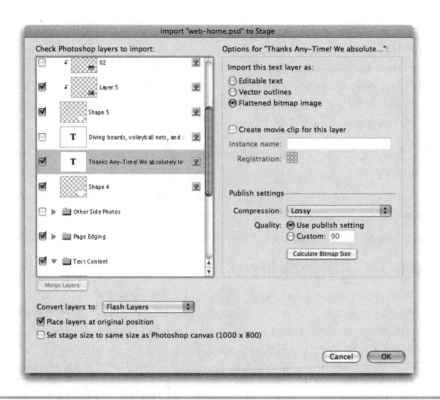

Figure 6-9 Importing a Photoshop file into Flash

3. To maintain layer effects (such as drop shadows) for text, choose the Flattened Bitmap Image option.

4. If you plan to animate an element, import it as Editable Paths And Layer Styles or Bitmap Image With Editable Layer Styles, depending on whether your element is a shape or image. This causes Flash to save the layer as a movie clip automatically, ready for animation.

5. Always choose Lossless compression for image layers with layer masks, to maintain your transparency using the PNG-24 file format.

Finally, as of this writing, there is no easy way to update the Flash file after changes have been made to a .psd already imported into Flash. This means you need to make sure your Photoshop files are approved by the client before importing them into Flash. In the event you must make a change to a Photoshop element after it's already been transferred into Flash, I suggest saving that element individually out of Photoshop as a PNG-24 with transparency. Then import it into Flash to replace the outdated element.

Learning More About Flash

Like any custom design, the development of Flash animation has its own process that may or may not be applicable to you, depending on the type of team in which you're working. Instead of confusing you with a less-than-adequate introduction here, I prefer to point you in the direction of some excellent books and online resources.

The first place you should look to learn more about Flash is the Web. Adobe has an excellent introduction on its site at **www.adobe.com/flash** and more tips for developers at **www.adobe.com/devnet/flash/**. Also consider the following resources at jumping off points for your study:

- **Flash Kit**   A Flash developer resource site: **www.flashkit.com**

- **Smashing Magazine**   Flash: **www.smashingmagazine.com/tag/flash/**

- **About.com**   Flash Web Design: **http://webdesign.about.com/od/flash/Macromedia_Flash.htm**

- **Tutorialized**   Photoshop and Flash tutorials: **www.tutorialized.com**

- **Newgrounds**   Flash tutorials: **www.newgrounds.com/collection/flashtutorials.html**

- *Flash CS4: The Missing Manual*, by Chris Glover (May 2009)

- *Learning Flash CS4 Professional*, by Rich Shupe (May 2009)

Ask the Expert

Q: I've only just gotten started designing for the Web. Should I learn Flash?

A: In the first few years of the Web, designers did it all, from the site architecture to the animation, writing, and production. As web design has matured, many designers have chosen to focus on certain elements of the craft. Some designers work solely in Photoshop, creating 2D graphics, while others work more regularly in Flash, providing the interactive and motion-driven elements of sites.

To any new web designer, I suggest identifying where your passion lies. Do you want to direct the overall look and feel of a site (perhaps as a designer or art director), or would you rather work with how elements move across the page and react to the user? If it's the latter, you might be a good candidate to focus on Flash development.

As with any new software, you shouldn't expect to learn Flash by reading a single book or taking one online tutorial. It's a very involved application, with many layers of complexity, which means it's also extremely powerful. But if you practice enough and have a lot of passion for your work, you'll surely be successful.

Q: So what if I don't want to learn Flash, but I do want to use it in my web design?

A: You have a few options. First, you could choose to partner with someone who is skilled in Flash development. Second, lots of stock Flash elements are available online. iStockPhoto (**www.istockphoto.com**) is one popular stock image company that offers premade Flash elements at reasonable costs. ActiveDen (**www.activeden.net**) is another stock company with plenty of inexpensive options for the non-Flash designer.

Finally, you might consider other software titles that make creating Flash animations simple for non-Flash designers. One such program that I have used for several projects is called BannerZest Pro (**www.aquafadas.com/en/bannerzest**). This tool allows you to drop a folder of images into a premade Flash template and then export as a Flash file, complete with the necessary HTML code.

Summary

At this point in a typical web development process, the bulk of the design work has been completed and produced. This chapter walked you through the process of saving out individual elements for use in the final HTML pages, as well as transferring the layered mockups to Flash for production.

The next step is to create the HTML code to tell the browser where to display each of the individual elements. While I covered a little bit of that in this chapter, when discussing how Photoshop and Fireworks export HTML, it's doubtful you'll be able to use that code without making any edits. Therefore, it is important for you to understand how code works. Part III, which includes Chapters 7–11, covers coding HTML and CSS for web pages.

Part III

Coding

Chapter 7

Getting Started with the Code

Key Skills & Concepts

- Create the file structure for the site
- Define the required HTML and CSS code elements for the page
- Define the header content for the page

After you design the look and feel of the web pages, and anyone who needs to (such as your client) has signed off on them, it's time to begin coding the pages and integrating the pieces. Depending on the size and structure of your web team, the task of coding pages may or may not fall upon your shoulders.

This section of the book covers how to code web pages, from a high level. This discussion is not meant to teach you extensive skills in HTML and CSS. Instead, I want to give you enough knowledge to help you understand how pages are coded and decide how much you want to be involved.

If you are planning to code all your own designs (as I typically do), this section serves as a "Cliff Notes" for my *HTML: A Beginner's Guide* book. I recommend picking up a copy of that book or enrolling in an HTML class to develop your skills further.

If you are not planning to code all your own designs, don't skip these few chapters! In fact, this section of the book just might be even more important to you. It is essential that you comprehend the methods used to code pages, so you can create successful designs.

Creating the File Structure

In Chapter 1, I discussed web servers. It's important for designers and developers to know a little about the web server before ever coding a bit of the page. The reason is this: each server has specific characteristics that might affect your coding.

The most basic aspect of your development that could be affected is probably the page name and folder structure. Most web servers are set up to recognize *index.html* as the default index of a folder on a web site. You can't assume your server is set up this way, however, because some servers default to using *welcome.html* or *default.html* as the default index page.

NOTE

Some servers are set up to look for another file extension (such as .asp or .htm) instead of .html. Check with your system administrator about this.

You want to set up your page names and folder structures as early as possible in the development process because changes made later affect any links to those pages already created. Ideally, you got this information during the proposal and information gathering process. But to confirm the specifications of your web server, check with the system administrator or the person in charge of maintaining that computer.

Here's a quick reminder of things you probably need to know about the web server:

- What operating system is the server running (for example, Windows, Mac, UNIX, Linux, and so on)? This might affect file naming conventions, or even the type of scripting used (because some server-side scripting works only on certain systems).

- How will you access the server to load your web files? For example, will you use an FTP program to transfer the files, or will you access the computer across your internal network and then simply copy and paste the files there? Do you need a user name and password to access the server and transfer files?

- How will you access the server to view your web files? For example, can you type the web server's domain name into your web browser (for example, **http:// testmachine.company.com**), or do you need to use a special IP address (for example, http://207.71.86.32)? Do you need a user name and password to access the server and view the files?

- What filename and extension is the server set up to recognize as the default index page in each folder (for example, index.html, index.htm, index.asp, default.html, default. htm, and so on)?

When I first start the coding aspect of a project, I typically create a new folder on my hard drive to house all the related files. Then, within that folder, I create a few additional subfolders. The most important of these is my images folder. It is a good idea to place all the images for a site within a particular folder, instead of leaving them strewn about in various places. This makes is easier to locate and reference images later.

Another folder I typically create contains all the non-HTML code files. The files in this folder might include my site's style sheet (which is a .css file) and any JavaScript files (saved with a .js extension). To help explain how I typically set up sites, take a look at the following illustration, which shows an example of the file structure for one of my client sites:

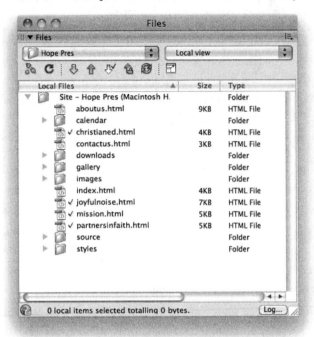

You can see that I have six folders and seven HTML files. The index.html file is the home page that will load when the site's address is visited in a browser. The other HTML files are pages linked from the site's home page. The calendar folder contains the files necessary to display the site's schedule of events to users. (This was placed inside its own folder because the calendar page required more than one file to display.)

The downloads folder holds files meant to be downloaded instead of displayed within the browser. For example, a school might include an enrollment form in this folder.

The gallery folder contains images specific to this organization's photo gallery. These are different from the files in the images folder, because they are uploaded through a browser-based photo gallery tool.

The images folder contains all the images required to display the web site in the browser. These include navigational buttons, graphical headlines, and any other images necessary to build the site.

The source folder holds the Photoshop source files used to develop the web site. The only time I include these within the web site file structure is when the site has multiple maintainers, located at multiple sites. In situations like this, it can be helpful to store the layered Photoshop files on the web server, so they can be "checked out" when edits are necessary.

Most file management tools work much like the public library, where a book can be checked out by only one patron at a time. Did you notice the little green check marks next to a couple of files in the structure? That is Dreamweaver's way of reminding me those files are checked out to me. When another person tries to edit those files, she will be notified that I have them checked out. She can either override my checkout (and therefore override any changes I've made) or request that I check the file back in before she makes any edits.

The final folder, called styles, is where I store the site's style sheets. Keeping them all in one location makes it quicker and easier to make changes later.

Opening and Saving Files

Now that I've talked about how to structure your files, let's look more closely at what constitutes an HTML file. At their very core, HTML files are simply files with two additional features:

- *HTML files have an .html or .htm filename extension. A filename extension* is an abbreviation appended to the filename that associates the file with the appropriate program or tool needed to access it. In most cases, this abbreviation follows a period and is three or four letters long.

- *HTML files have tags.* Tags are commands or code used to tell the computer how to display the page content. Choose View | Page Source, Page | View Source, or View | Source in your web browser to see the current page's HTML.

When you open HTML files in a browser, the code is translated behind the scenes to display the page accordingly. If you instead open that same HTML file in a development tool such as those discussed in Chapter 1, you see only the code. You might think of HTML files as being two-faced, in that they look completed different depending on how you approach them.

To clarify this, consider the following illustration, which shows an HTML page viewed in Dreamweaver. In this case, the page is viewed using Dreamweaver's Split Frame option, which displays both the HTML and design of the page at the same time (in different frames).

Naming Conventions

If you use a web development tool like Dreamweaver to create and save your HTML files, the program will automatically prompt you to save in the correct format. Even so, remember the following few points when saving your HTML files:

- Although in most cases it doesn't matter whether you use .html or .htm, you should be consistent to avoid confusing yourself, the browser, and your users.

NOTE

Wondering why some people use .html and some use .htm? Older systems such as Windows 3.1 and DOS could not understand four-letter file extensions, so anyone creating web pages on those systems used .htm as the extension. In any case, because the first three letters of .html and .htm are the same, those systems simply ignored the letter l and recognized the file type without any problems.

● Some web servers are case-sensitive, so remember this when naming and referencing filenames and try to be consistent. If you name your file MyPage.html, and then reference it later using mypage.html, you may end up with a broken link. One good technique is to use only uppercase or lowercase to name your files. This way, if you see a file with a letter in it that doesn't match, you know instantly that file is probably the problem. Even the pros run into case-sensitivity problems on an almost daily basis.

● Use simple filenames with only letters and numbers. Don't use spaces, punctuation, or special characters, other than hyphens (–) and underscores (_). Good examples might be home.html, my-story.html, and contactme.html.

TIP
While it's perfectly acceptable to use an underscore (_) in a file or folder name, I suggest using a hyphen instead. Underscores can easily become confused with an underline, especially when displayed as a link on a web page (because links are usually underlined).

These same recommendations hold true for any folder names you use. If you were creating a web site that had your favorite links, family photos, and résumé, you might find it useful to put each of those things in a separate folder.

TIP
If you decide to use Microsoft Word or WordPad to type your HTML, you need to choose the file type Text Document or Text Only and add an .html extension to the filename the first time you save it. This is because both of those programs default to saving "Word for Windows" or "Microsoft Word" documents with a .doc or .docx extension.

Preview an HTML File in a Browser

You can view HTML files located on your personal computer within your own web browser. It isn't necessary for your files to be stored on a web server until you are ready to make them visible on the Internet.

The most basic method of previewing a web page is to open it in your web browser. To do so, open your web browser and choose File | Open (or Open Page or Open File, depending on your browser), and then browse through your hard drive until you locate the HTML file you want to open. (If you don't see any File menus in IE, try pressing the ALT key to reveal them.)

If you're going to make frequent changes to the HTML file in a text editor, switch back to a web browser to preview the page, keeping both programs (a text editor and a web browser) open at the same time. Alternatively, you can use the built-in preview tools available with most web development applications. For example, in Dreamweaver, you choose File | Preview In Browser and select the browser you'd like to use.

Non-HTML Files

I've already mentioned a few types of non-HTML files you might use in web development. In particular, style sheets and scripts are two of the most common types of non-HTML files you'll encounter. As a reminder, here are the various reasons for using each type of file:

- **HTML**   Marks which bits of content are paragraphs, lists, images, tables, forms, and so on

- **CSS**   Specifies how each marked-up section should be displayed

- **JavaScript (or some other type of scripting language)**   Adds functionality by indicating how the page should react to user input

Both style sheets and scripts can be opened, edited, and saved in most web development tools. For example, the following illustration shows the different types of files you can create in Dreamweaver:

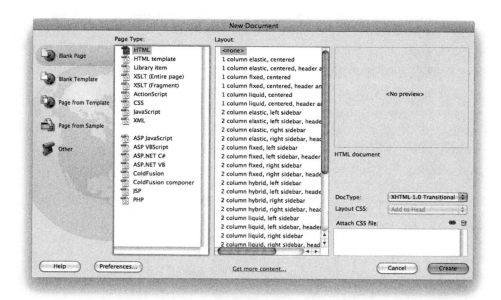

When you create a CSS file in Dreamweaver, the program knows this type of file is not meant to be displayed. As such, the Design feature is disabled, and you can access the file only in Code View. The same is true for scripts.

After they have been created, both of these files (style sheets and scripts) are then linked to the applicable HTML files. This means you can have one style sheet linked to all the pages on a site, as well as different style sheets for each section of a site. Likewise, you can offer one set of styles for use when the page is printed and another set to dictate how a page should be displayed on screens. I'll cover more about style sheets and scripts later in the section titled, "Header Content."

Basic HTML Page Code

Now that you know how to open and save an HTML file, let's look at adding some actual HTML code. An *HTML entity* or *tag* is a command used to tell the browser how to display content on a page. This command works in a way that's similar to what happens behind the scenes when you highlight some text in a word processor and click the Italic button to make the text italicized.

With HTML, instead of clicking a button to make text italicized, you can type a tag before and after the text you want to emphasize, as in the following:

```
<em>Reminder:</em> There will be no band practice today.
```

You can easily recognize tags because they are placed within *brackets* (< >), or less-than and greater-than symbols.

NOTE
If you've been around the web design scene for some time, you might wonder why I'm not using the i tag to italicize text, as in i. That tag was retired by the World Wide Web Consortium (W3C—the governing authority on HTML) in favor of the emphasis (<em>) tag.

Did you notice that the tag to emphasize text is <em>? Given that piece of information, can you guess the tags to add a paragraph or create items in a list?

Purpose	Tag
Create paragraphs	<p>
Create list items	<li>
Add a line break	

Page Tags

In HTML, both *opening* and *closing* tags are usually included. For example, if you use <p> as an opening tag to signify where to start a new paragraph, you have to use a closing tag to signify where that paragraph ends (unless you want your entire page to be contained within one paragraph). To do so, use the same tag with a forward slash placed before it: </p>. Table 7-1 shows a list of basic HTML page tags.

Attributes

Many tags have additional aspects that you can customize. These options are called *attributes* and are placed after the tag but before the final bracket. Specific attributes for

Opening Tag	Closing Tag	Description
!DOCTYPE	n/a	Tells the browser to which set of standards your page adheres.
\<html\>	\</html\>	Frames the entire HTML page.
\<head\>	\</head\>	Frames the identification information for the page, such as the title, that is transferred to the browser and search engines.
\<body\>	\</body\>	Frames the content of the page to be displayed in the browser window.
\<title\>	\</title\>	Provides the name of the page that will appear at the top of the browser window and be listed in search engines.

Table 7-1   Basic HTML Page Tags

each tag are discussed as we move through the next few chapters. But to give you an idea of how attributes work, let's look at an example using the tag for images:

```
<img src="mypicture.jpg" width="100" height="100" alt="A photo of me" />
```

In this example, the base tag is img, which tells the browser I want to insert an image at this spot. The attributes are src, width, height, and alt. Each attribute has a *value,* which comes after an equal sign (=) and is placed within quotation marks.

Required Tags

All HTML pages need to have the html, head, and body tags, along with the DOCTYPE identifier (more on that shortly). This means, at the very least, your pages should include the following:

```
<!DOCTYPE html PUBLIC "-//W3C//DTD XHTML 1.0 Transitional//EN"
"http://www.w3.org/TR/xhtml1/DTD/transitional.dtd">
<html>
<head>
     <title>My First HTML Page</title>
</head>
<body>
This is a very basic HTML page.
</body>
</html>
```

Here are the results of these tags displayed in a browser.

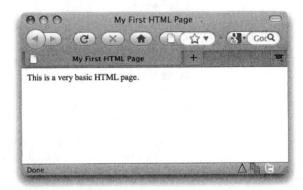

Specifying the Document Type

The first tag in any HTML file is the `doctype` tag. This is a required tag used to tell the browser which version of HTML is used in the document. When the W3C released HTML4 and XHTML, it specified three possible flavors, or versions:

- **XHTML Transitional**   For documents that contain a combination of old and new HTML code.
- **XHTML Strict**   For documents that don't contain any outdated code and are structurally "clean"
- **XHTML Frameset**   For documents that contain frames

As of this writing, HTML4/XHTML is still the current recommended specification. This means you should select one of those flavors for your pages. I suggest using the easiest one to work with (transitional) to validate your current web pages. To validate your pages against this flavor of XHTML, use this:

```
<!DOCTYPE html PUBLIC "-//W3C//DTD XHTML 1.0
Transitional//EN" "http://www.w3.org/TR/xhtml1/DTD/transitional.dtd">
```
This link tells the browser where to find the specification ⎤
against which you are validating your page.

NOTE
To see a glimpse as to what the future holds, after HTML5 is adopted, you'll simply have to use a `doctype` that identifies whether your page is HTML or XML. For example, HTML files will use `<!doctype html>`. Simple, huh? In general, HTML5 looks to be a great next step for this powerful language.

Validating Against These Doctypes

Wondering why you even need to *validate* your HTML against a particular document type? The purpose of validation is to help identify potential problems a browser might encounter when displaying your page. Because browsers render pages according to the official HTML specifications (as dictated by the W3C), it makes sense to double-check your pages against those specs as part of your testing.

The official W3C validation service can be found at **http://validator.w3.org**. Once you get there, you'll notice you can use several different methods to test or validate your pages.

- **Validate by URI**   If your page is already live on the Internet, you can simply enter the page's URI/URL (address), and the tool will seek to validate your page.

- **Validate by file upload**   If you're working on pages currently stored on your hard drive (but not live on the Internet), you can upload those pages to the online validator.

- **Validate by direct input**   Alternatively, you can simply copy and paste the code into an online form at the validation service.

Regardless of which method you choose, the results will be the same. The validator will give you a passing or failing grade. If your page fails to validate against the standard you've listed in your code, the tool will also tell you why the page fails. For example, it might tell you if you've used a particular attribute in the wrong tag or if you've used a tag that's not in the spec.

NOTE
I discuss validation more in Chapter 12, particularly as it relates to testing your pages before and after launch.

Meta Data

After the `doctype` tag tells the type of HTML document being presented, and the `html` tag officially opens the page, the next portion of code you might see is called *meta data*. Meta data, added to a web page through *meta tags,* is information about a document, as opposed to the document's content, which is transferred to applications such as search engines, web servers, and web browsers. For example, you can use `meta` tags to list the author of a particular web page or its copyright information.

```
<head>
<title>Welcome to Chop Point--a summer camp for co-ed teens
 and a K-12 school for day and boarding students</title>
<meta name="author" content="Wendy Willard">
<meta name="copyright" content="2010, Chop Point Inc.">
</head>
```

Perhaps the most popular use of meta data is to add a list of keywords to help search engines index the page. The following code shows the keywords specified for Chop Point's home page:

```
<meta name="keywords" content="camp, summer camp,
teenagers, teens, co-ed, trips, tripping, adventure trips,
residential camp, residential program, k-12, k-12 school,
k-12 private school, boarding school, resident students,
day program, boarding students, spanish, public service,
service projects, christian, non-profit, maine, new england">
```

You can also add a brief description via meta tags, which are used by some search engines in cataloging your page. If the value of your content attribute contains text in a certain language, you can add the `lang` attribute to your meta tag, as in the following example:

```
<meta name="description" lang="en" content="Chop Point, Inc.
is a non-profit organization operating a private k-12 school
for boarding and day students, and a co-ed summer camp for teenagers.">
<meta name="description" lang="fr" content="Chop Point, Inc.
est une organisation à but non lucratif actionnant une école
k-12 privée pour des étudiants d'embarquer et de jour, et une
colonie des vacances co-ed pour des adolescents.">
```

Chop Point draws a large number of campers and students from France each year, it makes sense to offer both French and English versions of important information, such as the page description. Table 7-2 lists the most common types of meta tags.

The `description` meta tag should properly explain the purpose of your site in a sentence or two (25 words is a good place to start). The number of keywords you can use in the `keywords` meta tag varies according to the search engine or directory reading it, so make sure your most important keywords are listed first.

Type of Meta Tag	Usage Example
author	`<meta name="author" content="name of author">`
copyright	`<meta name="copyright" content="year, owner">`
description	`<meta name="description" content="brief description">`
keywords	`<meta name="keywords" content="list of keywords">`
robots	`<meta name="robots" content="none">`

Table 7-2   Common Types of Meta Tags

NOTE

Be aware that some search engines and directories ignore meta tags altogether, while others support only a few types of meta data. For these reasons, they shouldn't be used as the only method of preparing your site for the search engines.

Avoid repeating words too often in the keywords meta tag. Some search engines are known for dropping sites from their listings because of suspected *spamming*—a word repeated over and over again on a single page is a big red flag for spamming. Be realistic and honest. Use words wherever them seem appropriate and you'll be fine.

In addition, don't use irrelevant keywords just to draw people in, and don't include keywords that aren't appropriate for your site. Users will get annoyed and complain, causing your site to be dropped from the search engine altogether.

You can also use the `robots` meta tag to restrict a page from being indexed by a search engine or directory. This might be useful for a private page or a work in progress.

TIP

Visit **http://searchenginewatch.com/2167931** for more tips on using the latest meta tags.

Header Content

After any meta data, the next portion of the code is referred to as the header content. This section of code (starting and ending with the head tag) gives additional instructions to the browser about the page itself, as opposed to the pieces of content on the page.

Page Title

The most common aspect of the header content is the page title. This is not the title that appears printed on the page within the content. Instead, this title is printed at the top of the browser window, as show in the following illustration:

The title tag specifies what's printed here.

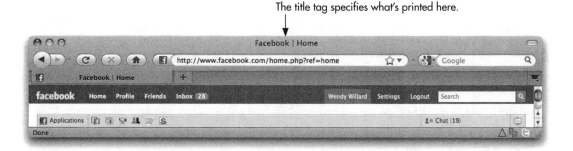

A few different methods exist regarding what text you should include in the title of your page. First and foremost, however, you should always include some descriptive text that gives users an idea of what the page is about. Remember that the contents of your title tag are used by default as the name of a bookmark if the user adds your page to his list of favorites.

With this in mind, you want to pick titles that will mean something to users when they look at their favorites two weeks or two months after they've visited your site.

As another example, consider how using the title "Dates and Fees" wouldn't be as effective as "Dates and Fees for Chop Point Summer Camp."

You also want to select something that helps your users identify their location on your site. For example, suppose you were coding a page describing one of several products offered. Instead of simply providing the name of the product in the page title, also providing the company name and any other pertinent information, such as the product category, would be more effective. Many people then separate the names of the company, category, and product with characters such as slashes (/), hyphens (–), or vertical pipes (|).

```
<head>
      <title>Amy's Flowers | Roses | Amy's Blooming Dozen Bouquet</title>
</head>
```

TIP
Because long titles can get truncated both in the browser window and in the favorites/ bookmarks lists, it's important that you keep the most important part of your titles at the beginning.

Scripts
When discussing the file structure, I mentioned scripts are used to add functionality to the web page that is not possible using basic HTML. You can add scripts in two different ways. First, you can create separate script files, which are then linked from within the header content of the HTML page. The following example shows how one such script might be referenced:

```
<head>
<title>Bay State Land Services &gt; Our Services</title>
<script src="insertmovie.js" language="JavaScript"
type="text/javascript"></script>
</head>
```

In this case, the script tells the browser to look for a file called insertmovie.js, written in JavaScript. When the browser loads the web page, it also loads this JavaScript and uses it as needed on the page.

Scripts are typically added with the `script` tag, using the language and type attributes to define which type of script is being added. The `src` attribute is used to tell the browser where to find the script.

TIP
Scripts are instructions to the browser written in some language other than HTML. As such, they cannot be included within a web page without your first giving the browser a little more information, including the script language and the location of the actual instructions.

Scripts can also be added to the header content on a page, meaning the script itself is placed in between the opening and closing `head` tags. Here's an example where the script tells the browser to display an alert box when the page is loaded:

```
<head>
<title>Bay State Land Services &gt; Our Services</title>
<script type="text/javascript">
function message()
    {
    alert("This alert box was created with JavaScript");
    }
</script>
</head>
```

Style Sheets
Finally, the last thing you probably need to add to the header content of your web page might be a style sheet. Two types of style sheets—internal and external—can be added to the header content, while the third (embedded) is added to an HTML tag within the body content of the page. Because the styling of a page is so important, the next section provides more details about style sheets.

Basic CSS Code
I've already mentioned the phrase "style sheets" a few times, but I haven't really given them a full explanation yet. Part of the reason is that style sheets weren't really a part of HTML until it was rewritten as XHTML. The purpose of *cascading style sheets* (CSS) is to separate the *style* of a web page from its *content*.

The current HTML "rules" dictate that we use HTML only to identify the content of the page, and then use a style sheet to specify the presentation of that content. This not only makes web pages more accessible and usable to all users (regardless of their browsers, platforms, operating systems, physical limitations, and so forth), but also to search engines and other types of software.

TIP

If you've ever used the style drop-down menu in some versions of Microsoft Word, you've already used a style sheet of sorts. The most basic style sheet might include a style called Body Text that specifies how the body text of the web page should look—which font and color to use, how much space to leave around it, and so on.

Types of Style Sheets

After you know a little about the individual parts of CSS, you can put them together to create a few styles. The organization of these pieces depends a bit on which type of style sheet you are creating. CSS offers three types of style sheets:

- **Inline** Styles are embedded right within the HTML code they affect.

- **Internal** Styles are placed within the header information of the web page and then affect all corresponding tags *on a single page*.

- **External** Styles are coded in a separate document, which is then referenced from within the header of the actual web page. This means a single external style sheet can be used to affect the presentation on a whole group of web pages.

You can use any or all of these types of style sheets in a single document. However, if you do include more than one type, the rules of *cascading order* take over: these rules state that inline rules take precedence over internal styles, which take precedence over external styles.

In a nutshell, CSS styles apply from general to specific. This means a ruleset in the `head` tag of a document overrides a linked style sheet, while a ruleset in the body of a document overrides one in the `head` tag. In addition, more local (or *inline*) styles only override the parent attributes where overlap occurs.

Inline

Inline styles are created right within the HTML of the page, hence the name. Inline declarations are enclosed in straight quotes using the style attribute of whichever tag you want to affect.

```
<h2 style="font-family: verdana;">
```

You can separate multiple rules by semicolons, but the entire declaration should be included within quotes:

```
<h2 style="font-family: verdana; color: #003366;">
```

Inline styles are best for making quick changes to a page, but they aren't suited for changes to an entire document or web site. The reason for this is that when styles are added to a tag, they occur only for that individual tag and not for all similar tags on the page.

TIP

Inline styles overrule internal and external styles when multiple types of style sheets are found on the same page.

Internal

When you want to change the style of all the h2 tags on a single page, you can use an internal, or embedded, style sheet. Instead of adding the style attribute to a tag, use the style tag to contain all the instructions for the page. The style tag is placed in the header of the page, in between the opening and closing head tags. Here's an example of what an internal style sheet might look like:

```
<head>
<title>CSS Example</title>
<style type="text/css">
h2 {font-family: verdana; color: blue;}
h3 {font-family: verdana; color: red;}
</style>
</head>
```

As this example shows, the selector is placed before the declaration, which is enclosed in curly brackets. This entire ruleset can be contained on a single line or broken up into multiple lines, as in the following example:

```
h2
{font-family: verdana;
color: blue;}
```

You can write styles in several ways. The following example is just as valid as the preceding one and is preferred by some people because it is easier to read:

```
h2 {font-family: verdana;
    color: blue;}
```

In addition, you can use certain shorthand properties to reduce the amount of coding necessary. For example, instead of specifying both font family (Verdana) and font size (12 point), you could type the following because both properties begin with font:

```
h2 {font: verdana 12pt;}
```

TIP
Chapter 9 discusses how to style text in more detail.

External

An *external* style sheet holds essentially the same information as an internal one, except an external style sheet is contained in its own text file and then referenced from within the web page. Thus, an external style sheet might look like this:

```
/* Basics and Typography */

body {
    margin: 0px;
    padding: 0px;
    display: block;
    background: #fff url(images/bg.jpg) no-repeat fixed;
    font-size: 12px;
    font-family: "Trebuchet MS", Trebuchet, Verdana, Arial, sans-serif;
    color: #330;
    position: relative;
    z-index: 0;
}
p {
    font-size: 1em;
    line-height: 1.5em;
    margin: 1.2em 0;
    font-family: georgia, trebuchet, arial, sans-serif;
}
ol, ul {
    font-size: 1em;
    line-height: 1.5em;
    margin: 1.2em 0 1.2em 2em;
    padding: 0;
}
```

Notice that external style sheets don't use the `style` tag or attribute but simply include a list of rulesets as instructions for the browser. Once you create your external style sheet, save it as a text file with the .css filename extension.

Then return to your HTML file and add the `link` tag to the page header to reference the external style sheet, as in the following example:

This is where the name of your style sheet is placed.

```
<head>
<title>Using an External Style Sheet</title>
<link rel="stylesheet" type="text/css" href="styles.css">
</head>
```

In this case, I needed to write only `styles.css` because the style sheet is in the same folder as my HTML page. However, if the style sheet is in a folder that doesn't also contain your HTML page, you should be sure to reference that path appropriately. (Link references are discussed more in the next chapter.)

NOTE

External style sheets can be overruled by internal and inline style sheets.

Coding Etiquette

If you view the source code for several different web sites, you will see a few similarities. This is not a coincidence; you should keep in mind the following HTML etiquette rules as you start coding your pages:

- HTML4/XHTML is case-sensitive and requires all tags to be lowercase.
- HTML4/XHTML also requires all values to be placed within straight quotation marks, as in the following example:

```
<p style="font-family: verdana;">
```

You also want to observe proper spacing within tags. Let's look more closely at some example code to identify where proper spacing should occur:

```
No space is between the        No space should come between a tag and the text it affects.
<body> ◄——— brackets and the tag.
<a href="http://www.google.com" title="Search Google">Search Google</a>
   ▲                                 ▲
A single space should come         A single space should come between attributes.
between tags and attributes.
```

Finally, you must consider how to nest tags properly. The term *nesting* refers to the process of using one HTML tag inside another. The easiest way to understand this concept is to see it in action:

```
<strong><em>These tags are nested properly.</em></strong>
<strong><em>These tags are not nested properly.</strong></em>
```

You should always be able to draw semicircles that connect the opening and closing versions of each tag. If any of your semicircles intersect, your tags are not nested properly.

Indenting Code

Upon checking out other designers' code, you will likely see many lines of code that are indented. In most cases, pressing the SPACEBAR or TAB keys will have little, if any, impact on the code itself. So, if you're using the TAB key to indent certain lines of code, as the designer did in this example, and it doesn't affect the code, why do it?

```
Source of: http://www.foxnews.com/story/0,2933,554920,00.html?test=faces

<a name="top"></a>

        <div id="header">
        <div id="right-head">
                <ul>
                    <li><a href="/video/index.html" style="width:55px;">Video</a></li>
                    <li><a href="/radio/index.html">Radio</a></li>
                    <li><a href="/mobile/index.html">Mobile</a></li>
                    <li><a href="/ureport/index.html">U-Report</a></li>
                    <li><a href="http://www.fncimag.com/">iMag</a></li>
</ul>
        </div>

Line 200, Col 35
```

The answer lies in a concept you just learned: nested tags. Whenever a tag is nested inside another tag, it can be helpful to indent the nested tag in your code, just to set it apart visually. This helps you clearly identify which tag is functioning as the container tag, also called a *parent* tag.

TIP
Indenting nested tags can also make it easier to ensure that all tags are closed.

Summary

This chapter is the first of five chapters covering coding techniques used in web design. I am a firm believer in the concept that all web designers (even those who won't be doing much of their own coding) need to understand how HTML works to create a truly successful web design.

We just covered the very basics of HTML, mostly focusing on the header content of the page. Next, we'll move into the body of the page, to set up the structure for the page's content.

Chapter 8

Structuring Content

Key Skills & Concepts

- Set up appropriate container blocks for content on the page.

- Use HTML to organize content within each container block.

- Add links and images to define the content.

To re-create your designs using code, you first need to set up the structure of the page. The structure must be set before the pieces of your page are styled and positioned. You can think of it as being like adding a new bookcase in your house. First, the shelving unit must be built (structure). Then it is painted or stained (style), before being installed in your house (position).

Setting Up Content Areas

You've heard me say it before…. An important aspect of coding a web page is planning—especially when it comes to organizing sections of content on that page. A great strength of style sheets is that they let you apply groups of formatting characteristics to whole sections of text. But the key to all this is first setting up the content areas with the `div` tag.

Amazingly, adding a simple `<div>` to the code on your page will cause no outward change in appearance when the page is viewed in the browser. In fact, the `div` tag does *nothing* by itself—it doesn't even cause a line break. It is simply used as a container, allowing you to manipulate its contents later with style sheets. As you begin coding your pages, you want to identify the most appropriate "boxes," or sections, to house the content on the page.

Identifying Natural Divisions

It's normal for a web page to have natural divisions according to the type of content found in each area of the page. A few common divisions or sections of a page might include the navigation, the body copy, the header, and the footer. The code used to separate each section might look similar to the following:

```
<body>
<div id="header">
Header content goes here.
</div>
<div id="bodyCopy">
Body copy goes here.
```

```
</div>
<div id="footer">
Footer content goes here.
</div>
</body>
```

NOTE

Notice I didn't use any spaces when assigning names to my divs. Instead, I added a capital letter to help readability when multiple words were used in a single div name.

To identify your own content areas, return to the approved mockups and any divisions you already created when you added guidelines to the page. How do those guidelines separate the page? Does the primary navigation fit in one area? Are there clear header and footer sections? Perhaps you also have content areas for advertisements. Whatever the sections may be, now is the time to create content area blocks within the code to house each one.

Once you've set up basic divisions like this, the possibilities are endless. Need to move the navigation from the top of your page to the bottom…on ten different pages? If you put all of it into its own div, it's a piece of cake! Not only is it easy to move that entire navigation bar, but you have to edit only the style sheet—and not the individual HTML pages—to do so. I'll talk more about editing the style sheet in Chapter 9, but for now let's look specifically at different methods of structuring the content with HTML.

DIV + ID

When using the div tag to separate content areas, you also need to add the id attribute to give each division a name (as I did with header, bodyCopy, and footer in the preceding code example). In the same way that a unique Social Security number is assigned as identification—ID—for each person living in the United States, so should a unique name be given to each division on a web page. Once you've named your divisions, these content areas can easily be formatted in the site's style sheet, which might look something like the following:

```
#header {border: 1px;}
#bodyCopy {font-family: Verdana; font-size: 12pt;}
#footer {font-size: 10pt;}
```

In the style sheet, the # before each content area name is necessary because this isn't a normal style sheet selector. Instead of using a tag as my selector, such as p, I've essentially made up my own selectors and given them names like header and footer. And because I used the id attribute to do so, I prefaced my selector name with a hash mark (#).

SPAN + CLASS

Similar to the `div` tag, the `span` tag doesn't have any distinct HTML characteristics of its own. The difference with the `span` tag is that it is best used to style *inline*—as opposed to container-level—bits of content.

So while you might use the `div` tag to add a colored background behind whole sections of your page, you would use the `span` tag to highlight a single word or phrase within a paragraph. The following shows some code that illustrates this:

```
<head>
<style type="text/css">
#introCopy {background-color: #cccccc;}
.highlight {background-color: #ffcc66;}
</style>
</head>
<body>
<div id="introCopy">
<p>Paragraph 1</p>
<p>Paragraph 2</p>
</div>
<p>Paragraph <span class="highlight">3</span></p>
<p>Paragraph 4</p>
</body>
```

This tells the browser how to display text contained in the "`highlight`" class.

The `class` attribute identifies which set of instructions in the style sheet apply to this bit of text.

You'll notice I added a hash mark (#) before "`introCopy`" and a period before "`highlight`". The difference is simple: "`introCopy`" was created with an id attribute, whereas "`highlight`" was created with the class attribute. Even though I named them both, they need to be prefaced by specific characters to let the browser know where to find them in the rest of the code (in other words, they should follow `id` or `class` attributes). So, when you use the class attribute, you always preface the class name with a period in your style sheet. Likewise, you use a hash mark or pound sign before your `id` names.

TIP

While there are many people in a *class*, your personal identification (ID) is unique to you. This holds true in CSS—`id` selectors can be used only once on a page, whereas classes can be repeated as many times, and in as many tags, as necessary.

Using HTML to Contain the Content

After you've organized your page into the key content areas, you can further organize the text in those content areas using some basic HTML container tags.

Paragraph Breaks

HTML is different from traditional word processors because you cannot simply press the RETURN or ENTER key to end a paragraph, and then press the TAB key to indent a new one. Instead, you have to use tags to tell the browser where to start and end paragraphs, as well as any other types of breaks.

The p tag functions specifically as a container for paragraphs. This means you use an opening p tag at the beginning of your paragraph, and a closing p tag at the end. If you had two paragraphs of text on your page, the structural might look like this:

```
<p>Far far away, behind the word mountains, far from the countries
Vokalia and Consonantia, there live the blind texts. Separated they
live in Bookmarksgrove right at the coast of the Semantics, a large
language ocean.</p>

<p>A small river named Duden flows by their place and supplies it
with the necessary regelialia. It is a paradisematic country, in which
roasted parts of sentences fly into your mouth. Even the all-powerful
Pointing has no control about the blind texts it is an almost
unorthographic life One day however a small line of blind text by
the name of Lorem Ipsum decided to </p>
```

Even though the p tag is most often used to contain paragraphs of text, it doesn't automatically indent them. Why not? Remember that HTML is meant to structure the content, not style it. So the blank lines separating each paragraph on the page serve to set the paragraph apart from the text around it. You can add the indent (if desired) using a style sheet.

Line Breaks

You can also use the br tag to add a line break in your HTML page. Typing the br tag in HTML is the same as pressing the RETURN or ENTER key on your keyboard in a word processor program. It causes the browser to stop printing text on that line and drop down to the next line on the page. If you want to force a line break at a particular point in a paragraph, you might use code like this:

This tells the browser to stop and add a line break.

```
<p>Far far away, behind the word mountains, far from the countries
Vokalia and Consonantia, there live the blind texts. <br />Separated
they live in Bookmarksgrove right at the coast of the Semantics, a
large language ocean.</p>
```

NOTE

Some HTML tags that don't have closing versions. The tag used to add line breaks, br, is one such tag. To close the br tag, you add a space and a forward slash before the final bracket, as in <br />.

Headings

One of the earliest means of structuring text was the heading tag. It is available in six levels of importance from `<h1>` down to `<h6>`, as shown in the following illustration. You use the heading tags to tell the browser which pieces of text function as headings, and then specify how to style them with CSS.

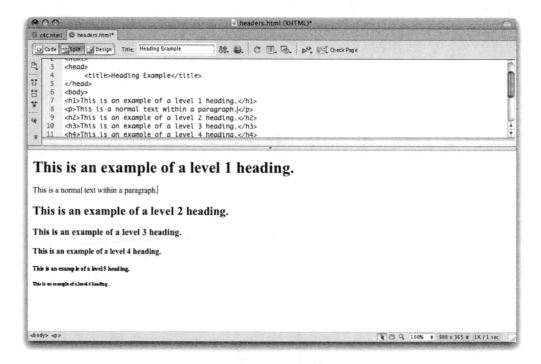

Heading tags are similar to the headings you might use in a word processor such as Microsoft Word. They are also similar to headings in outlines, because they should be used only in the proper order, from `h1` down to `h6`.

```
<h1>This is an example of a level one heading.</h1>
```

For example, you wouldn't create an outline that began with a small letter *a* and was followed by the Roman numeral *I*. Instead, you would begin with the Roman numeral *I*, follow that with a capital *A*, and, most likely, follow it with a number *1*. In like manner, an `<h1>` should be followed by an `<h2>`, as opposed to an `<h3>`.

While the heading tag does change the size of the font, it is primarily used as a structural element to identify the headings of various content areas. So at this point, don't try to change or alter the font characteristics of your headings. We'll do that with a style sheet in Chapter 9.

Lists

Lists are everywhere—on your refrigerator, in schoolbooks, next to the telephone, on bills, and in all sorts of other documents. That's why special HTML tags are used to create three types of lists, as outlined in Table 8-1.

As with heading tags, these HTML tags are not intended to style the lists. So if you want to change the look of your list bullets or adjust the indentation a bit, keep that thought. We'll get to some related styling methods in the next chapter.

TIP

Lists are especially useful in web pages to draw attention to short pieces of information. Remember this when you create your lists and try to include short phrases, instead of long sentences, in each list item.

Tables

Quite simply, a *table* is a section of information divided into columns and/or rows of blocks, called *cells*. Those of you who use Microsoft Word may be familiar with the Table menu item in that program, which enables you to create tables just like those used in web pages. Microsoft's word processor isn't the only one with tables; most word processors are capable of enabling you to format content in tables.

Type of List	Sample Code	Sample Browser Display
Ordered—each list item is preceded by a number or letter	```Homework: <ol> <li>Read pgs. 4-10</li> <li>Do the exercises on pg. 11</li> <li>Select a science fair project</li> </ol>```	Homework: 1. Read pgs. 4–10 2. Do the exercises on pg. 11 3. Select a science fair project
Unordered—each list item is preceded by a bullet	```Homework: <ul> <li>Read pgs. 4-10</li> <li>Do the exercises on pg. 11</li> <li>Select a science fair project</li> </ul>```	Homework: • Read pgs. 4–10 • Do the exercises on pg. 11 • Select a science fair project

Definition—contains terms, which are flush left, and definitions, which are indented	```<dl>
	<dt>HTML</dt>
	    <dd>Hypertext Markup Language</dd>
	<dt>FTP</dt>
	    <dd>File Transfer Protocol</dd>
	</dl>```
		HTML
		   Hypertext Markup Language
		FTP
		   File Transfer Protocol

Table 8-1 Types of HTML Lists

Another form of a table, either printed or electronic, is the spreadsheet. Along these lines, you might think about a table as a large piece of grid paper, in which you get to decide the size of the cells that will hold the information.

Basic Table Tags

To create tables with HTML, you need to know about four basic table tags, as described in the following list. With these tags in mind, you can create both basic and complex table structures according to your needs.

- **<table>...</table>** The table tag is a container for every other tag used to create a table in HTML. The opening and closing table tags should be placed at the beginning and the end of your table.

- **<tr>...</tr>** The tr tag stands for *table row*. The opening and closing tr tags surround the cells for that row.

- **<th>...</th>** The th tag stands for *table header*. An optional tag used instead of the td tag, this tag defines a cell containing header information. By default, the content in header cells is boldface and centered.

- **<td>...</td>** The td tag stands for *table data* and holds the actual content for the cell. An opening and closing td tag for each cell is in each row.

Opening and closing table tags surround the entire section of code. This tells the browser that everything inside these tags belongs in the table. Opening and closing tr tags for each row are included in the table. These surround td or th tags, which, in turn, contain the actual content to be displayed by the browser. For example, suppose you wanted to create a table with three columns and three rows, like this:

Row 1, Cell 1	Row 1, Cell 2	Row 1, Cell 3
Row 2, Cell 1	Row 2, Cell 2	Row 2, Cell 3
Row 3, Cell 1	Row 3, Cell 2	Row 3, Cell 3

Here's how you might accomplish that in HTML:

```
<table>
    <tr><td>Row 1, Cell 1</td>
        <td>Row 1, Cell 2</td>
        <td>Row 1, Cell 3</td>
    </tr>
    <tr><td>Row 2, Cell 1</td>
        <td>Row 2, Cell 2</td>
```

```
        <td>Row 2, Cell 3</td>
    </tr>
    <tr><td>Row 3, Cell 1</td>
        <td>Row 3, Cell 2</td>
        <td>Row 3, Cell 3</td>
    </tr>
</table>
```

You can include nearly any type of content in a table cell that you might include elsewhere on a web page. This content should be typed in between the opening and closing td tags for the appropriate cell. All tags used to format that content should also be included in between the td tags.

Tables, by nature of their design, have internal and external borders. By default, most recent browsers set the border size to zero, making them invisible. However, borders can be quite useful for tables of statistical information, for example, where seeing the columns is necessary to understand the data better.

When the borders are visible for a table, it's easier to see how much space is around the content and in between the cells. We will adjust that space with a style sheet when the time comes.

Table Uses

Before style sheets existed as a way to position elements on a web page, the most common method of web page layout involved the use of many complex tables. Thankfully, those days are behind us, and now tables are used primarily as they were originally intended: to display tabular data.

Figures 8-1 and 8-2 show examples of different uses of tables on a web page. In most cases, tables work best to display information that might otherwise appear in a spreadsheet. Using a table allows the designer to display the information in an organized fashion that might not be possible with basic HTML.

In Figure 8-1, the space in between the individual cells isn't apparent, while Figure 8-2 allows for a 1-point white border around each cell. In each case, the designer made choices based on which styling effects presented the information in the most readable and understandable manner. Keep that in mind when we style page elements in the next chapter.

Forms

Another type of HTML container is the form. In Chapter 4, I discussed the usability of forms, as it related to web design. After you've created a usable set of criteria for your forms, the next aspect of form creation to consider is the structure and layout.

Figure 8-1 An example of a basic table on a web page

Figure 8-2 Another example of a table on a web page

Form Container

Even the most basic forms have the same structure. This includes opening and closing
`form` tags, input controls, and processing methods. The `form` tags surround the entire
form, just as `html` tags surround the entire HTML document.

```
<form>
... content goes here ...
</form>
```

All the other `form` tags listed in this section must be placed in between the opening
and closing `form` tags to display properly. Figure 8-3 shows visual examples of each of the
form elements you likely need to include in your pages. The next few pages outline only
how to add these elements to your pages. I'll focus on styling form elements in Chapter 9.

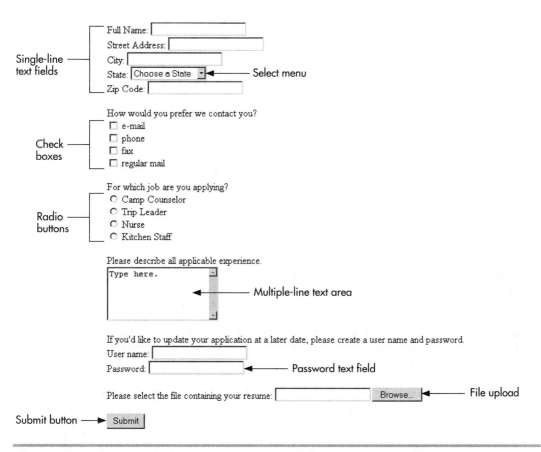

Figure 8-3   This sample form contains each of the most common form elements.

NOTE

While you can't nest `form` tags (include one `form` tag within another), you can use two or more sequential forms on a single page.

Single-Line Text Fields

The most basic type of input control is the single-line text field. This control is a space, that looks like a box, and that can contain a single line of text. Usually, text fields are preceded by descriptive text telling the user what to enter in the box. Here's an example:

```
Full Name: <input type="text" size="20" name="FullName" /><br />
Street Address: <input type="text" size="20" name="StreetAddress" /><br />
City: <input type="text" size="20" name="City" /><br />
```

As shown in Figure 8-3, *text fields* are single-line, white spaces that appear slightly indented on the page. Unless you specify otherwise with the `size` attribute, text fields are usually 20 pixels in length.

NOTE

Because the `input` tag doesn't have a closing version, use a space and a forward slash to terminate it: `<input type="text" />`.

Several attributes can be added to this `input` tag to customize the text field. Of these attributes, perhaps the most important is `name`.

To process all the controls in your form, each one must be identified with a name. For example, when the form is processed, you could tell it to take whatever the user entered in the control you named `FirstName`, and print that text at the top of an e-mail message.

TIP

Blank spaces between words in a value can cause problems in HTML and other coding methods. To avoid such problems when using the `name` attribute, many developers like to run phrases together, capitalizing the first letter in each word. For example, instead of using `"Middle Initial"` as the value of your name attribute, use `"MiddleInitial"` or `"middle_initial"`. Remember that these values are case-sensitive, which means whenever you reference that control later, you must also capitalize the first letters of each word. In addition, be sure to use unique names to avoid confusion when the form is processed.

HTML enables you to create two types of text fields: one for regular text (as you just learned) and a second for passwords. The main difference between the two is that password text fields show text that's displayed as bullets or asterisks instead of straight text.

You use `password` as the value of the `type` attribute in your `input` tag to create this type of control. Here's an example of the code from Figure 8-3:

```
<p>If you'd like to update your application at a later date,
please create a user name and password.<br />
User name: <input type="text" name="UserName" /><br />
Password: <input type="password" name="Password" /></p>
```

NOTE

Although this may seem as if it adds a level of security to your page, it's only a way to prevent those looking over the user's shoulder from seeing a password. The actual password isn't encrypted in any way when the form is processed and, therefore, this control shouldn't be implemented as the only means of security for pages with passwords.

Multiple-Link Text Areas

When you need to allow your web site visitors to enter more than a single line of text, use a text area instead of a text field, as shown in Figure 8-3. To specify the size of the text area, use the `cols` and `rows` attributes:

- The `cols` attribute identifies the visible width of the text area, based on an average character width.

- The `rows` attribute identifies the visible height of the text area, based on the number of text lines.

NOTE

Although the attributes refer to columns and rows, this might be a bit of a misnomer, as you're really specifying the height and width of the text area, respectively.

```
<p>Please describe all applicable experience.<br />
<textarea name="Experience" cols="20" rows="5">Type here.</textarea></p>
```

Radio Buttons

Radio buttons are small, round buttons that enable users to select a single option from a list of choices. This is accomplished with the `input` tag and the `radio` tag for the `type` attribute. Radio buttons are particularly useful for questions requiring a yes or no answer. When the user selects one of the options by clicking the radio button, the circle is filled in with a black dot.

```
<p>For which job are you applying?<br />
<input type="radio" name="Job" value="Camp Counselor" /> Camp Counselor<br />
<input type="radio" name="Job" value="Trip Leader" /> Trip Leader<br />
<input type="radio" name="Job" value="Nurse" /> Nurse<br />
<input type="radio" name="Job" value="Kitchen Staff" /> Kitchen Staff</p>
```

Check Boxes

Check boxes are similar to radio buttons because they don't let users enter any data and can be clicked only on or off. However, check boxes do let the user select more than one choice from a list of options. For example, you might use check boxes for selecting how job applicants might want to be contacted. When a check box is clicked, a small *x* or check mark typically appears in the box, depending on the browser.

To include a check box in your online form, use the input tag and type attribute with checkbox specified (note that *checkbox* is one word when used as an HTML value). Just as with radio buttons, the text used in the name attributes for all the options should be the same. Use the value attribute to identify what's different about each option, as in the following code from Figure 8-3:

```
<p>How would you prefer we contact you?<br />
<input type="checkbox" name="ContactMe" value="e-mail" /> e-mail<br />
<input type="checkbox" name="ContactMe" value="phone" /> phone<br />
<input type="checkbox" name="ContactMe" value="fax" /> fax<br />
<input type="checkbox" name="ContactMe" value="mail" /> regular mail</p>
```

When the form is processed, the values of any check boxes clicked by the user are transmitted to the server, along with the value of the name attribute. So, in the previous example, if I clicked the check boxes next to "e-mail" and "phone," the appropriate name and values would be transmitted: ContactMe: e-mail, phone.

Select Menus

Whenever you want to let users select from a long list of options, you might consider using a select menu instead of check boxes or radio buttons. Select menus are lists that have been compressed into one or more visible options, similar to those menus you find at the top of other software applications.

This type of menu, also called a *drop-down menu,* enables users to click an option initially visible and then pull down to reveal additional options. Only a single option is visible when the page loads, unless a number greater than *1* is specified in the size attribute. When the size attribute is *2* or more, that number of choices is visible in a scrollable list.

The select element is used to create the menu initially, while option tags surround each item in the menu. A menu asking users to choose the state in which they live, as shown in Figure 8-3, might be coded like this:

```
State: <select name="state">
<option value="">Choose a State</option>
<option value="AL">Alabama</option>
```

```
<option value="AK">Alaska</option>
<option value="AZ">Arizona</option>
<option value="AR">Arkansas</option>
... the rest of the states would be listed here ...
</select>
```

By default, users can select one item from the list. If you want them to be able to choose more than one option, add the `multiple` attribute to your opening `select` tag. The way users select more than one menu item depends on their computer system. For example, Macintosh users typically hold down the COMMAND key while clicking, while Windows users hold down the SHIFT key, or the CONTROL key, while clicking to select noncontiguous choices in the list.

File Uploads

Some online forms might require a file to be transmitted, along with any data from the form. For example, you might provide the option for potential employees to submit a photo with a job application being filled out online. This can be accomplished in part by using `type="file"` with the `input` tag.

```
<p>Please select the file containing your resume:
<input type="file" name="ResumeUpload" /></p>
```

For document uploads, most browsers display a text field followed by a button typically labeled *Browse...*, as shown previously in Figure 8-3. By clicking the button, users can locate the file they want to send with the form on their computers. After doing so, the browser prints the location and name of the file in the text field provided.

Buttons

Buttons enable users to interact with a form. For example, to tell the browser you're finished filling out a form and are ready to process it, you might click a Submit button. You can create buttons with two different HTML tags: `input` and `button`. The most common method of adding a button to a form is through the `input` tag, as with the following code:

```
<input type="submit" value="Send Message" />
```

The `type` attribute identifies this is a normal submit button, while the `value` attribute specifies the text to be displayed on the submit button. You can also use an image as a button with the `input` tag, by changing the type to `image`, as in the following example:

```
<input type="image" src="sendmessage.gif" name="Submit" alt="Send Message" />
```

Ask the Expert

Q: You've told us the basic methods used to add forms to web pages, but what happens when our users click the submit button? Where does the information go?

A: This question is referring to the form's processing method. Is the form's data e-mailed to the site administrator or stored in a database? Is it, perhaps, written to another web page on the site, such as occurs with blog comments? Many possibilities exist, and they ultimately depend on the purpose of the form.

But you really want to know about what happens behind the scenes. The most successful web forms use some sort of scripting (such as ASP, PHP, or CGI) to process the forms. When a user clicks the submit button, the contents of the form are sent to the script. The script then determines what to do with the data: send it, store it, or display it.

In larger web teams, programmers typically handle the processing of web forms. If you don't have access to such a person, first check with the site's hosting provider, since they sometimes offer free scripts to customers. Or, you could search the thousands of free scripts available at sites like these:

- **www.scriptarchive.com**
- **www.hotscripts.com**
- **www.cgi-resources.com**

Pay attention to the documentation offered with each script, because it should tell you how to customize the script for your needs and how to install it on your server.

TIP

All buttons have gray background colors by default. If you want to customize the look of the button, specify the desired characteristics in your site's style sheet, as discussed in Chapter 9.

Adding Links

By now you probably noticed that the crux of HTML is its ability to reference countless other pieces of information easily on the Internet. This is evident because the first two letters in the acronym HTML stand for Hypertext, or text that's linked to other information.

HTML enables us to link to other web pages, as well as graphics, multimedia, e-mail addresses, newsgroups, and downloadable files. Anything you can access through your browser can be linked to from an HTML document. In fact, one of the easiest ways to identify the URL of a page you want to link to is to copy it from the location or address toolbar in your web browser. You can then paste it directly into your HTML file.

Links are a big part of any web page. As such, they will likely fall within several different content areas. At this point, I want to talk about the HTML of links. Later on, I'll address styling questions, such as how to change link colors.

The a tag, short for *anchor* and used to add links to HTML files, doesn't serve much purpose without its attributes. The most common attribute is href, which is short for *hypertext reference* and tells the browser where to find the information to which you're linking. This and other popular attributes are listed in Table 8-2.

The text included in between the opening and closing a tags is what the person viewing your web page can click. In most cases, this text is highlighted in a different color from the surrounding text and is underlined. For this reason, it's important that you select easily recognizable link names.

Link Paths

The value of the href attribute is the actual path of the file you're linking to. Two basic types of paths exist—absolute and relative—depending on where the file being linked to is located.

Relative links are so called because you don't include the entire pathname of the page to which you're linking. Instead, the pathname you use is relative to the current page. This is similar to saying, "I live on Summershade Court, about three miles from here," which is relative to wherever "here" is. A more *absolute* way to say this might be "I live at 410 Summershade Court in Anytown, USA 55104."

Relative links are most commonly used when you want to link from one page in your site to another. Here's an example of what a relative link might look like:

```
<a href="contactme.html">Contact Me</a>
```

Attribute="Value"	Description
href="url"	Tells the browser where to find the information you're linking to
name="link_name"	Gives that spot in the page a name, so it can be linked to by another link
title="description"	Gives a brief description of the link
accesskey="character"	Assigns a keyboard shortcut to the element
tabindex="number"	Assigns the tab order of an element
target="window_name"	Specifies the browser window in which the link should be loaded

Table 8-2   Commonly Used Attributes of the a Tag

This link looks for the contactme.html file in the same folder that contains this page. If you were linking to a file in another folder below the current one, the value of your `href` might look like this:

```
<a href="wendy/contactme.html">Contact Me</a>
```

This link looks for the contactme.html file in a folder called *wendy*, located one level below the current folder in the site's directory structure.

Whenever you're linking to a page *that isn't contained in your web site,* you'll probably want to use an absolute pathname. When using an absolute pathname, remember to include the protocol prior to the domain name, as I did with the `http://` in the following example:

```
<a href="http://www.yahoo.com">Visit Yahoo!</a>
```

Interior Links

When you link to a page, the browser knows what to look for because each page has a name, but it's also possible to link to a section of text *within* a page on your web site. Before you can do so, you must first give that section a name, using the `name` attribute of the `a` tag. Because you're only labeling a section at this point, you can forgo the `href` attribute.

```
<a name="section1">Section 1</a>
```

Then, after the section is named, you can link to it with the `href` attribute. To tell the browser you're linking to a section within the page, precede your link with a pound sign, or hash mark (#).

```
<a href="#section1">Link to Section 1</a>
```

Other Links

Thus far, I mentioned only links to other web pages. When you want to link to other types of files, the process is almost the same. In fact, the only part that changes is the actual value of the `href` attribute. Here's an example of a link to an e-mail:

```
<a href="mailto:name@company.com">Email me!</a>
```

When linking to a file other than a standard web page, be sure to make this information clear to users. For example, e-mail links work only if the user is on a computer that has an e-mail program with a working e-mail address.

TIP

If you're linking to a downloadable file that is any larger than typical web pages, also provide the size, so users can decide whether or not to download it.

Using HTML to Add Images

Images are used in a variety of ways on the Web. A photograph located within a news article, for example, is part of the actual page content. In other cases, such as when applied to the background of a navigation bar, photographs are used as decoration. This section covers how to add images that are part of the actual page content. (Other images, added to dress up the page, are inserted via the page's style sheet, as discussed in the next chapter.)

You can easily add images anywhere in the foreground of your web page by using the img tag, where img is short for *image*. Add the src attribute (short for *source*) and its appropriate value to specify the actual filename and path of the image.

```
<img src="/images/lk_camp.gif" />
```

When you use the img tag, you're telling the browser to display the image directly within the web page, wherever you placed the tag. In doing so, remember the following:

- The image must be in a web-friendly file format, such as GIF, JPEG, or PNG; it must also be very small in file size and quick to download, as discussed in Chapter 5.

- The value of your src attribute should include the correct pathname and location of your file. So if the image you want to use isn't located in the same folder as the HTML page you're working on, you need to tell the browser in which folder that image is located.

- It's a good idea to use one folder (perhaps named *images*) to store all the images for your site. This makes it easy to locate and reference images, regardless of which page you're coding.

Image Height and Width

You can help speed the display of your web pages by telling the browser the size of your images within the img tag, using the height and width attributes. When the image height and width aren't specified in the HTML code, some browsers actually wait until the images are all loaded before displaying the web page.

```
<img src="/images/lk_camp.gif" width="122" height="18" />
```

NOTE

The value of both the width and height attributes should be in pixels—not in inches or centimeters.

By giving the height and width of an image in the HTML code, the browser is able to leave a space the proper size for the image and continue drawing the page. In addition, this enables the browser to avoid moving elements around after the page is loaded to make room for an image whose size it does not know.

Alternative Text

As discussed in Part I, because some people visiting your site won't be able to see the images on your pages, including alternative text with images is important. A variety of reasons exist why this might be the case, but here are a few of the most common ones:

- *They turned images off in their browsers.* Most browsers have a setting in the preferences that enable you to disable images on pages. By turning off images, visitors can view web pages more quickly and then choose which (if any) images they want to see.

- *They're using text-only browsers.* Although a minority of people using desktop computers have text-only browsers, many of those who have handheld devices do use text-only browsers on a daily basis. These devices might include web-enabled phones, gaming devices, and handheld computers. In addition, those who are vision impaired often use text-only browsers with additional pieces of software that read the pages to them. In these cases, your alternative text may be the only way vision-impaired people can understand the purpose of your images.

- *The image doesn't appear.* Sometimes, even though you have coded the page properly, a visitor to your site won't be able to see every single image on the page. This could happen if too much traffic occurs or the visitor clicks the stop button in her browser before the page has fully loaded.

You can do something to help visitors to your site understand the content of your images, even if they can't see them. You can use the `alt` attribute of the `img` tag to provide alternative text for an image. The text value of the `alt` attribute is displayed in the box where the image should be located, if the browser can't find the image or if it isn't set to display images.

```
<img src="/images/lk_camp.gif" alt="LINK: Chop Point Co-ed Summer Camp
for Teens 12-18" width="122" height="18">
```

TIP

Remember to be descriptive with your alternative text. For linked images, I like to begin the alternative text with the word *LINK:*, to make sure there's no question the image is linked.

You can also use the `title` attribute to add what's commonly referred to as a *tool tip* for images and links.

```
<img src="/images/lk_contactus.gif" alt="LINK: Contact Chop Point"
width="67" height="18" title="LINK: Contact Us">
```

While the `alt` attribute's text is typically covered when the image itself is loaded, the contents of the `title` attribute are displayed whenever the user moves his mouse over the image. Note that the individual browsers display tool tips a bit differently—some display the `title` value the same as the `alt` value (a small box with the text inside), while others such use something similar to a quote box in a cartoon.

TIP

The `title` attribute can also be added to other elements in HTML. For example, if you add it to the `a` tag for a text link, you are, in effect, creating a rollover for the text link.

Progress Check

At this point, I want to show you the status of my practice page, to help you visualize what a page might look like with the content areas in place. No styling has been applied, so things do quite match up with the mockup just yet. But that's OK. After we add some style in the next two chapters, this page will be right on target.

Figure 8-4   Status of practice page after content areas are added.

TIP

You can see the working code by visiting my web site: **www.wendywillard.com/blog/ my-books/design-files**.

Summary

By the end of this chapter, you've learned basic methods for containing text and image content within a web page. At this point in the process, your web pages won't look pretty, but they should have all the necessary content blocked out. The next two chapters will outline styling and positioning methods, to bring it all together.

NOTE

If you find yourself enjoying the code and looking for more in-depth explanations, consider picking up my book *HTML: A Beginner's Guide* (McGraw-Hill, 2009), or research the tags online.

Chapter 9

Styling Content

Key Skills & Concepts

- Use HTML tags as selectors to define styles.

- Use CSS to customize font characteristics.

- Use CSS to style links.

- Use CSS to style web forms.

This chapter is your chance to spruce up the look of your coded pages. Thus far, I've focused on helping you understand the code used to structure and contain content on web pages. After you have properly structured that content, you can style it—add color; change font characteristics; reformat content within lists, tables, and forms; and move content right where you want it.

Of course, that's a bit too much to fit into a single chapter, so I'll continue the discussion in Chapter 10. This chapter covers everything except positioning, which is discussed in the next chapter. Keep that in mind as you read both chapters, because formatting and positioning work together to help you add style to your web pages.

Setting the Style

You can style loads of different aspects of your web pages, from individual letters of text to the page itself. But first things first: you must know where to put your styling information. Chapter 7 discussed the three places you put style instructions:

- Embedded within the HTML code (inline styles)
- Placed within the header content of the page (internal styles)
- Coded in a separate document, and then linked to the affected pages (external styles)

NOTE
Refer to the end of Chapter 7 for a refresher about each type of style sheet.

If you're just getting started coding a single page, it's fine to start by placing all of your styles within the header content of your page. This makes it easy to edit, proof, edit, and proof, without having to switch between multiple files.

But, ultimately, if you are coding a site with multiple pages that follow the same basic styles, it's much more efficient to place all the style instructions in one external style sheet. Then you simply link to that style sheet from each of the affected pages. I typically start off with an internal style sheet, and then I copy and paste those styles into an external style sheet after I've gotten the styles set.

Selectors

Once you know where you're placing your style sheet instructions, it's time to consider the method by which you'll access the content on the page. In other words, how will you apply your styles?

With CSS, you use *selectors* to apply styles to page elements. Selectors allow you to style a particular piece of content, or whole sections of content, depending on the original mockup. A selector can be an HTML tag (such as p or div), or even custom words you create for the sole purpose of apply styles.

To put this in other terms, let's compare it to building a house. After you've completed the basic construction, it's time to decorate each room. You might specify to your crew that all walls be painted blue, with white moldings. If we were using CSS to tell your painters what to do, the code might look like this:

```
walls {
    color:blue;
    molding:white;
    }
```

In this example, walls is my selector; it's what aspect of the page (or house) we want to style. Now that you've got a basic understanding of what a selector is used for, let's move on to the different types of selectors available with CSS.

Tag Selectors

Suppose you wanted to cause all the level two headlines on your page to display in the Trebuchet font and to be colored blue. The simplest way to accomplish this would be to add a style declaration using the h2 tag as your selector, like this:

```
h2 {font-family:trebuchet;color:blue;}
```

NOTE
Notice that although the tag looks like this, <h2>, in your HTML code, you remove the brackets when using it as a selector in CSS.

Any tag can be used as a selector. So if you want to style all the paragraphs on your page, you could use p as your selector. Or, if you wanted to style *all* of the text on your page (regardless of whether it is contained in paragraphs, lists, tables, or what not) you could even use body as your selector.

Likewise, using div as a selector adds style to everything contained within divs on your page. But what if you wanted to style one particular div differently than another? Here's where you need custom selectors.

Custom Selectors

There are two types of custom selectors: classes and ids. These two have very different uses in CSS. Classes can be used multiple times throughout your pages. For example, a class might be used to apply a style called "highlight" that adds a yellow background color behind various important bits of text on multiple pages.

In the HTML code, use the class attribute to specify the class's name:

```
<span class="highlight">This text is highlighted.</span>
```

The class attribute can be added to any existing tag in the code, or you can use the span tag with the class attribute to apply a class to a section of text not already affected by another tag.

In the style sheet, classes are preceded by periods. This tells the browser that the selector is not an HTML tag, but a custom name used throughout the code:

```
.highlight {background-color:yellow;}
```

Conversely, ids can only be applied once per page. These are most commonly used to separate the content divisions of a page. In the same way that a unique Social Security number is assigned as identification—ID—for each person living in the United States, so should a unique name be given to each content division on a web page.

NOTE

If you need a refresher on setting up content divisions using the div and id tags, refer to the beginning of Chapter 8.

In the HTML code, use the id attribute to specify the id's name:

```
<div id="header">
```

The id attribute can be added to any existing tag in the code, so long as it is used just once in each page. Because of that limitation, it is most commonly used with the div tag to separate the page content.

Once you've named your divisions, these content areas can easily be formatted in the site's style sheet, which might look something like this:

```
#header {border:1px;}
#bodyCopy {font-family:verdana;}
#footer {font-size:10pt;}
```

Descendent Selectors

Sometimes you want to be more specific with your selectors, so that they affect only those paragraphs that fall within a certain content division, for example. Suppose your page has three content divisions (header, bodyCopy, and footer). You want to cause all the paragraphs in the bodyCopy to display using one font size, while those paragraphs that display in the footer to be a smaller font size. To accomplish this, you might set up your style sheet like this:

```
#bodyCopy p {font-size:12pt;}
#footer p {font-size:10pt;}
```

TIP

These types of selectors are called "descendent selectors" because they match elements that are descendents (children) of other elements in the document's family tree. When you separate two selectors with a space, you are telling the browser to look first for the first selector, and then find the second selector inside the first selector within the code. So in this case, these style declarations only affect paragraphs within the bodyCopy division and the footer division.

Combining Selectors

You can also apply styles to multiple selectors quickly and efficiently by combining selectors. When you do this, you simply separate them with a comma. Here's an example in which I change the font size for all paragraphs and table cells at once:

```
p,td {font-size:12pt;}
```

But what if you want to use the same font size for all paragraphs and table cells, but different font colors? Here's one way to do just that:

```
p,td {font-size:12pt;}
p {color: black;}
td {color: blue;}
```

Overwriting Selectors

One last thing to keep in mind about selectors is this: if you apply a particular style using the p tag as a selector, *all* paragraphs will carry that style. The only way to overwrite that style is to create a custom selector and apply it to whichever paragraph you want to display differently. Here's an example in which I specify all paragraphs should use a certain size text, except for one paragraph styled with a custom selector:

```
p {font-size:12pt;}
p.footer {font-size:10pt;}
```

Changing Font Characteristics

Well, now that you know how to target specific aspects of your page (using selectors), let's move on to what you can do with styles. You alter aspects of your page through the use of CSS properties. So if the selector tells the browser you want to focus on level one headlines, for example, the properties tell the browser exactly what to do with those headlines.

The first, and most commonly used, properties I want to discuss are the font properties. The following seven properties all affect aspects of fonts used on web pages:

- **font-family**   Changes the font family (for example, verdana, arial, times)
- **font-size**   Changes the font size (for example, 12px, 14pt, 1.2em)
- **font-size-adjust**   Adjusts the font size up or down, relative to its current size (for example, 1, -2)
- **font-stretch**   Changes the horizontal width of the font (for example, wider, narrower, condensed, expanded)
- **font-style**   Adjusts whether the text is italicized (such as italic, oblique)
- **font-variant**   Adjusts whether the text is displayed in small-caps (such as normal, small-caps)
- **font-weight**   Adjusts the heaviness of the text (such as normal, bold, bolder)

Here's an example to help you see these properties in action:

```
p {
    font-style: italic;
    font-size: 1em;
    font-weight: bold;
    font-variant: small-caps;
    font-family: arial;
}
```

TIP

Want to read more about these font properties? Check out **www.w3.org/Style/Examples/007/fonts** to see them in action.

But that's a lot to write! Thankfully, these can also be grouped together using CSS shorthand, via the `font` property. In other words, you can adjust all five of the characteristics shown in the preceding code sample at once with a single property, like this:

```
p {font: italic 1em bold small-caps arial;}
```

Ask the Expert

Q: **I see you are using different units for font sizes. Can you explain those?**

A: That's right. You can specify font sizes in a variety of ways, including keywords (small, medium, large), relative sizes (smaller or larger), or absolute sizes (using numbers followed by units).

The most common units used to specify fonts for screens are *px* (short for pixels) and *em* (short for eighteen millimeters). Two less popular, but never-the-less possible, units are *pt* (short for points) and *%* (percentage). Here's a little more information about each of these units:

- **em**   Em is a scalable unit of measurement, which means it can increase or decrease depending on the user's browser settings. One em is equal to the current font size. So if you specify in your `body` tag that a document's font size is 12 points, then for that document 1em = 12pt. If you later specify that a headline should be 2em, the headline would display at 24pt.

- **px**   Pixels are the common unit of measure for screens. Depending on your computer and monitor, web pages may display at 72 or 96 pixels per inch (ppi). Unfortunately, pixels are not scalable, which means users cannot increase the font size if you code a page using pixels for font measurements.

- **pt**   Points are the common unit of measure for print. Seventy-two points make up one inch on the printed page. Just like pixels, points are fixed and not scalable.

- **%**   You can also specify font sizes by percentage. Just like ems, percentages are scalable. In addition, they are dictated by the current font size (either in the page, or if that's not specified, then for the browser). So if the current font size is 12pt, then 100% is equal to 12pt, while 150% would be 18pt.

There is much debate as to the best unit of measure for web font sizes, so I won't crack open that can of worms. I do suggest you do your own research to identify the best unit of measure for your target audience. For what it's worth, I have found that a mixture of fixed and scalable units can often be the best of both worlds. So I use ems and pixels quite a bit.

Font Families

One of the biggest decisions you'll make has to do with the fonts used for your web pages. In Chapter 3, I discussed the difference between text created by the code and that which is included in images. At this point, I need to clarify the method used to render text with code.

Whenever you type text content into an HTML file, it will be rendered by the browser in the default font unless you specify otherwise. For most browsers, the default font is something like Times New Roman, which is not exactly a very easy-to-read font for screens. So most designers choose to change the default font to something a bit more screen-friendly.

To do so, you use the `font-family` style sheet property. Thankfully, this property can be applied to virtually any aspect of your web page. That means you are free to ban Times New Roman from your pages altogether, if you so choose.

TIP

Refer to Table 3-3 (in Chapter 3) for a list of the most popular and widely supported web fonts.

Because it's common for some fonts not to be available on certain users' machines, you can include multiple fonts in your `font-family` specification. This process is referred to as "cascading." Consider the following example:

```
p {font-family: verdana, arial, helvetica;}
```

In this case, the browser first looks for the font called Verdana on the user's system. If that is not available, it looks for Arial and then Helvetica. If none of those three fonts are available, the text will be displayed in the default font.

Here are a couple of points to remember about specifying font families:

- Some font names include two words, such as Gill Sans. Whenever a style sheet value includes a space, use single quotes to contain the value, like this: `'gill sans'`.

- The capitalization of font names varies according to the operating system. Therefore, I recommend always using lowercase letters in the font names.

- The actual font names may be a bit different across computer systems. To compensate, I suggest including any possible names for a font commonly known by multiple names. For example, the font Comic Sans can sometimes be installed as Comic Sans or Comic Sans MS. You can code your page to allow for both instances by using this: `'comic sans','comic sans ms'`.

● You can end your list of fonts with a generic font, such as serif, sans-serif, monospace, cursive, and fantasy. That way, if all of the other fonts you specify aren't available, the browser will at least know what type of font you were shooting for and will display something similar.

Other Font Styles

Aside from the CSS properties listed so far (which all begin with `font-`), a few more properties are available to customize your text. Here's a brief overview:

● **color**   Changes the color of the text.

● **direction**   Sets the direction in which the text will be read (left-to-right or right-to-left).

● **letter-spacing**   Changes the spacing between the letters, which is similar to kerning in print design.

● **line-height**   Changes the spacing between lines, which is similar to leading in print design.

● **text-decoration**   Lets you add underlines, overlines, and line-throughs.

● **text-transform**   Changes the case of the text.

● **word-spacing**   Changes the spacing between words, which is similar to tracking in print design.

● **text-indent**   Specifies the amount text is indented.

● **text-shadow**   Allows for text to have a drop-shadow effect.

The next chapter will also discuss `text-align` and `vertical-align`, which have to do with the alignment of text on the page.

NOTE
You can find more about these properties in the appendix, in my HTML book, or through online resources such as **www.w3schools.com/css/css_text.asp**.

Setting the Base Font Characteristics

As you've probably noticed, a great way to add style characteristics to many aspects of the page at once is to use the body tag as a selector. In fact, lots of designers style the body tag with a few key instructions right off the bat for all pages. I typically start with something along these lines:

```
body {
    font-family: verdana,arial,helvetica,sans-serif;
    font-size: 12px;
    color: black;
    }
```

This sets the tone for all text on the page. Then, if I need to alter the size or color for a particular section, I can do that with a more specific style declaration.

Styling Links

After you've styled the rest of your text, you'll undoubtedly want to move on to links. In fact, many beginners try changing the color, size, and format of links using standard font properties, only to find that doesn't work. Instead, you need to use special link properties for style sheets.

You actually use the a tag as your selector, as in the following example. You'll notice a colon follows the a, with additional specifications as to which type of link being styled.

```
a:link {color: blue;}
a:visited {color: purple;}
a:hover {color: orange;}
a:active {color:red;}
```

The a:link selector allows you to specify the style of the links before they're clicked, while the a:visited selector alters the links after they've been selected. The a:hover selector specifies the style of the link while the cursor is positioned over them. Finally, a:active states the style of the links while they are being clicked.

In most cases, the default link color for browsers is blue. The default visited link color is purple, and the active link color is red. Remember that, as with many other features of web browsers, the user ultimately controls these default colors.

At this point you need to refer to your mockups to determine how the text links on the page should be handled. Are they all the same? Or are there different sections (such as a header and footer), each with different link colors? One way to handle this is to create a custom selector (a class) with a different color link, as in the following example:

```
a.navlinks:link {color: white;}
a.navlinks:visited {color: gray;}
a.navlinks:hover {color: yellow;}
a.navlinks:active {color: orange;}
```

After you create these instructions in your style sheet, you just need to apply the class to the links you want affected. Remember that we use the `class` attribute to do so:

```
<a href="home.html" class="navlinks">Home</a>
```

Alternatively, if you have already set up content divisions (such as `#header`, `#bodyCopy`, and `#footer`), you can use descendent selectors to specify which links should display with each style:

```
#header a:link {color:white;}
```

In this example, the browser is instructed to change links within the header content area to white. As a reminder, here's how that content area might be defined:

```
<div id="header">Links go here</div>
```

Beyond Colors

You don't have to stop at just changing the colors of your links. You can format links using other properties, just like those discussed previously in this chapter. For example, you might cause all links to appear in boldface, except for those that have been clicked. And perhaps you add a yellow highlight in the background when the user's mouse hovers over a link.

The possibilities are endless. If you haven't already done so during the mockup process, I encourage you to experiment with creative ways to style your links. Having said that, I have a few words of caution:

- Avoid using different size fonts in each link state, unless the size change in no way affects the surrounding content. (It can be very annoying to a reader to move his mouse across a page and then not be able to read the content because the links become large enough to block the text around them.)
- Avoid making any changes that cause text to move or jump around on the page when a link is activated.
- Make sure to choose colors that complement the rest of the page. While you want your links to be visible, you don't want them to distract the reader.

NOTE

What about links with images? I'll cover creating image-based rollovers at the end of Chapter 10.

Styling Lists

In Chapter 8, I outlined the basic HTML code used to format text content in list form. Once you have formatted the content as a list, you can use a couple of style sheet properties to style it. Here's a brief overview of each of these properties:

- **list-style-image**   Changes the appearance of the bullet by replacing it with an image.

- **list-style-position**   Identifies the indentation of additional lines in list items.

- **list-style-type**   Changes the appearance of the bullet or characters at the beginning of each list item.

So with the `list-style-type` property, you can change the default bullets from circles to squares or adjust the numbering from decimal numbers to uppercase Roman numerals or even letters. And with the `list-style-image` property, you can actually replace the default bullets found in unordered lists with custom images.

TIP

Learn more about these properties in the appendix, an HTML book, or online through a resource such as **www.w3schools.com/css/css_list.asp**.

Using Lists for Navigation

While you were working on your mockups, I encouraged you to consider the many different types of navigation used by popular web sites. You may be surprised to learn that many of those types of navigation are actually based on basic HTML lists. To give you an idea how this might work, check out Figure 9-1 to see an example of one type of horizontal navigation bar.

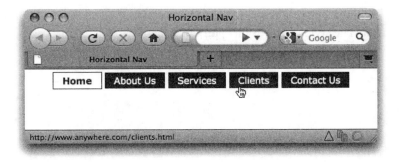

Figure 9-1 Common type of horizontal navigation bar

Here's the HTML used to code this bar, minus the CSS (we'll look at that in a minute):

```
<ul id="navlist">
<li class="active">Home</li>
<li><a title="LINK: About Us" href="aboutus.html">About Us</a></li>
<li><a title="LINK: Services" href="services.html">Services</a></li>
<li><a title="LINK: Clients" href="clients.html">Clients</a></li>
<li><a title="LINK: Contact Us" href="contactus.html">Contact Us</a></li>
</ul>
```

Notice I added a special class called `"active"` to the first item in the list. This helps set apart the page currently being viewed in the navigation. In this case, that means the home page link will be styled a bit differently than the other links, to help remind the user that this is the page currently being viewed.

Without the CSS, this really is just a regular list. When I remove the style sheet from the code, here's how that list displays:

- Home
- About Us
- Services
- Clients
- Contact Us

It's the style sheet that causes the list to go from looking like a list to looking like a navigation bar. The style sheet for this particular navlist looks like this:

```css
body {
    font-family: verdana, arial, helvetica, sans-serif;
    font-size: 10pt;
    }
#navlist {
    margin: 0;
    padding: 0;
    text-align: center;
    }
#navlist li {
    list-style: none;
    display: inline;
    }
#navlist li a {
    color: #fff;
    background-color: #900;
    padding: .2em 1em;
    text-decoration: none;
    }
#navlist li a:hover {
    color: #ffffff;
    background-color: #333333;
    }
.active {
    border: 1px solid #900;
    color: #900;
    font-weight: bold;
    padding: .2em 1em;
    }
}
```

Here, I turn off the bullets and tell the browser to display the list inline (one after another, horizontally across the page).

This specifies how the links in each list item should display.

This specifies how the colors should change when the user rolls over each link in the list item.

The final declaration styles the "active" button with a red border and bold, red text.

NOTE

Some of the CSS properties used to style this list have not been covered yet in this book, but we're getting there. In the next chapter, you'll learn more about those properties as we cover positioning and spacing.

I'm showing you this to help you consider the many possibilities that exist with regard to coding navigation. While a mockup might call for navigation to be contained in boxes, such as those shown in Figure 9-1, you may not have realized they could be created with a basic list. If you plan to code all your own web pages (or even those of other designers), I encourage you to delve deeper into HTML and CSS to discover the creative ways you can use coding better to serve your users.

Customizing Form Fields

Form fields can be styled, just like any other aspect of a web page. This means you can do away with those boring white and gray text boxes and color them all green if you'd like! Most of your form elements can be styled by using the `input` tag as a selector, like this:

```
input {
    border: 1px solid #fc0;
    background-color: #fc3;
    }
```

This will add a yellow background and a 1-pixel red border to each element that uses the `input` tag. Obviously, you can use a variety of other properties to customize your form fields, but hopefully you get the idea.

You can also style select menus and text areas, using the `select` and `textarea` tags as selectors. So, if I wanted to cause *all* the form elements to have the same red border and yellow background, I could use all three of the selectors:

```
input, select, textarea {
    border: 1px solid #fc0;
    background-color: #fc3;
    }
```

Compare Figures 9-2 and 9-3 to see how styling like this can drastically alter the appearance of web forms.

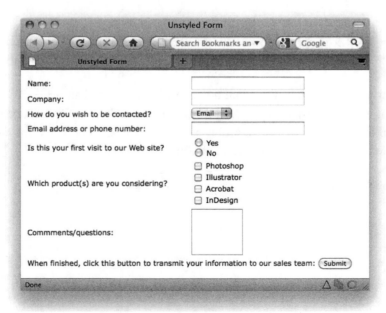

Figure 9-2   Web form without a style sheet

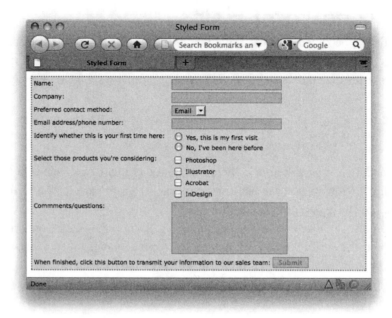

Figure 9-3 Web form after style sheet has been applied

If you want to customize individual form fields, you can add an `id` to each field, and then reference that `id` in your style sheet. Here's an example in which I added an `id` called `"submit"` to the `input` control used to create the submit button for a form. First, let me show you the HTML used to create the submit button:

```
<input type="submit" name="Submit" value="Submit" id="submit" />
```

Next, here's the part of the style sheet that applies to this input control:

```
input#submit {
    color: #f60;
    font-weight: bold;
}
```

In this case, I am telling the browser to look for a specific instance of the input tag, one in which an id attribute is added, with a value of "submit". Then, when it finds that button, I instruct it to display the text as bold, with an orange hue. That's how it works when you use HTML in conjunction with CSS to code web pages: first you build the page in HTML, and then you style it in CSS.

In the next chapter, you'll read about how to adjust the spacing in and around elements. Those properties (border, margin, and padding) will prove quite useful if you want to customize your forms further. Here are a few online resources to help you envision how creatively forms can be styled:

- **www.noupe.com/css/form-elements-40-cssjs-styling-and-functionality-techniques.html**

- **http://speckyboy.com/2009/07/02/20-resources-and-tutorials-for-creative-forms-using-css**

- **www.1stwebdesigner.com/inspiration/91-trendy-contact-and-web-forms-for-creative-inspiration**

Progress Check

It's time to check in on the status of the page I've been building as a teaching tool. In the last chapter, I set up the content areas, but they had no style. Now, I've added the style declarations to customize the font family, size, and color. I also specified that the list-style is none (to remove the bullets), but I haven't done anything else to change the format from vertical to horizontal. Compare Figures 8-4 (from the previous chapter) and 9-4 to see how the page has changed with these new styles.

TIP

You can see the working code by visiting my web site: **www.wendywillard.com/blog/my-books/design-files**.

Figure 9-4 Status of practice page after content areas are styled

Summary

When coding web pages, styling happens in two pieces. One is the way the content looks—color, size, weight, and so on—which was covered in this chapter. The other is its position on the page. The next chapter delves into positioning content within web pages using CSS.

NOTE

If you find yourself enjoying the code and looking for more in-depth explanations, you can read my HTML book or simply research the tags online.

Chapter 10

Positioning Content

Key Skills & Concepts

- Understand cascading style sheets (CSS) box properties.

- Understand how elements are positioned with CSS.

- Recognize uses of layering and backgrounds in web design.

Thus far, our coding has focused on formatting various types of content, from bits of text to images. This chapter seeks to close the loop, so to speak, by discussing how to put it all together into effective, user-friendly web pages. That, in this chapter, is all about the coded layout.

You've already created a layout in a graphic program, but that was the easy part (relatively speaking, of course). Now you have to re-create that layout without the help of a Layers palette, Blending Modes, and Alpha Channels. Instead, it's all code!

To summarize my earlier discussions on CSS, style sheets were created as a way to separate the content of a web site from the design. The theory is that content is king (as it should be), so anything else is simply icing on the proverbial cake. So we keep the content in the main HTML document and pull the design aspects into the accompanying style sheet.

The most striking benefit to this arrangement is in maintenance of the site. It used to be an expensive and exhaustive process for businesses to redesign their web sites every few years. If the content is separated from the design with style sheets, the site can be redesigned much more quickly, at a mere fraction of the cost. The reason for this is simple—instead of recoding every page on the site, the developer has to recode only the site style sheet (provided it was coded correctly in the beginning).

So how do you go about laying out pages with style sheets? Well, it all starts with a box....

Understanding Box Properties

Every element on a web page—text, photographs, logos, drop-down menus, and so on—is contained within a box of sorts, or at least it's considered to be a box in coding terms. This is important to realize, because you must code each element on the page as if it had four corners and four sides, even if it doesn't look like that when it's displayed in the browser.

Two basic types of boxes are used in web development: *block* and *inline*. By default, each type of element falls into one of those two categories. However, the box type can also be changed as needed. For example, boxes created by `paragraph`, `heading`, `div`, and `blockquote` tags are block boxes by default. This means they have certain characteristics, such as the following:

- Block-level elements can contain other blocks.

- Block-level elements fill all the available horizontal space unless specific width attributes are assigned.

- Block-level elements typically begin just below the previous block (which means they often start new lines of text).

By contrast, other elements, such as those created by the `strong` or `span` tag, are called inline boxes. These carry different characteristics than block boxes:

- Inline elements don't usually contain other blocks.

- Inline elements don't start new lines or extend beyond their contents.

TIP

An example of an inline element might be a link inside of a paragraph, a bolded sentence, or any other piece of content that flows inside of other content.

Also, all nested boxes (that is, boxes placed inside of other boxes) inherit certain characteristics of their containing (block) boxes. This is important because it affects how you define styles for your pages. To clarify, suppose you were coding a page with two copy sections. One contains black text, and the other contains white text on a black background. Then, inside of each copy section are multiple paragraphs of text. Instead of coding a color style for each paragraph, you can contain all the paragraphs in each section into a single division (using the `div` tag). That containing box will hold the color style, which is inherited by all the boxes (paragraphs) nested inside.

TIP

You can change a box type from block to inline, and vice versa, with the `display` property. Use `display: block`, `display: inline`, or even `display:none` to hide the content altogether.

Box Properties

All block-level elements use five basic spacing properties:

- height
- width
- margin
- padding
- border

As mentioned previously, all block-level elements will fill the available horizontal space by default. This means that unless you specify a smaller width, paragraphs will always run all the way across the page. The margins, padding, and border you specify for any box are always added to your height and width dimensions. So if you define a paragraph to be 500 pixels in width, and then add a 5-pixel border, your entire box will actually take up 510 pixels of horizontal space on the page (500 + 5 for the left border + 5 for the right border). Here's an illustration to help explain:

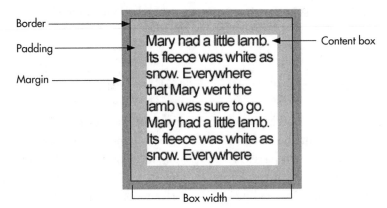

Margin and Padding

The amount of space in and around each box's edges are (for the most part) dictated by the `margin` and `padding` properties in your style sheet.

In the preceding illustration, notice how the padding is actually contained *within* the borders of the text box. This means you can use the `padding` property in a style sheet to give the content a buffer zone of white space on one, two, three, or all four sides, as I did for the `blockquote` tag in the following example:

```
blockquote {
    padding-bottom: 25px;
    padding-top: 25px;
    padding-right: 25px;
    padding-left: 25px;
}
```

When all four sides need the same amount of padding or margin, you can use shorthand to specify that quickly. For example, instead of typing out all four sides, as shown in the preceding example, you could simply add code: `padding: 25px`. When no side is specified, the browser applies the padding or margin value to all four sides equally.

If you do specify a certain amount of padding, such as `padding-right: 25px`, those 25 pixels are subtracted from the total width of the content box. So if your box is 200 pixels wide by 200 pixels tall, and you code a 25-pixel padding on all four sides, you are left with 150 pixels across and 150 pixels down for the actual content.

The `margin` property affects the buffer space *outside* the box properties, so it won't subtract space from the overall size of the content box. As with the `padding` property, you can define the margins for one, two, three, or all four sides of the box, such as in the following example:

```
p {
    margin-bottom: 25px;
    margin-top: 5px;
    margin-right: 15px;
    margin-left: 5px;
}
```

TIP

You might think of margins and padding in terms of a framed painting. The padding affects how far the paint is from the edge of the canvas, while the margin corresponds to how wide the matte and/or frame is.

Border

Another associated style sheet property is `border`. This property identifies the color, size, and style of each element's border. Suppose your mockup called for a pull-quote within each page's text content, and the pull-quote with a thin, colored border on top and bottom. Thankfully, there's a style sheet property for that.

The following CSS declaration might be added to a style sheet to get the ball rolling:

```
p.pullquote {
    border-width: 1px;
    border-color: #0066FF;
    border-style: solid;
}
```

This bit of code would create a 1-pixel, solid blue border on all four sides of any paragraph assigned to the class named "pullquote". Here's how the related HTML might look:

```
<p class="pullquote">Did you know we can accomplish this task is just
1/8 of the time it took 2 years ago?</p>
```

So the combination of the CSS and HTML I just showed you would combine to produce the following display in the browser:

Latest Product Release

Lorem ipsum dolor sit amet, consectetuer adipiscing elit, sed diam nonummy nibh euismod tincidunt ut laoreet dolore magna aliquam erat volutpat. Ut wisi enim ad minim veniam, quis nostrud exerci tation ullamcorper suscipit lobortis nisl ut aliquip ex ea commodo consequat. Duis autem vel eum iriure dolor in hendrerit in vulputate velit esse molestie consequat, vel illum dolore eu feugiat nulla facilisis at vero eros et accumsan et iusto odio dignissim qui blandit praesent luptatum zzril delenit augue duis dolore te feugait nulla facilisi.

Did you know we can accomplish this task is just 1/8 of the time it took 2 years ago?

Mirum est notare quam littera gothica, quam nunc putamus parum claram, anteposuerit litterarum formas humanitatis per seacula quarta decima et quinta decima. Eodem modo typi, qui nunc nobis videntur parum clari, fiant sollemnes in futurum.

Not bad, except the left border runs right up to the edge of the text, and wasn't the intention to have it display only on the top and bottom of the pull-quote? Plus, with the use of some CSS shorthand, we can shorten up our code a bit. Check out the revised CSS to see how it has changed:

```
p.pullquote {
    border-top: 1px solid #0066FF;
    border-bottom: 1px solid #0066FF;
    padding: 8px;
    color: #0066FF;
}
```

I used shorthand to condense the `border-width`, `border-style`, and `border-color` properties into one statement each for the top and bottom borders. Next, I added some padding to move the text away from the border a bit. Finally, I changed the color of the text to help it stand out a bit more. Here's the resulting display:

Latest Product Release

Lorem ipsum dolor sit amet, consectetuer adipiscing elit, sed diam nonummy nibh euismod tincidunt ut laoreet dolore magna aliquam erat volutpat. Ut wisi enim ad minim veniam, quis nostrud exerci tation ullamcorper suscipit lobortis nisl ut aliquip ex ea commodo consequat. Duis autem vel eum iriure dolor in hendrerit in vulputate velit esse molestie consequat, vel illum dolore eu feugiat nulla facilisis at vero eros et accumsan et iusto odio dignissim qui blandit praesent luptatum zzril delenit augue duis dolore te feugait nulla facilisi.

Did you know we can accomplish this task is just 1/8 of the time it took 2 years ago?

Mirum est notare quam littera gothica, quam nunc putamus parum claram, anteposuerit litterarum formas humanitatis per seacula quarta decima et quinta decima. Eodem modo typi, qui nunc nobis videntur parum clari, fiant sollemnes in futurum.

NOTE

In these examples, after the initial HTML code was set, I did not have to make any changes to the HTML. Instead, when I needed to add some padding and change the border characteristics, I edited only my style sheet.

A whole slew of options are available when you play with the border width, color, and style choices. While those are discussed more thoroughly in my HTML book, or online in one of the many HTML tutorials, I have included the options for each CSS property in this book's appendix.

Adjusting Basic Alignment

You just saw how easy it is to add spacing and borders to any sort of element on a web page. But what about alignment? In the last few chapters, you added all sorts of elements to your pages, but I've been silent on the topic of alignment. That's because alignment with CSS is so complex.

You know how the most basic method of alignment in a word processor is to click a button for align left, align right, and center? That used to be all we had in HTML as well. But CSS opens up a whole slew of possibilities, including the option to position any element in a specific location on the page.

We'll get to that—absolute positioning—shortly. In the meantime, here's how you can accomplish those basic forms of alignment. Two properties can be used for basic alignment: `text-align` and `vertical-align`. Both affect the way text is aligned, relative to the edge of the page. Here's what the style sheet might look like if I were to center the text in my pull-quote:

```
p.pullquote {
    border-top: 1px solid #0066FF;
    border-bottom: 1px solid #0066FF;
    padding: 8px;
    color: #0066FF;
    text-align: center;
}
```

But what if I wanted to justify *all* the paragraphs on my page, aside from the pull-quote? I'd simply add the text-align property (with a value of justify) to my style sheet declaration for the p tag:

```
p {
    text-align: justify;
}
```

Using Floats

Experience has shown that we all definitely want to be able to move other elements around on our web pages, in addition to from basic text alignment. So bring on the floats! As opposed to large trucks that slowly move down the street during a parade, CSS floats are stationary objects that allow other elements to move freely alongside them.

The `float` property essentially tells the browser to place the floated element nearest whichever browser edge is specified (left or right) and then flow the rest of the page's content around it. To say it another way, content automatically flows along the right side of a left-floated element, and to the left side of a right-floated element.

For example, if you wanted to place an image in the upper-right corner of several paragraphs of text. You could use the `float` property on that image, and set the value to `"right"` to tell the browser to keep the image on the right side of the text.

NOTE

When coding floats, your floated content must be placed in the HTML code *before* any other content to wrap around it.

Take a look at Figure 10-1 to see why floats are rarely used without some additional bit of coding. In this example, the floated image runs right up against the text at its left and covers part of the pull-quote below. To fix that, I can add some margin spacing along the left and bottom edges of the image. Then I use the `clear` property to tell the browser where to stop floating the image. Figure 10-2 shows the updated display, using the following styles:

```
p.pullquote {
    border-top: 1px solid #0066FF;
    border-bottom: 1px solid #0066ff;
    padding: 8px;
    color: #0066FF;
    text-align: center;
    clear: right;
}
img.globe {
    float:right;
    margin: 0 0 10px 10px;  ◄——— When using shorthand to specify margin values,
}                                always assign those values clockwise: top right
                                 bottom left.
```

Latest Product Release

Lorem ipsum dolor sit amet, consectetuer adipiscing elit, sed diam nonummy nibh euismod tincidunt ut laoreet dolore magna aliquam erat volutpat. Ut wisi enim ad minim veniam, quis nostrud exerci tation ullamcorper suscipit lobortis nisl ut aliquip ex ea commodo consequat. Duis autem vel eum iriure dolor in hendrerit in vulputate velit esse molestie consequat, vel illum dolore eu feugiat nulla facilisis at vero eros et accumsan et iusto odio dignissim qui blandit praesent luptatum zzril delenit augue duis dolore te feugait nulla facilisi.

Did you know we can accomplish this task is just 1/8 of the time it took 2 years ago?

Mirum est notare quam littera gothica, quam nunc putamus parum claram, anteposuerit litterarum formas humanitatis per seacula quarta decima et quinta decima. Eodem modo typi, qui nunc nobis videntur parum clari, fiant sollemnes in futurum.

Figure 10-1   The `float` property is used to move this image to the right side of the text.

Figure 10-2 Additional coding allows the floated image to maintain a 10-pixel buffer zone, away from text around it.

Ask the Expert

Q: What if I want to float the pull-quote instead of the image? When I try to add the `float` property to the `pullquote` class, the results aren't what I expected.

A: Images are easy to float because they carry defined height and width values. But by default, paragraphs of text fill the entire width available. So in this case, you must first assign a `width` value before the element can be floated properly. This allows the browser to estimate how much space is needed for the pull-quote, and to then flow the remaining elements around it in the leftover space. Use the `width` value in your style sheet to specify how much space you want the pull-quote to fill.

Using CSS Positioning

At this point, you understand how to use basic left-right-center alignment, and how to float elements along the left or ride side of the page. But what about more specific positioning? As promised, here's the part where I talk about the complex, powerful, and custom positioning available with CSS.

There are four basic flavors of positioning with CSS. *Normal* (also called *static*) is the default type of positioning that happens when no other type of positioning is specified. With normal positioning, items are placed one after another, starting at the upper-left of the page.

Relative Positioning

Relative positioning starts off using the normal positioning, but then allows certain elements to be moved up, down, left, or right, from the original position. In other words, boxes are moved relative to where they would normally be placed on the page. Here's an example of a level-two headline that is moved 50 pixels to the right of its normal position:

```
h2 {
    position:relative;
    left: 20px;
}
```

But wait? Didn't I say we moved it to the right? Then why did I use the left property to do this? With relative positioning, we're moving the box relative to its current location. So if we want to move a box to the right, we actually do that by asking the browser to look at the left edge, and push it 20 pixels over (to the right). To move it back toward the left edge, we'd instead specify a value of -20. With relative positioning, we have to think of this whole page as a big grid, with the zero point at wherever the box's edge would normally be placed.

TIP

Want to try this yourself to understand what's happening with relative positioning? Visit **www.w3schools.com/Css/tryit.asp?filename=trycss_position_relative** to do just that.

Fixed and Absolute Positioning

The remaining two types of positioning both place an element on the page in a firm, concrete spot. However, the difference lies in how the spot is determined. In the case of fixed positioning, the element is positioned relative to the browser window. With absolute positioning, the element is placed relative to its parent object.

So how exactly does this work? Consider Figure 10-3, which shows two elements, each of which is contained inside a box (signified by the colored and dotted outlines). One of the elements (APPLES) uses fixed positioning, and the other (ORANGES) uses absolute positioning. Even though both are set to be 20 pixels below the top edge and 10 pixels off the left edge, they don't end up in the same spot.

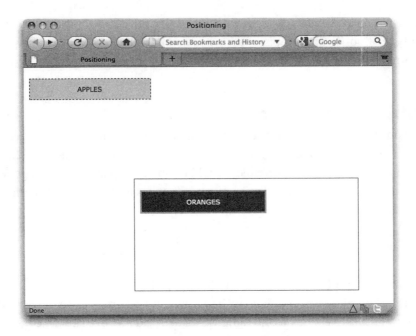

Figure 10-3 Comparing fixed and absolute positioning

Why? Because the ORANGES element (which is positioned absolutely) is placed 20 pixels below the top edge *of its container box*, but the APPLES element is placed 20 pixels below the top edge of the browser window. The style sheet and HTML for this page is included here:

```
<!DOCTYPE html PUBLIC "-//W3C//DTD XHTML 1.0 Transitional//EN"
"http://www.w3.org/TR/xhtml1/DTD/transitional.dtd">
<html>
<head><title> Positioning </title>
<style type="text/css">
#apples {
    position: fixed;
    top: 20px;
    left: 10px;
    width: 200px;
    padding: 10px;
    text-align: center;
    background-color: #ccc;
    border:1px dashed black;
}
```

```
#oranges {
    position: absolute;
    top: 20px;
    left: 10px;
    width: 200px;
    padding: 10px;
    text-align: center;
    background-color: #333;
    color: #fff;
    border: 3px solid #999;
}
#container {
    width:400px;
    height:200px;
    position:absolute;
    left:200px;
    top:200px;
    border:1px solid red;
}
</style>
</head>
<body>
<div id="container">
    <div id="apples">APPLES</div>
    <div id="oranges">ORANGES</div>
</div>
</body>
</html>
```

When you begin working with the different types of CSS positioning, you will undoubtedly have to encounter some "on the job training." Don't let that frustrate you, because it happens to the best of us. Figuring out the nuances of relative, fixed, and absolute positioning can be tricky at first, but it does become easier the more layouts you develop.

My *HTML: A Beginner's Guide* book provides more information about the different types of layout you can achieve with CSS. You can also find a lot of layout templates online, at sites like these:

- **http://layouts.ironmyers.com/**

- **www.smashingmagazine.com/2007/01/12/free-css-layouts-and-templates/**

- **www.freecsstemplates.org/**

Browser Behavior

It should be noted that the positioning I describe comes from the Worldwide Web Consortium's (W3C) specifications for CSS. However, only well-behaved browsers will actually render pages according to that specification. Certain older browsers, such as Internet Explorer 5, behave poorly when elements are positioned with CSS. Therefore, it is important that you do thorough testing before launch to ensure the pages display properly in all your target browsers.

Don't forget to specify the unit when assigning positioning values. If you want to move a box 50 pixels from the left edge, but you forget to specify **px** as the unit, the browser won't know what unit to use and will instead ignore the statement. The one exception is 0 (zero); it's not necessary to specify the units when assigning a value of 0.

Layering

In the preceding section, I showed you two elements that might have been positioned on top of each other if both had used absolute positioning. When that happens, which element is displayed and which is hidden behind the other?

While you might think it depends on how the two elements are placed within the HTML, that's not entirely the case. You can include a specific CSS property to tell the browser which element goes where in the stacking order.

CSS functions in three dimensions: height, width, and depth. The z-index property specifies the depth of an element, or more specifically, the layering of elements that overlap. If two elements overlap, the one with the higher z-index value is placed on top. This means you can actually use negative z-index values to force a layer to drop behind others. Take a look at the following sample styles to see what I mean:

```
#apples {
    position: absolute;
    top: 20px;
    left: 20px;
    width: 200px;
    padding: 10px;
    text-align: center;
    background-color: #ccc;
```

```
         border:1px dashed black;
         z-index: 1;
}
#oranges {
         position: absolute;
         top: 50px:
         left: 50px:
         width: 200px;
         padding: 10px;
         text-align: center;
         background-color: #333;
         color: #fff;
         border: 3px solid #999;
         z-index: 2;
}
```

The two elements in this sample overlap. However, the `z-index` value of the `oranges` element is set to 2, which is higher than the value given to the `apples` element. This places the `oranges` element above the `apples` element when viewed in a browser (as shown in Figure 10-4).

NOTE

The `z-index` property works only on elements that use relative or absolute positioning with CSS.

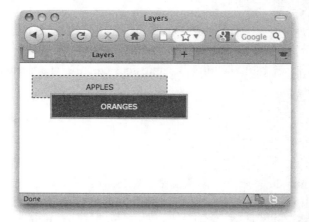

Figure 10-4   The `z-index` property specifies the layers when elements overlap.

The layering of elements in a web page can be a very powerful way to add depth and interactivity. This can happen when layers are hidden temporarily (using "visibility: hidden" in the style sheet) and then made visible based on user action. Here are just a few of the ways layers might be used:

- **Advertising** Ever click a link in a banner ad, only to have that ad appear to grow larger without the actual web page changing? Very likely, the larger version of the ad was a hidden layer set to appear when you click the link.

- **Games** While many online games use Flash for interactivity, some use a combination of JavaScript and CSS called Dynamic HTML. These games often place different elements on layers so they can easily be moved around on the page, independently of one another.

- **Navigation** You've likely visited a web site and used navigation that had submenus or drop-down menus. These types of navigation systems can be accomplished by placing the drop-down menu content into a layer that is brought forward and made visible by the user clicking a particular link.

Centering

One of the most common uses of CSS positioning is to center content on a page. For example, suppose your layout is contained within an 800-pixel–wide box. You'd likely want that box to be centered within the browser window, regardless of how wide or narrow the browser is.

The most efficient way to do that is to set the margins on the box to fill the available space automatically on both the left and right sides equally. That's the long way of saying you do this:

```
#container {
    width: 800px;
    margin: 0 auto;
}
```

If you remember how shorthand works in CSS, you recognize that whenever two values are specified, the first one applies to the vertical sides and the second to the horizontal sides. So in this case, there will be no margin (0) on the top and bottom, and an equal amount (auto) on the left and right. This, in effect, centers the box.

NOTE

While this works excellently in well-behaved browsers, versions of Internet Explorer prior to version 7 did not respond properly to this method. So there is a workaround for those browsers. Check out this page for details: **www.bluerobot.com/web/css/center1.html**.

CSS Backgrounds

With all this talk of positioning and layouts, I need to cover one more key aspects of most designs: the background. For most designers who work in graphics programs such as Photoshop, layering is a very important tool. Photoshop allows you to place images, colors, and textures "below" other elements through the use of semi-transparent layers.

I covered how the z-index property can be used to layer elements in a web page. Other tools available to help with this task are the five background properties:

- **background-color** Used to add a solid color in the background
- **background-image** Used to add an image in the background
- **background-position** Specifies where an image sits in the background
- **background-repeat** Specifies whether an image is repeated (tiled) in the background
- **background-attachment** Specifies whether an image scrolls with the page

Each of these properties can be used to customize the background for the entire page or for specific elements. For example, you could add a colored background to a paragraph, and a repeating image to the background of a table cell.

When you want to use more than one background property for a single element, you can use CSS shorthand to avoid coding them all longhand:

```
p {background: url(star-bg.gif) no-repeat;}
```

In this case, the first part of the statement tells the browser to use a file called star-bg.gif in the background of the paragraph, and the second part specifies not to repeat that image in the background.

So how can you use backgrounds to accomplish your design goals?

- **Create "faux" columns** You can quickly and easily give the appearance of different colored columns by creating a single background image containing each of the column colors. Read more here: **www.alistapart.com/articles/fauxcolumns/**

- **Customize bullets** The default bullets typically used for unordered lists sometimes don't fit a client's design scheme. An easy way to replace them with custom images is to turn off the default bullets and add the images to the list's background. Check out this page for more: **http://css.maxdesign.com.au/listamatic/vertical05.htm**

- **Add shadows** Designers frequently like to add drop-shadows to various page elements, if for no other reason that to add a little depth to an otherwise flat page. Many sites use partially transparent images in an element's background to achieve a drop-shadow affect in web design. Refer to **http://nontroppo.org/test/shadow .html** and **www.projectseven.com/tutorials/images/gradient_tiles2/index.htm** for two different examples.

Take a look at the following illustration, which shows a small image with a slight horizontal gradation:

When repeated vertically, this image helps give the appearance of a shadow along the left side of the main content box, as shown in Figure 10-5. Visit **www.anytimespasandpools .com/history.html** in your browser and choose File | View Source (or similar) to see exactly how I accomplished this shadow affect.

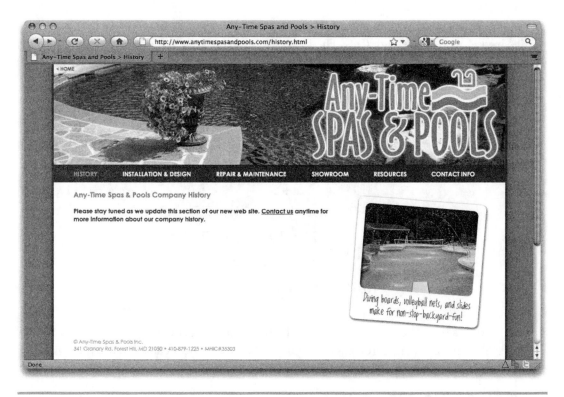

Figure 10-5   When a small image is tiled in a background, great shadow effects can be achieved.

Image Rollovers with CSS

You can also use the same concept to style image-based links, by adding different images to the background of text links.

Suppose you wanted to create a navigation bar with a series of images, and you wanted those images to change when the user's mouse rolls over them. Before the advent of CSS, designers had to use complicated JavaScript to code image-based rollover effects. Thankfully, it is now possible to achieve the same effects with some background images and a few CSS instructions.

I've already told you it's best to keep links as text whenever possible. But what happens when you want to add a stylized background not possible with pure HTML? With CSS, you can have the best of both worlds.

We'll create the written portion of the image with plain text in HTML. Then we'll add the background image with CSS. The first step is to create the background images. I know this might sound strange, but we want to create all three versions (normal state, rollover state, active state) within a single image, like this:

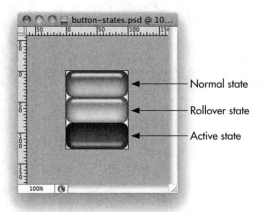

Next, it's time to code the HTML for the links. Remember that we're using text for the links. This ensures that search engines and text-based browsers can still access the links. The only other addition is a `div` tag surrounding the links.

```
<div class="imageRollovers">
<a href="home.html" id="homeButton" title="Home">Home</a>
<a href="aboutus.html" id="aboutButton" title="About Us">About Us</a>
</div>
```

The last step is to add the CSS, to tie it all together. We'll add the background image behind each of the links and position it according to which state we want to display at any given time. In other words, we'll move the image around in the background so as to display the appropriate button state. The following code is included in the style sheet attached to this page:

```
.imageRollovers a {
    display:block;
    width:100px;
    padding: 12.5px 0;
    font-family:verdana;
    font-size:10pt;
    color: #003;
```

```
        background: url("button-states.jpg") 0 0 no-repeat;
        text-decoration:none;
        text-align:center;
        text-transform: uppercase;
}
.imageRollovers a:hover {
        background-position: 0 -42px;
        }
.imageRollovers a:active {
        background-position: 0 -84px;
        color: #fff;
        }
```

Check out Figure 10-6 to see how the buttons look when positioned in the browser. Then, let's look a bit more closely at the style sheet used to accomplish this task.

The `display` property tells the browser to fill the available space with this link, which, in this case, should be 100 pixels wide because of the `width` property settings. (That size will vary according to whatever image you use.) The `padding` is set next, to prevent the text from sitting along the edges of the button. I've set a 12.5-pixel padding along the top and bottom edges, but no padding along the left and right edges.

Next I specify the font settings and colors, before finally adding the background image. I set the initial position of the image to 0 0, which essentially places it right in the middle of the box I've created.

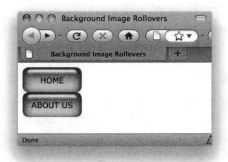

Figure 10-6   Status of practice page after content areas are positioned

I use the `text-decoration` property to turn the underline off for the text link, align the text to the center of the button, and then force each text link to display in uppercase with the `text-transform` property.

Moving on to the hover state, the only change necessary is to move the background image down a bit. Because each button is 42 pixels tall, I position the background for the hover state at `-42px` to move it up by 42 pixels. (Remember that the hover or rollover state is the second button in my background image.)

TIP

To think about this a different way, suppose we're looking through the address window on a business envelope. The clear window is the box we've created to hold our button. Inside the envelope, we've placed the background image. Only one "button" shows through the window at any time. When we move the background image around, different button states are visible.

For the active state (the state visible when the user actually clicks the link), I move the background again and change the text color to white. This time, the background is moved up 84 pixels, to display the bottom button in my background image. Whenever we move "up" the page in positioning, we use a negative number. So, the vertical position of the image changes to `-84px`.

Want to see some more examples online, to help you solidify this concept in your mind? Check out these links:

- **http://monkeyflash.com/tutorials/css-image-rollover-navbar**
- **www.alistapart.com/articles/sprites**
- **www.websiteoptimization.com/speed/tweak/cssrollovers/**

Progress Check

In this chapter of the coding section, we covered how to move elements around on the web page. This is undoubtedly the trickiest aspect of coding web pages. As such, a single chapter hardly does it justice. Nevertheless, Figure 10-7 shows you the final page design, as viewed from the web browser.

Figure 10-7 Status of practice page after content areas are positioned

If you visit my web site and view the live page, you can also view the final code. You'll notice lots of adjustments for the padding and margins of various elements, and several floated items. All in all, we've come pretty far from a bunch of text plopped on the page and displaying in Times New Roman.

Summary

CSS positioning is an extremely powerful tool for the web designer, because it allows us to achieve highly customized page layouts that were previously impossible. This chapter was meant to give you a basic understand of positioning with CSS, to help you when planning your mockups. If you will also be creating the code for your mockups, I suggest you pursue the links listed throughout the chapter for more information. In addition, check out these other resources:

- **http://css.maxdesign.com.au**
- **www.westciv.com/style_master/house/index.html**
- **www.yourhtmlsource.com/stylesheets**

Chapter 11

Integrating Dynamic Content

Key Skills & Concepts

- Identify whether additional dynamic content meets the site goals.

- Describe how to embed various types of multimedia files into web pages.

- Understand how to syndicate pages with RSS.

- Recognize the uses of JavaScript to extend the capabilities of HTML.

- Understand how blogging software can benefit web designers.

While basic HTML enables you to create static, or unchanging, web pages, certain other add-ons allow you to include elements that *do* something.

On the Web, the term *multimedia* refers to presentations of various types of media, such as audio, video, text, graphics, and animation, which are used to produce a certain effect, mood, or feeling. You may have seen multimedia presentations on news or weather sites, where they are used to display audio and video to viewers. Other sites use multimedia to entertain viewers, such as in the form of a movie or animated story.

Many forms of multimedia enable visitors to interact with the presentations. For example, a visitor might be watching an animated story, and can click the individual characters to learn more about them.

Anytime you incorporate elements that move or change, they are called *dynamic* content. This chapter discusses how to integrate dynamic content into your web page. Sometimes you'll need to step beyond HTML even to add just dynamic content to your pages. In such cases, a scripting language such as JavaScript can be used in conjunction with cascading style sheets (CSS).

Other times, dynamic content can be added to a page without additional coding methods. For example, HTML contains all the code necessary to integrate dynamic content created by Adobe Flash.

Meeting the Site Goals

Before I go too much further, we need to have a brief discussion about how multimedia and dynamic content can help you achieve your site's goals. Regardless of which type of multimedia or dynamic content you plan to add to your site, it's important that you first consider your reasons for adding it. Getting caught up in the exciting possibilities on the Web is easy, and you can forget the main purposes of the web site.

Table 11-1 includes a checklist to help you verify the need for multimedia or dynamic content on a specific site. Generally speaking, if something can be accomplished using plain text or static images, why not use those?

If multimedia and dynamic content can help you achieve the goals for a site better than plain text or static images could, you need to determine the most appropriate way to incorporate such content into your site. For example, suppose you decide that including an animation or video of one of your products is necessary because it's the only way that product can be realistically experienced on the Web. With all the different types of animation and video available, which do you select?

You can accomplish multimedia and dynamic content on the web in many different ways. The next few sections outline some of the most popular methods of doing so. Because this topic is so vast and its content changes so frequently, tips are included in "Where to Learn More" at the end of each section. This way, if you decide you want to implement a Flash solution, for example, you know where to look for more information.

Ask yourself...	Yes	No
Does the new content potentially delay users from getting to the real reasons for visiting the site?		
Does the new content prohibit users from controlling their viewing experience on your site in any way?		
Is the navigation for the site contained only in the multimedia element or dynamic content?		
Is the navigation used in the multimedia different from most other types of navigation schemes used in computer design (such as standard text links and buttons)?		
Does the new content prohibit the use of the back button on the site?		
If your site reaches international users, does the new content provide for other language translations?		
Could the new content be displayed using plain text or images and achieve the same or similar effect?		
Does the new content require a certain browser/plug-in/technology that less than 50 percent of your users might have?		

Table 11-1   Checklist for Verifying the Usability of New Multimedia/Dynamic Content

If you answered yes to any of the questions in the table, consider whether you need to remove or alter this new content before adding it to the site. Remember that your goal is to get users to the content they want in a timely and efficient manner, and anything you do to inhibit that might cause your site to fail.

TIP
Don't overuse motion on a page. The best instances of motion on a web page reinforce the site's goals, tell a story, or aid in navigation. Repeated moving elements on text-heavy pages distract the eye from the message of the page.

Adding Multimedia Content

In Chapter 6, I talked about the use of Flash in web design and how to transfer graphics files to Flash for production. Now it's time to talk about embedding those Flash files, as well as other types of multimedia, into your HTML.

Even though you can integrate many different types of multimedia to a web page, you add them in two primary ways: You can embed media so it appears within the web page or you can link to it.

Linking to Multimedia

A link to a multimedia file is essentially the same as any other link. This means you use the a tag, as in the following example:

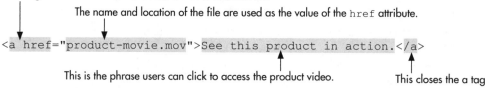

The a tag and `href` attribute are used to link to a media file.

The name and location of the file are used as the value of the `href` attribute.

`<a href="product-movie.mov">See this product in action.</a>`

This is the phrase users can click to access the product video.

This closes the a tag.

Viewers of this page could click the link "See this product in action." to access the file. Depending on how their system is set up, one of the following things might happen:

- It may prompt the user to download the file and either view it now or save it for later.
- If the browser recognizes the file as one it is set up to display automatically, it may take over and do just that.

Knowing that many systems may handle your multimedia files differently, try to offer your visitors as much guidance and instruction as possible. For example, list the size of the file you're asking them to download, so they can consider whether they want to wait for it to download. In addition, provide alternative ways of getting the information for users who cannot access your multimedia files.

Embedding Multimedia

When you embed multimedia files, they appear directly within the context of your page. As long as the appropriate plug-in is installed on the user's computer, the file loads and plays along with anything else that might appear on that page.

The original method for embedding multimedia was to use the embed tag. However, that tag was a proprietary tag created by Netscape (which means it worked only in the Netscape browser). As a result, the W3C created the object tag as a method for embedding various types of media, from static images, to Flash files and more. It is supported by version 3 (and later) of Internet Explorer, as well as all current versions of Mozilla-based browsers (such as Safari and Firefox).

The object tag can contain other HTML tags and attributes, including other object tags. If the browser is capable of interpreting an object tag, it does so and ignores the HTML contained within the opening and closing object tags. If it doesn't understand the object tag, it uses the HTML included in it instead. This is beneficial because you can offer a plug-in–free alternative to visitors who may not have or want to use the plug-in. Here's an example of how this might look, where I use the object tag to embed a Flash file into an HTML page:

```
<object type="application/x-shockwave-flash" data="movie.swf"
height="60" width="200">
    <param name="movie" value="movie.swf" />
    <param name="bgcolor" value="#ffffff" />
    <a href="http://www.adobe.com/products/flashplayer"
title="You must install Flash to access this movie">
<img src="movie-pic.jpg" width="200" height="60" alt="Screen
shot of movie - need Flash to view" /></a>
</object>
```

Let's look a bit more closely at this code. When you use the object tag, you must tell the browser what type of file you are embedding and where to locate that file. The type and data attributes are used for this process. Then, after the opening object tag, you add any additional properties you want to specify using the param tag (short for parameters). Finally, you close the object tag.

In this example, I also included a link to Adobe's site, with a tool tip (using the title attribute) explaining that the user needs to download Flash prior to viewing this file. Then I added a screen capture of the movie to give users an idea what they might see after downloading the appropriate plug-in. Notice the link and image were added after the `param` tags but before the closing `object` tag.

Table 11-2 lists some optional attributes for the `object` tag. Tables 11-3, 11-4, 11-5, and 11-6 list some other parameters you might use when embedding Real Media files, other types of sound files, QuickTime movies, or Flash files. The plug-ins and parameters listed here aren't exhaustive, but are meant to give you an idea of some of the possibilities you have when using them. For more information about any of these, visit the web site of the corresponding plug-in's manufacturer.

Attribute	Possible Values	Description
`width="#"`	Number of pixels	Specifies the width of the window (video/animation) or controller (sound)
`height="#"`	Number of pixels	Specifies the height of the window (video/animation) or controller (sound)
`border="#"`	Number of pixels	Defines the width of the border, in pixels
`name="name"`	*Name*	Gives a (case-sensitive) name to the file so that it can be referenced by a script or other method
`type="value"`	MIME type (refer to http://en.wikipedia.org/wiki/MIME-Type for a list)	Specifies the type of file being embedded, which then defines the plug-in needed
`standby="Text goes here"`	Text to be displayed	Specifies text to be displayed while the object is loading
`tabindex="1"`	Numeric value	Specifies where the element appears in the tab order of the page

Table 11-2 Attributes for the `object` Tag

Parameter Name	Possible Values	Description
autostart	true false	Defines whether the file immediately starts playing when the page is loaded
backgroundcolor	hexadecimal code or color name	Changes the background color of the embedded file; the actual effect varies according to the plug-in used
center	true false	Centers the embedded file in the window
console	name	Identifies this and other embedded controls by naming them
controls	all controlpanel controlpanel, statusbar controlpanel, infovolumepanel playbutton stopbutton	Specifies the style of the controller displayed in the web page
Loop	true false	Defines whether a file repeats
nojava	true false	Stops the Java Virtual Machine from running, causing your embedded file to run only with the plug-in (and not Java)
nolabels	true false	Stops the presentation of label information (such as the author, copyright, and title) on the controller
nologo	true false	Prevents the RealLogo from displaying
numloop	number	Specifies the number of times a file will repeat
shuffle	true false	Plays multiple sounds in random order

Table 11-3 Optional Parameters for Real Media Files

Parameter Name	Possible Values	Description
bgcolor	hexadecimal code	Changes the background color of the embedded file; the actual effect varies according to the plug-in used
controls	console playbutton pausebutton smallconsole stopbutton volumelever	Specifies the style of the controller displayed in the web page
loop	true false # (number of times)	Defines how a file repeats: true tells the browser to loop the file infinitely, and false specifies to never loop. Alternatively, you can specify the exact number of times it should loop.
volume	number between 0 and 100	Specifies the volume of the sound file

Table 11-4 Optional Parameters for Most Sound Players

Parameter Name	Possible Values	Description
base	URL	Specifies the base directory for all included links
play	true false	Defines whether the file begins playing when the page is loaded
quality	best high autohigh autolow low	Defines the quality level of the embedded file
scale	showall noborder exact fit	Defines how the embedded file fits within the rest of the web page

Table 11-5 Optional Parameters for Flash

Parameter Name	Possible Values	Description
autoplay	true false	Defines whether the file immediately starts playing when the page is loaded
bgcolor	hexadecimal code	Changes the background color of the embedded file; the actual effect varies according to the plug-in used
controller	true false	Turns on the movie controller (when true, you need to add 16 pixels to the height of the movie)
kioskmode	true false	When true, disables the pop-up menu for the movie so that users cannot copy or save it
loop	true false	Defines whether a file repeats
qtnext qtnext#	URL	Identifies a URL for the movie to load when it finishes playing the current one; if you want to list multiple movies to play in sequence, use qtnext#, where # is the order to play the movie
qtsrc	URL	Forces the browser to use the QuickTime plug-in to load the file instead of any other video plug-in
scale	tofit aspect #	Defines how the embedded file fits within the rest of the web page
volume	whole number between 0 and 100	Defines the beginning volume for the movie

Table 11-6   Optional Parameters for QuickTime Movies

TIP
You can learn much more about embedding Flash files by visiting an online tutorial, such as **www.w3schools.com/flash**.

Testing Your Skills

The most common type of multimedia embedded in the average web site are files from YouTube. Thankfully, this online video megasite offers lots of help for anyone trying to embed their files on other pages. This makes for a great place to test your embedding skills.

To get started, visit **www.youtube.com** and locate a video you'd like to use. Then look for a toolbar with additional options for the video (as shown in the following illustration). Click the word "Embed" to see how you can customize the way the file will appear after being embedded in your page. This allows you to specify whether to show related videos, add a border, change the size, or select an alternate color scheme.

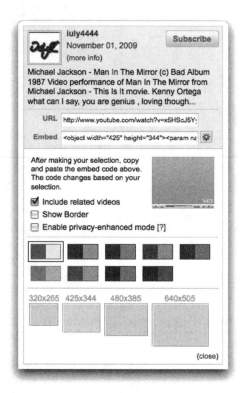

After you've made any necessary customizations, simply copy the code included in the Embed text field, and paste it into your HTML file at the appropriate location. Here's an example of the type of code YouTube creates for you:

```
<object width="425" height="344">
    <param name="movie" value="http://www.youtube.com/v/x5HScJ5YyaQ&hl=en&fs=1
&"></param>
    <param name="allowFullScreen" value="true"></param>
    <param name="allowscriptaccess" value="always"></param>
    <embed src="http://www.youtube.com/v/x5HScJ5YyaQ&hl=
en&fs=1&" type="application/x-shockwave-flash"
allowscriptaccess="always" allowfullscreen="true"
width="425" height="344"></embed>
</object>
```

You'll notice YouTube includes both the embed and object tags. While this practice used to be required to reach the widest possible audience, it is no longer necessary given that all modern browsers support the object tag.

NOTE

If you intend to validate your pages against the current HTML specifications, you'll want to remove the embed tag. The embed tag is not part of the specification and will cause your page not to validate.

Adding Scripts

In previous chapters, I mentioned how scripts can be added to accomplish tasks that are not possible with plain HTML. The most popular scripting method used to add dynamic content to web sites is JavaScript. While HTML enables you to create static, or unchanging, web pages, JavaScript lets you create dynamic pages, which either change or react to users' input. The combination of JavaScript and CSS is commonly referred to as Dynamic HTML, or DHTML.

TIP

When I need to perform a function on my site that I think might require a script, my first stop is usually a site such as **www.scripts.com** or **www.scriptsearch.com**. From any of these sites, you can search for the type of script you want, or, more specifically, for what you want the script to do.

JavaScript Quick Primer

The following sections use JavaScript to show you two examples of making a page more dynamic. If you already have some experience with different scripting languages, picking this up should be easy; if this is the first time you've looked at JavaScript, if might be a bit challenging. Don't worry, though, because JavaScript isn't difficult to use, once you learn a few basic concepts.

If you're new to this, the following quick primer is intended to give you a brief introduction so you can follow along. I encourage you to practice adding these scripts to your page, and with enough practice, I'm confident you'll begin to understand. Because this quick introduction can't teach you everything, if you really want to learn the nuts and bolts of JavaScript, I suggest picking up a copy of *JavaScript: A Beginner's Guide* by John Pollock (McGraw-Hill).

When you write JavaScript, it's actually placed in the HTML on your page. This means you can learn JavaScript from your favorite web sites, just as you can with HTML, by viewing the HTML source from within the browser.

You should learn several new terms before you use any JavaScript. Given that scripts are essentially a set of instructions to the browser, you can often read them logically as a series of commands. The most common type of command is an *if... then* statement, also called a *conditional*, which tells the browser to do one thing if *x* is true and to do something else if *x* is false. In JavaScript, you actually write these instructions as *if... else*.

Notice the actual instructions on what to do are included within curly brackets { }. The spacing here is important because the opening curly brackets should be on the same line as the `if` or `else`. The closing curly bracket is on a line by itself, after the instructions end. In addition, all statements (instructions) end with semicolons. Here's a simple example of the layout:

```
if (something) {
    do this;
}
else {
    do this;
}
```

In the following example, `document` is acting as a JavaScript object. Quite simply, an object is anything that can be manipulated or changed by the script. In this case, it tells the browser the word directly following this object is referring to the HTML document itself. So, I'm saying, write "I can write JavaScript!" into the current document.

```
<script language="JavaScript" type="text/javascript">
document.write("I can write JavaScript!");
</script>
```

Objects can have methods, which are actual things that happen to the objects (in this case, a document is written to). Methods are following by a set of parentheses containing any specific instructions on how to accomplish the method. In the preceding example, the text inside the parentheses is written into the current document.

Just as an object, such as a car, has features (tires, brakes, and so forth) in the real world, JavaScript objects can have properties. Objects and properties are separated by periods. For example, HTML documents can have frames, images, forms, background colors, and so on. When you want to specify the value of a property, such as the color of the background, you add the value after the property, as in this example:

```
document.bgColor="333333";
```

In JavaScript, a *variable* is something you specify for your own needs. You might think of variables as labels for changeable values used within a single script. To define a variable, type `var`, followed by the one-word name of the variable. Remember that JavaScript is case-sensitive. If you capitalize a letter when you first define a variable, you must also capitalize that letter every time you refer to it.

```
var VotingAge;
```

Likewise, a *function* is a group of commands to which you give a name, so you can refer to the group later in the page. To create a function, type `function`, followed by the function name and a set of parentheses. Then, type the commands that are part of the function below the name enclosed in curly brackets, as shown here:

```
function functionName()
    { commands go here
}
```

Different from other terms discussed here, *event handlers* needn't be placed within the opening and closing script tags. These pieces of JavaScript can actually be embedded within HTML to respond to a user's interaction and make a page dynamic. For example, placing the event handler `onClick` within the a tag (`<a>`) causes the event to occur when the user clicks the link. So if I want to change the page's background color when a link is clicked, I could use the following code:

```
<a href="home.html" onClick="document.body.style.backgroundColor='#333333'";>
Home</a>
```

Sample Script: Automatically Adding the Date to a Page

The following script shows the most basic way to add the current date and time to a web page. I've included it here because it is a very easy way to try out some JavaScript code.

Place this script into the body of your web page wherever you want the date and time to appear.

```
<script language="JavaScript" type="text/JavaScript">
document.write(Date());
</script>
```

Sample Script: Creating a Dynamic Navigation Bar

In Chapter 10, I discussed how you can actually have hidden layers of content within your web page. While the layers can be created and hidden with CSS and HTML, you use JavaScript to make them visible when a user interacts within the web page. The most common use of this in web pages is for dynamic navigation bars, in which a submenu or drop-down menu appears after you click a link, providing additional link choices without refreshing the HTML page itself.

These dynamic navigation bars can become extremely complex, but the core concept is relatively simple, and that's what this section discusses: a bare-bones method for invoking submenus. For more on how to make your navigation bar "bigger and better," refer to the online resources listed at the end of this section.

To try this out, place this JavaScript in the header of your page (between the opening and closing head tags). The boldface text highlights pieces of the script you should customize.

```
<script language="JavaScript" type="text/javascript">
function showLayer () {
    document.getElementByID('aboutus-sub').style.visibility='visible';
}
function hideLayer () {
    document.getElementByID('aboutus-sub').style.visibility='hidden';
}
</script>
```

Next, adjust your style sheet to format the visible navigation button/link and the hidden submenu. Be sure to set the positioning so that the submenu displays below the top menu. What follows is the style sheet I used to create the menus shown in Figures 11-1 and 11-2.

```
body {
    font-family: verdana;
}
#aboutus {
    position: absolute;
    top: 20px;
    left: 20px;
    width: 100px;
    padding: 10px;
    text-align: center;
    background-color: #ccc;
    border:1px solid black;
    cursor: pointer;
}
#aboutus-sub {
    position: absolute;
    visibility: hidden;
    top: 60px;
    left: 20px;
    width: 100px;
    padding: 0px 10px;
    text-align: center;
    background-color: #333;
    color: #fff;
    border: 1px solid #999;
    cursor: pointer;
}
ul {
    padding: 0px;
    margin: 0px;
}
li {
    list-style: none;
    padding: 5px 0px;
    border-bottom: 1px dashed white;
}
li a {
    color: #fff;
    text-decoration: none;
}
.last {
    border: 0px;
}
```

◄————— This changes the cursor to a pointer, to help indicate that the content is linked.

◄————— I set the visibility to hidden so the submenu is not visible when the page first loads.

The final piece to this DHTML is the actual HTML code for the content, which is placed between the opening and closing `body` tags:

The `onclick` JavaScript event handler tells the browser to display the `"aboutus-sub"` layer when the user clicks anywhere within the `"aboutus"` content area.

```
<div id="aboutus" onClick="showLayer('aboutus-sub');">ABOUT US</div>
<div id="aboutus-sub">
<ul><li><a href="history.html">History</a></li>
    <li><a href="location.html">Location</a></li>
      <li class="last"><a href="team.html">Team</a></li>
</ul>
</div>
```

As mentioned, this is just the tip of the iceberg regarding what is possible with DHTML. If it has inspired you to want to do more with JavaScript and CSS, don't miss the section "Learn More" at the end of this chapter.

Figure 11-1 This shows the navigation button before it's been clicked.

Figure 11-2   This shows how the hidden layer is made visible after I clicked the About Us button.

Additional Resources

While I didn't expect this section would teach you everything you need to know about JavaScript or DHTML, I hope it gave you a basic understanding of what types of things these scripts can do. If you'd like to learn more, many sources of additional information are available on this topic. The following list shows some of the most popular web sites.

The sites listed here offer many free scripts that you may borrow and use on your own site. This is considered perfectly normal, so long as you give credit to the original author(s) in your code.

- **SitePoint.com**   This site contains DHTML and JavaScript articles (**www.sitepoint .com/subcat/javascript**), as well as a whole blog about this stuff (**www.sitepoint .com/blogs/category/dhtml-css**).

- **Web Reference JavaScript Articles**   This web site (**www.webreference.com/ programming/javascript**) includes tutorials, tips, and reviews of tools.

- **Mozilla Developer Center**   This section of the Mozilla Developer Center (**http:// developer.mozilla.org/en/docs/DHTML**) is specifically geared toward anyone developing DHTML and includes helpful documentation and support communities.

- **www.javascripts.com**   You can find thousands of free scripts and information about how to use them.
- **DHTML Center**   This site (**www.dhtmlcentral.com**) has thousands of free scripts you can download and customize, as well as tutorials and help forums.

NOTE

Always look for the most recent references you can find when working with JavaScript and DHTML. Older scripts were written for older browsers and may or may not be valid today. Often, those older browsers required web developers to use special workarounds, called hacks, in their JavaScripts and DHTML. Many of those hacks are no longer necessary, and in some cases they can even "break" in modern browsers.

Spreading the Word with RSS

Another way to add dynamic content to your site is by pulling information from other sources, such as news outlets and media publishers. RSS, Really Simple Syndication, has grown so quickly in recent years that even though you might not have known what it meant, you've likely seen it referenced at one web site or another. Many news sites and web blogs include little orange or blue rectangular buttons near a story that is available for syndication by the general public. For example, visit **www.foxnews.com/rss** to see a list of the Fox News content available for syndication.

TIP

To "read" such syndicated content, you need to open the RSS feed in a news reader (also called an aggregator). Check out **http://blogspace.com/rss/readers** for a list of some popular news readers.

Anyone can create his or her own RSS feeds. (Refer to **www.mnot.net/rss/tutorial** for a great tutorial on doing just that.) In fact, it's quite popular for anyone who updates a site regularly to publish that content in an RSS feed as well. Once you've created your own syndicated content, you probably want to put a link on your page to advertise that content (similar to those little orange buttons you've probably seen at other sites). Links to RSS feeds look similar to other HTML links with a few minor variations:

```
<a type="application/rss+xml" href="feed.rss">RSS feed for this page</a>
```

What about situations where you want to embed an RSS feed into your page? Suppose you were building a web site for a law firm that wants to include a legal news section. First you need to visit the site offering news, and click the link to access its RSS feed.

Then you can embed the feed within your own site's HTML to allow it to display within your page's framework.

You'll need to use another tool to help you embed the feed, because HTML doesn't have such a mechanism on its own. Have no fear, because hundreds (if not thousands) of options are available to help you with this task. To try one out for yourself, follow these steps:

1. Visit **www.rssinclude.com** and sign up for a free account.

2. Click the Create a New RSSbox link.

3. Select the template you want to use to display the RSS feed on your site. (Don't like any of the existing templates that come with the free service? Upgrade to a paid account for additional options.)

4. On the next page, you're presented with a place to paste the RSS feed. (If you haven't yet found one and want to test out this service, try **http://rss.news.yahoo.com/rss/topstories**.) Paste the feed address and click Add Feed.

5. Click the Content and Styling Options tab to customize the display of the feed, as shown in the following illustration:

6. Click the Include! tab to access the HTML code you'll need. Copy it and then paste it into your web page wherever you want the feed to display.

This is just one way to incorporate RSS feeds in your web pages. Visit **www.rss-specifications.com/display-rss.htm** to see a lot more options.

Using Blog Templates

This final section is reserved for a very hot topic in web design: blogs. Once reserved for individuals who wanted to create an online "journal" of sorts, blogging has gone mainstream for businesses and individuals alike.

In fact, it's gone so mainstream, that many companies have taken advantage of blogging tools to manage their web sites. Why? The answer lies in the real power of a blog, which is its ability to allow the author to write, edit, and publish web content quickly without using any HTML code.

You might think that this sounds a lot like the CMS, content management system, tools I mentioned earlier. Indeed, this is why a lot of small businesses turn to blogging tools to help build and maintain their web sites. Blogs are essentially mini content management systems. The best part is that some really great blogging tools are free!

Ask the Expert

Q: Wait a minute. Why is this section about blogging included in a chapter titled "Integrating Dynamic Content"?

A: I've included this blogging section for a couple of reasons. First, many web sites without content management systems remain static. In other words, without an easy way to update their web site, most businesses just don't do it. The result is a stale site with outdated content.

By contrast, businesses with content management systems—even those as basic as the blogging tools discussed here—tend to update their content much more frequently, making their site more dynamic in nature. In addition, many blogs offer add-ons that easily integrate things such as stock tickers, weather updates, and news reports into your site.

If you're looking to create a dynamic, user-centered site, don't underestimate the power of basic blogging tools.

As a freelance web designer, I can give many of my clients sites they can easily manage without the added cost of a third-party or custom CMS. Of course, not every site lends itself to being built with blogging software, so this is not an option for everyone. But because it has worked so well for plenty of my clients, it's probably worth at least considering for yours.

So where you do you start? Visit the two most popular blogging tools to get a handle for how each one works.

- Google's Blogger (**www.blogspot.com**)
- WordPress (**www.wordpress.com**)

Before we go any further, you need to understand a key difference between Blogger and WordPress. Both are available as free *hosted* blogging tools for anyone wanting to use them. The hosted part refers to the fact that someone else (Google or WordPress) maintains the server on which the blog is housed.

However, only WordPress is also available to be installed and completely customized on your own web server. This means you (or your system administrator) can download all the source files necessary to run the blogging software and install them on your own server for free. This downloadable WordPress is found at **www.wordpress.org** (as opposed to wordpress.com).

Comparing the Hosted Blogging Options

If you don't need control or access to the web server, a hosted option from Blogger or WordPress is probably a great choice for you. Table 11-7 compares the most basic features of each tool.

Beyond the basic features listed in Table 11-7, both tools boast thousands of additional features called widgets. Most of these have been created by other people throughout the world and made available for installation through the blog administrator settings.

What can you do with blog widgets? Almost anything. You know those iPhone commercials that say "There's an app for that"? Well, the same is true for blogs. If you have an idea for a way to extend the capabilities of your blog, there's probably a widget for that. For example, if you want to earn money with ads on your blog, there's a widget for that. Or if you want to display clips from YouTube on your blog, there's a widget for that. Need to add a slideshow or a poll? There are widgets for that, too.

NOTE

The one caveat to widgets is that you can use only official Blogger or WordPress widgets on the hosted blogs. If you find another widget out on the Web somewhere and want to install it on your blog, you'll need to consider hosting the blog on your own server, as discussed in a later section.

Feature	WordPress	Blogger
Ability to import content from another source	Yes (from a variety of blog tools)	Yes (only from another blogspot. com blog)
Ability to use different themes (designs)	Yes (but you can't edit the style sheet for a theme without a paid subscription)	Yes (you can also edit the style sheet for each template)
Ability to add static pages (that are not part of the blog system)	Yes	No
Ability to add a built-in contact form	Yes	No (but you could create your own and host it elsewhere)
Ability to make the blog content private	Yes (but you are limited to 35 readers of private pages, unless you upgrade to a paid subscription)	Yes (but you can restrict access only to those with Google accounts)
Ability to allow others to author content	Yes (four levels of access: Administrators, Editors, Authors, and Contributors)	Yes (two levels of access: Administrators and Non-Administrators)
Ability to upload and add images	Yes (3 gigabytes of storage with free account)	Yes (1 gigabyte of storage with free account—uses Picassa Web Albums)
Ability to moderate comments	Yes	Yes (but you can't edit comments)
Ability to use custom domain name (www.myblog.com)	Yes (only with paid subscription)	Yes

Table 11-7 Comparison of the Two Most Popular Hosted Blogging Options

Creating a Blog

After you decide which blog software to use, it's easy to get started. Both WordPress and Blogger offer video tutorials to help walk you through the process:

- **http://wordpress.tv/2009/08/05/videopress-com-basics** Getting Up & Running on WordPress.com
- **www.youtube.com/BloggerHelp** How to Create a Blog with Blogger

Regardless of which software you select, you can be blogging within minutes of setting up the account. The real time-intensive process is not in the initial setup, but the customization of the template. The extent of how much you can edit the template depends on which tool you're using (as shown in Table 11-7).

I encourage you to get creative when it comes to selecting and editing your theme. Browse the available options and research what others have done with each theme.

Now that you understand a bit of HTML and CSS, you can actually accomplish a lot more with your templates.

When you run into problems, check out the user community for your tool (WordPress, **www.forums.wordpress.com**, or Blogger, **www.google.com/support/forum/p/blogger**). You'll likely find others who have encountered the same issue, as well as more who have come up with solutions.

Hosting Your Own Blog

So, if the hosted blogs offer so much, why would anyone decide to host their own? Here are a few key reasons:

- **Custom themes** If you want to customize the layout, look, and feel of your blog completely, you'll need to host it yourself.

- **Custom plug-ins** If you want to upload third-party plug-ins (or widgets), you'll need to host it yourself.

- **Custom code** If you want to customize the PHP (Hypertext Preprocessor) code used to create the blog, you'll need to host it yourself.

TIP

For more information about comparing Wordpress.com to Wordpress.org, check out **http://en.support.wordpress.com/com-vs-org**.

When you encounter a project that needs a custom blog hosted on a server you (or your administrator) can manage, you can still take advantage of a free blogging tool. WordPress also offers a downloadable version you can install (free of charge) on any server that meets the basic requirements (as listed here: **www.wordpress.org/about/ requirements**).

If you're worried about whether you can actually install a powerful piece of software such as WordPress, let me offer a few words of encouragement. I will be the first to admit I went to art school partially to avoid math and science. I have always considered myself the creative type (that is, clueless when it comes to programming). However, I have successfully installed WordPress, without the help of any programmers, on more than one occasion.

Most hosting providers actually make the process quite painless. In fact, several (which are promoted at **www.wordpress.org/hosting**) offer "1-click" installations of WordPress for any sites hosted on their servers.

After the installation is complete, you'll want to focus your efforts on the template files. As of this writing, those are located in the wp-content\themes folder. You can download additional themes from developers all over the Web (simply Google WordPress themes to find a few), and paste them in this directory as well.

Each theme comes with multiple templates to handle the different types of pages displayed through the blogging tool. For example, here are a few of the template files contained within the default theme:

- archives.php

- comments.php

- footer.php

- header.php

- index.php

- page.php

- sidebar.php

- style.css

You'll need to edit each one to create your own theme with a custom layout. Or just edit the style sheet to change elements such as backgrounds and font characteristics.

To see an example of how a WordPress template can be completely customized to match an existing site's brand, compare Figures 11-3 and 11-4. The first one shows the Let's Dish! home page, as it was designed by its marketing group. The second figure shows the WordPress blog I created to match the corporate brand. The client is able to update and maintain the blog completely with little (if any) interaction from me, thanks to the WordPress software.

Figure 11-3   Original site

Figure 11-4   WordPress blog customized to match the original site's look and feel

Adding Other Third-Party Content

Throughout this chapter, I've outlined ways to extend the capabilities of your basic web site, such as using CNN's RSS feed to add the latest headlines to your site's news page. But the topics covered in this chapter aren't the only ways to add dynamic content to your site. In fact, tons of other options are available, many of which use code and/or software made available by other developers or companies.

One good example is loading the current weather forecast into a page on your site. If your business isn't weather, you're probably not going to store a large database of weather-related information on your own web servers. This doesn't matter, because plenty of other people are willing to store that information for you. In fact, The Weather Channel allows you to add its weather forecasts to your site for free. After you register, weather.com provides you with a chunk of code to copy and paste into whichever page you want the forecast to display. Visit **www.weather.com/services/oap.html** to learn more. (Note, if you need to customize the forecast beyond the basic settings available to free users, you can upgrade to a paid subscription for advanced options.)

Table 11-8 includes that and many other resources for adding this type of remote content to your site.

Content	Site
Applicant tracking: Post job openings and allow potential employees to submit applications. Tools offer sophisticated tracking, searching, and reporting features.	www.icims.com www.applicantstack.com www.mystaffingpro.com
Bulletin boards/communities: Lets users search and post content regarding a specific topic. You can find easily customized scripts to run your own bulletin boards or link to someone else's free bulletin board system.	www.vbulletin.com www.phpbb.com www.ubbcentral.com
Calendars: Post events in a detailed calendar or a simple list. After setup, use these tools to maintain the calendar without knowing/using HTML.	http://calendar.google.com www.phpjabbers.com/web-calendar www.coffeecup.com/web-calendar/
Daily quotes/jokes/tips: Everything from This Day in History and Quotes of the Day to Fresh (JPEG) Flowers, Cartoons, and Daily Recipes, all delivered free of charge to your web site.	www.quotationspage.com/useourquotes.php www.brainyquote.com/link www.quotesdaddy.com/widgets

Table 11-8   Resources for Common Types of Third-Party Content

Content	Site
Directions/maps: Provide site visitors with customized directions to your office/location, and/or maps of your offices.	**http://maps.google.com/help/maps/getmaps** **http://company.mapquest.com/map-widget.html** **www.mapme.com**
Event management: Beyond basic calendaring features, these tools offer advanced event management, including collecting RSVPs and e-mailing guests.	**www.cvent.com** **www.acteva.com**
Live chat: Allows site visitors to access customer service representatives instantly online.	**http://solutions.liveperson.com/live-chat** **www.everywherechat.com** **www.clickandchat.com** **www.boldchat.com**
Reference and search tools: Lets users search other web sites. (Most search engines let you add their search tools to your web site. Check with your favorite search engine for details.)	**www.google.com/cse/**
Shopping carts: Let users purchase items from an online store. This is an area of much variation—you could spend thousands of dollars on a custom-built solution or a few hundred dollars on third-party content. The options listed here are basic, inexpensive resources. Search for "shopping cart software" for more resources.	**http://store.yahoo.com** **http://checkout.google.com/seller/integrate.html** **www.shopify.com**
Stock quotes: Typically a small "ticker" cycling through popular and/or predefined stock quotes.	**http://finance.yahoo.com/badges** **www.cooltick.com** **http://moneycentral.msn.com/investor/external/invapps.asp**
Surveys: Poll users for feedback, and then view your results online or download to include in offline presentations.	**www.surveymonkey.com** **www.zoomerang.com** **www.checkbox.com**
Translation tools: Translate whole pages or sections of content into other languages, for supplying international content without the hassle of maintaining multiple versions of your site.	**http://babelfish.yahoo.com** **http://translate.google.com/translate_tools**
Weather: Text only or graphics based. Implementations vary greatly, from the current conditions to a five-day forecast.	**www.weather.com** **www.wunderground.com** **www.hamweather.com**

Table 11-8   Resources for Common Types of Third-Party Content (*continued*)

> ### NOTE
> I haven't used every product listed in Table 11-8, but I've included this information to give you an idea how much third-party content is available (tons!). I encourage you to do your own research as well so you can locate the most appropriate solution for your needs.

Summary

This chapter provided you with the ideas and tips necessary to help make your sites more dynamic in nature. This, in turn, helps keep visitors returning. Regardless of your programming skills, I encourage you step a little outside your expected comfort zone to try your hand at some of the concepts discussed throughout this chapter.

If you decide that using JavaScript or customizing WordPress blogs is not up your alley, you can still benefit from understanding what's involved, so you can better interpret your client's needs.

In the next chapter, we'll move on to publishing your content.

Part IV

Going Live

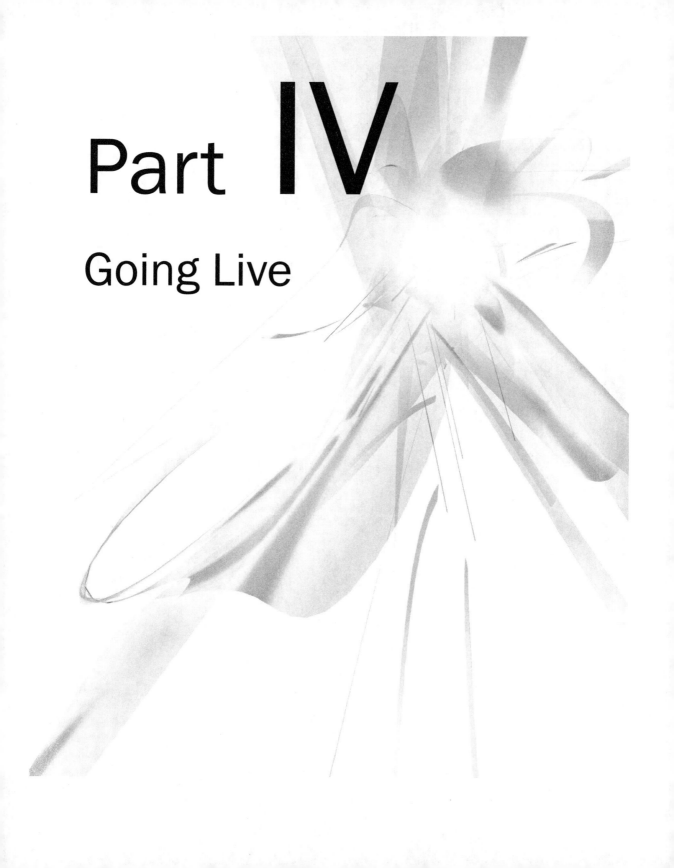

Chapter 12

Publishing Content

Key Skills & Concepts

- Thoroughly test the web site according to the target audience defined in the original specifications.

- Upload the site to the appropriate location, where it can be accessed by its target audience.

- Update the project documentation accordingly.

- Prepare the site for maintenance.

n Chapter 2, I outlined the basic steps in the typical Web development process:

- **Planning and Analysis**   The project is scoped out and defined. The contracts are written, reviewed, and signed.

- **Design**   The structure of the project is designed, as specified in the documentation. Storyboards, wireframes, and/or mockups are created for the various aspects of the project and presented to the client for approval.

- **Development**   The project is built and tested, according to the specifications approved in the first two phases. Images, multimedia, code, and so on, are developed and tested.

- **Transfer and Maintenance**   The project is uploaded to the final web server and tested. Ownership is then transferred to the client or another team for maintenance.

At this point in our development process, the site—or at least the home page—is completed and you're likely itching to transfer it to a location where everyone can see it. This chapter reviews how to do just that.

In some larger development teams, you might pass off the project now to another group of people who test and deploy the site, or if the site requires integration with a back-end system such as an online store or other web application, you transfer the site to the technical team.

But when you're working with smaller teams or even just smaller web sites that don't require additional integration or programming, you can likely handle much of the work yourself. What exactly is "the work"? Primarily testing to confirm that the site looks and functions like the approved mockups and specifications, and deployment, which is transferring the site to its final resting spot, updating the documentation, and preparing for maintenance.

Testing

Even when you think your site is ready for launch, you should double-check a few things before you upload the content. You should also confirm that all aspects of the site perform as expected in the target browsers and on the target platforms.

NOTE

No matter who is doing the actual uploading of the files, you must always test your own work thoroughly before you hand off the files to anyone else.

Test Environment

When building a site, you have a few options with regard to location:

- You can build the site in its final resting spot on the hosting server.
- You can build the site locally, perhaps on your personal computer.
- You can build the site in a special testing environment that mimics the final hosting environment.

Each of these three scenarios has its pros and cons. The first option (build the site where it will eventually live) is the most straightforward of the three. This option allows you to place all of the images and supporting files on the server where they need to live. You can also upload all the pages as well. When working with this type of setup, I usually name the home page something like "index-test.html" just so the whole world can't find it yet. Then, when the site is tested and ready for launch, I can simply rename the home page to "index.html".

The biggest drawback to building the site where it will live comes when making revisions after the site is launched. For example, suppose you created a site for a client in June, but need to make changes in September. Typically, you would want to get approval from the client for any changes you made before taking the page live. But if you're working on the live site, it can be difficult to get approval for changes before making them live. In fact, you'd have to put up a copy of the changed page (using a different filename) to allow the client to see your changes without making them public. This process can be time consuming and costly. Even worse, making changes to web applications and databases using the live site is dangerous because you risk "breaking" or bringing down the entire site.

The second option (build locally) provides the least opportunity for accurate testing. When you build a web site on your own personal machine, or on any machine that is not specifically set up to mimic the actual hosting environment, you risk building a site that won't work when it's transferred to the host server. Building a site locally is an option only for a very small web site containing only static HTML, and no interactivity or additional functionality.

Building a site in a fully-functional testing environment is the ideal situation. In such situations, you are able to test, edit, and finalize the site in an environment that is as close to the final hosting server as possible. This means, ideally, what works in the testing environment should also work in the live environment. Many large companies choose to maintain both testing and live hosting environments even after a site is launched. This makes maintenance of the site a breeze, because all edits can be made and approved on the testing server before going live.

The biggest drawback to using a testing environment is cost. Many small businesses simply do not have the budget to pay for multiple hosting environments at the same time. Some web development companies take care of this by hosting testing environments internally for their clients. Ultimately, you have to find the right situation for you and your client that meets your testing needs before launch as well as the maintenance needs after launch.

Test Checklist

The .zip archive for this module (which can be downloaded from **www.wendywillard.com**) contains an excellent testing checklist to help you complete this task.

The following lists highlight a few items from that document to get you started:

- **`<meta>` tags**   Are all the `<meta>` tags complete and current?
- **Page titles**   Have the page titles been updated according to the actual page content?
- **Alternative text**   Do all images and media elements have appropriate alternative text labels?
- **Links**   Do all links work?
- **Images**   Do all images display as intended?

- **Multimedia**   Do all multimedia elements load/play/display as intended?

- **Layout**   Does the layout stay consistent across multiple browsers and platforms?

TIP

Run your pages through an online validator, such as the one offered by the W3C at **http://validator.w3.org**. A service like this tests your pages against the HTML specifications and prints a list of errors, which makes locating problems easy.

After your site is uploaded to the (testing or live) server, you want to run through each page once more to verify that everything transferred as expected. In addition, test to make sure all the links work and images appear.

Once you make a cursory check, it's time to confirm cross-browser and cross-platform consistency. Throughout this book, I stress the importance of checking your pages in multiple browsers and on multiple computer systems to make sure they appear as you intended.

Even if you don't have more than one type of computer or browser, after your pages are live, you can ask friends to test them for you. You can also visit local libraries, schools, and sometimes even shopping malls to see how the site fares in different environments.

Each time you visit the site on a different computer, record the browser, monitor size, screen resolution, and operating system used, similar to the checklist shown in the .zip archive for this module. This way, when you see errors or bugs, you can get help in determining the problem.

TIP

Don't have access to lots of different browsers and/or computers? Try an online tool such as Browsershots, which shows you a screen capture of your site in various environments (**www.browsershots.org**). Litmus is a more comprehensive cross-browser and cross-platform testing tool. Check it out at **www.litmusapp.com**.

For added help, consider downloading a few very helpful free add-ons for your Firefox browser. (Don't have Firefox yet? Download it here: **www.firefox.com**.) I find the following two add-ons most helpful when coding HTML, especially for pesky details such as aligning CSS boxes or tweaking CSS styles. These and plenty of others are available by searching at **http://addons.mozilla.org**.

- **Web Developer**   Gives you a special toolbar filled with features that help you debug and test your pages right within the browser. For more information from the add-on's creator, visit **http://chrispederick.com/work/web-developer**.

- **Firebug**   Differs from Web Developer in that it actually lets you edit HTML and CSS live, while it is viewed in the browser. For more information from Firebug's creator, visit **http://getfirebug.com**.

Usability

A key aspect of a web site's success is how well it functions with users. Many designers fail to perform usability testing on sites before taking them live, leaving everyone to wonder whether the site will work. Instead, I encourage you to perform some simple, yet effective, usability tests on any site you build before it goes live.

TIP

Designers sometimes avoid usability testing because we are afraid the results might negate our designs or our work. On the contrary, usability tests should be part of the plan all along, so you are working them into the project at various stages—more of a series of checks and balances. With a few usability tests sprinkled throughout the process, you won't be surprised by anything scary at the end of the project. For more on how design choices can make or break a web site, check out this article: **www.alistapart.com/articles/designcancripple**.

People often think usability tests are expensive and time-consuming, when in fact they can be much more of a cost-saver when you consider how much time you might spend on a redesign to fix an unusable site. You don't need any fancy equipment or specialized training to test for usability.

In its most basic form, a usability test requires only three things: a web site, a tester, and a facilitator. In fact, those three things don't even need to be in the same room (although that is preferable). I have even performed usability tests over the phone, while watching the user's screen through a conferencing tool such as WebEx (**www.webex.com**).

Locate the Testers

So you have the web site to be tested. How do you find the users? In my experience, you need only ask. Let's face it, lots of us like to be watched...to be the center of attention...if for only a few minutes. You don't need a large number of testers either. As long as the tests you have are a good representation of the target audience, four to six people should be sufficient.

To locate potential users, first check with the client to identify current customers who might be able to help. If the client doesn't have an existing customer base, check out the competition. Look for people who currently patronize a competitor and ask if they might be willing to participate. You could offer a discount coupon as incentive or even a small payment to cover their time.

Consider a team working on a web site for a bank, for example: They set up a station in the bank lobby to ask for volunteers. The computers are all set up and ready to go, so it takes only about 10 or 15 minutes of each customer's time to get the results. The bank rewards each participant with a water bottle or other branded give-away. The users are pleased to have their concerns heard by the bank, and the bank is excited to test the web site before launch. The development team is happy to validate its work and see what still needs some tweaking. This type of situation is a win-win for everyone.

In general, you want to make sure the tester has not been involved in the design or development process at all, is completely new to the web site, and is not working for the client or web site owner. Beyond that, you can ask anyone who fits the site's target audience.

Create the Test

When planning your usability tests, refer back to the usage scenarios from the first two chapters. You likely used them to create your target audience. Now use them to write test scenarios for your users.

NOTE
A test scenario outlines a task for users to accomplish using the web site. Be sure to test them out yourself so you know what users will encounter when participating in the usability test.

You want to be prepared before the usability test, so as not to waste anyone's time. It's best to limit the actual test to 10 to 15 minutes, so you have time to debrief the tester afterward and he still gets out in less than 30 minutes.

With each test, you want to determine whether the user understands the page being tested and can use (successfully) the navigation to find information. General usability tests might evaluate whether the page is difficult to read, where users tend to get lost, and how easily accessible is the information. More detailed tests might seek to know whether a user can perform a specific task or locate a nugget of information.

Consider a trial run with a colleague before running the actual test. This can tell you whether your testing procedure is too long, too short, confusing, and so on.

Facilitate the Test

When you've found the users and created the test, you can set up a time (or times) to run the test. At that point, you'll need a facilitator to guide the users through the test and record the results. Because you might have a tendency to step in and correct a tester (because you know the answers!), it is best to find someone else to facilitate the test.

TIP

While I don't recommend you actually facilitate the test, I do suggest you observe so you can watch the user's natural progression through the site. This will undoubtedly provide you with ideas for any changes necessary.

At the start of the test, have the facilitator remind the user that she is not being tested—the web site is. Also, ask her to think out loud, so you can record her thoughts about the site. For example, with our bank scenario, you might ask, "What might you do if you are looking for information about a used car loan?" Then, do not direct the tester in any way. Simply let her show where she might click and what she might do to accomplish the task.

Avoid asking the tester to make suggestions about how to fix the site. This is your job! Do take notes, and if the budget allows, record the session with a video recorder. While obviously an additional cost, recording usability tests can save money down the road because you always have the video to refer back to when questions arise.

After the test is completed, you need only thank the tester and offer any payment or gift promised before compiling your results. The best part of usability tests is they provide instant access to how real users are interacting with the site.

Uploading to a Live Server

After your site is finished and you're ready to make it *live,* or accessible to visitors on the Web, it's time to transfer the pages to the host computer. You can use File Transfer Protocol (FTP) programs to do so.

The concept of using an FTP program is similar to moving things around on your own personal computer. Instead of moving files from one folder to another on your computer, you're moving them from one folder on your computer to another folder on a different computer.

Just as you can change settings and information about who has access to view or edit a file on your own computer, you can also make these changes on a host computer. For information about how these settings might work, check with your ISP or host company.

Depending on what type of computer you have and who's hosting your site, you may use one of many different types of desktop FTP programs. Or you might use an FTP tool that comes with your HTML editor, such as the built-in FTP capabilities with Adobe Dreamweaver. The next sections outline a few popular options.

Desktop FTP Programs

Tons and tons of desktop FTP programs (just Google FTP program to see what I mean) are free, and some are not. One of the most popular cross-platform free FTP programs is FileZilla. It is available for download from **www.filezilla-project.org**. The following overview outlines how to use this particular tool, but the basic steps are the same regardless of which FTP program you select.

After the program is downloaded and installed, double-click the app's icon to get started. The first screen you encounter after launching the program probably looks something like Figure 12-1 (depending on your operating system).

To begin, you must choose which computer you want to access. If you want to upload your files to your web server, enter that computer's information in the spaces provided at the top of the screen (Host, Username, Password) before clicking Quickconnect.

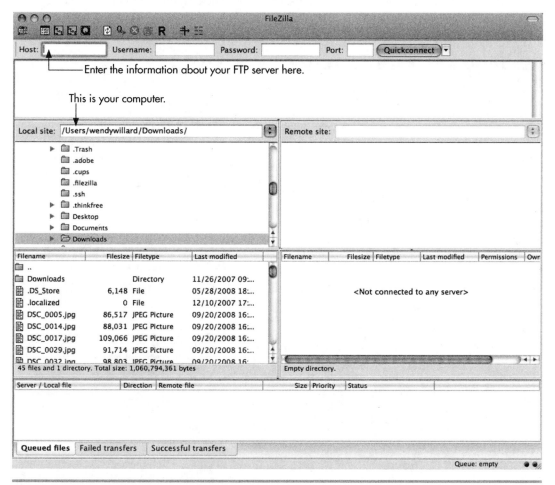

Figure 12-1   FileZilla start-up screen

NOTE

You should receive all the necessary information when you sign up for hosting service. If you're unsure, check your host company's web site or call its customer support line for assistance.

If your connection is successful, FileZilla displays the computer you're accessing, referred to as the *Remote Site,* in the right window. The files on your local computer are visible in the left window (as shown in Figure 12-1).

You can transfer files between these two computers in a couple of different ways. The simplest transfer method is to double-click the file you want to transfer. To be more specific with your actions, you can right-click (CTRL-click on the Mac) the file and select from one of the available options (Figure 12-2).

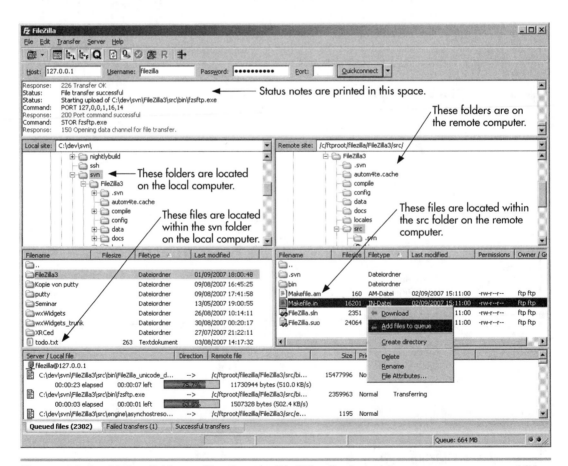

Figure 12-2 Right-clicking a filename in FileZilla displays this context menu, providing access to download the file or perform other necessary actions.

You can also navigate through the directory structure of either computer by clicking the folder names to expand or condense them. Right-click (CTRL-click on the Mac) to add a new folder quickly or to delete an existing one.

TIP

You can transfer files in two different ways: ASCII or binary. HTML and text files should be transferred in ASCII mode, while graphics, multimedia, and most other file types should be transferred in binary mode. FileZilla (and most FTP programs) uses the "auto" mode by default, whereby the program tries to determine the best transfer method for each file type.

That covers the most basic method of FTP—the transfer of files from one computer to another. If you have an FTP site you plan to visit often, you can store that server's login information in FileZilla's Site Manager to save you time (see Figure 12-3). To access the Site Manager, click the first button in the upper-left corner of the main FileZilla window. When the Site Manager displays, click New Site and type the necessary login information before clicking OK to save the information or Connect to save and also connect to the remote site immediately.

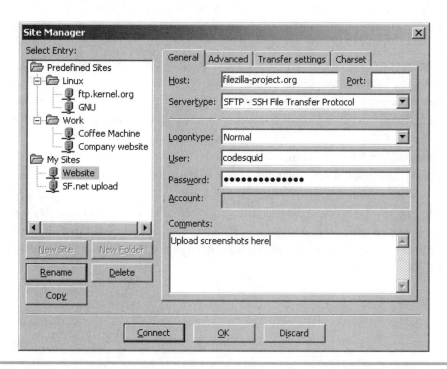

Figure 12-3 Use FileZilla's Site Manager to store usernames and passwords for frequently accessed FTP sites.

For more information about using FileZilla, visit **www.filezilla-project.org**. Or, if you prefer, try one of these other great FTP programs:

- CoffeeCup Free FTP **www.coffeecup.com/free-ftp** (Windows)
- SmartFTP **www.smartftp.com** (Windows)
- FTP Voyager **www.ftpvoyager.com** (Windows)
- WS_FTP **www.ipswitch.com** (Windows)
- YummyFTP **www.yummyftp.com** (Mac)
- Fetch **www.fetchsoftworks.com** (Mac)
- VicomsoftFTP **www.vicomsoft.com** (Mac)
- Transmit **www.panic.com** (Mac)

Web-based FTP

If you are using a free service to host your web page, you probably have FTP capabilities through that company's web site. This is called *web-based FTP* because you don't need any additional software to transmit the files—in fact, you transmit the files directly from within your web browser.

Even if your host company doesn't offer web-based FTP, if you use the Firefox web browser, you have an even better option. While I typically use the built-in FTP capabilities in Dreamweaver, since that's my preferred HTML development tool, I sometimes have a need for file transfer outside of Dreamweaver. If so, I use a powerful Firefox add-on called FireFTP.

To install FireFTP (or another web-based FTP tool for Firefox), open Firefox and visit **https://addons.mozilla.org**. Search for FTP. Locate the FTP app you want to add, and click the corresponding Download or Add To Firefox button.

After the FTP app is installed, you can locate it under the Tools menu in Firefox. Similarly to how the previously discussed FTP programs function, FireFTP displays your local files on the left and the remote files on the right. Take a look at Figure 12-4 to see what I mean.

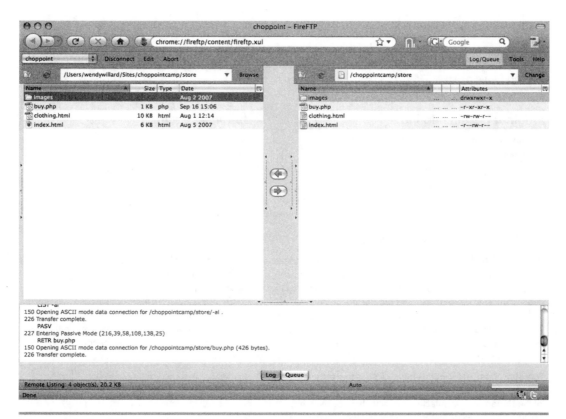

Figure 12-4 Web-based FireFTP is a super easy way to upload your files to a web server.

Updating the Documentation

As discussed in preceding chapters, the most successful web projects are thoroughly documented throughout the design and development phases. In addition, effective and efficient sites are continually redocumented after the site's launch and during its maintenance. While this may seem like the least enjoyable aspect of the project, it can often save immense amounts of time and money down the road.

In Chapter 2, I outlined some common types of documentation for web projects. At the end of the project, confirming that all appropriate documentation has been updated according to the final outcome is important. Table 12–1 reviews those types of documentation discussed and outlines how you might update each.

TIP

Recording all changes during the actual course of development is important—even if this is simply in the form of sticky notes—to avoid having to rely on your memory at the end of the project.

Original Documentation	Updates Required?
Request for Proposal (RFP): States the problem/need, as explained by the client.	No.
Proposal/ Statement of Work (SOW): Evaluates the problem/ need; states proposed solution (at a high level) or a way to meet the need(s), as well as estimated costs and timeline, as explained by developer(s). Also may be called a Requirements Definition, and/or Needs Assessment, and is usually considered a contract because the client signs off on it.	Perhaps. In most cases, any changes that need to be documented are entered into a file, often referred to as a Change Log, or an addendum on the Design and Architecture Specification.
Design and Architecture Specification: Details the exact course of action to be taken during the project's development phase, including the exact project schedule, scope, and cost; requires client sign-off prior to developing the document. Also may be called a Thick Spec and/or Technical Specification, and may be referred to as another contract. An addendum may be added to record changes made to this document during the development process.	Yes, in the form of an addendum. Any and all changes, regardless of how small, must be documented to avoid questions later. Many people use Change Logs within the specifications to document these. Note: a Change Log is essentially a tracking sheet of all changes requested, who made the request, when it was made, and what actions were taken.
Mockups/Comps: Gives visual descriptions or pictures of how the project will be implemented; these may be part of the Design and Architecture Specification, or they may be completed and delivered separately. Mockups must be extremely detailed because the clients will probably sign-off on them to give you authority to produce the final pages. You should develop mockups or comps for each major section/ aspect of the site.	Yes. Mockups should be updated according to any changes required throughout the development process. All changes must be approved by the client.
Usability Report: Specifies steps taken to test the usability and functionality of the site, as well as the results found and any changes made. Also may be referred to as the Testing Report and/or Quality Assurance Analysis.	Yes. A large portion of the report covers how the site responds to the testing and, consequently, how the site is updated accordingly. The client must review the report before and after any changes are made to the site.
Maintenance Plan: Outlines the process through which the site can be maintained; should include sections for each part or aspect of the site (for example, a Style Guide for updating the front end and a Technical Maintenance Guide for the back end).	Yes. Much of the maintenance plan will likely be written toward the end of the development phase of the project, once the actual details of the site have been ironed out. You should play a big role in the creation of this document, according to your client's needs. See "Creating a Style Guide."
Acceptance Letter: Delivers the final product to the client; requires sign-off to signal completion of the terms of the contract.	No.

Table 12-1 Updates to Documentation

You probably noticed that most of the documentation requires updates at some point. This means most documents work better as "living" docs, continually updated throughout the development process. For this reason, many teams choose to store project documentation in an online arsenal that can be accessed by all members of the team. Google Docs (**www.google.com/docs**) is a free solution that works great for small teams. More complete project management tools include:

- **www.basecamphq.com**   Basecamp
- **www.freelancesuite.com**   Freelance Suite
- **http://projects.zoho.com**   Zoho Project

Creating a Style Guide

Probably the most important aspect of the site documentation for web designs—aside from the actual mockups, of course—is the Style Guide. This document spells out the decisions made in designing the site. For example, what fonts were used? It's important to specify not only the font name, but also the point sizes used, as well as any other typographical details needed to reproduce all graphical and web-based text.

Style Guides needn't be fancy documents, but they must effectively transfer style information from the original designer to whoever might need to maintain or edit the site. In fact, because you—the original designer—might not even know who will make changes to the site in the future, it's best to err on the side of caution and record as much information about the site's creation as possible. Table 12–2 gives a brief example of some of the information you might include.

Element/Selector	Specifications		Color			Styling
	Font family	Size	Name	RGB	Hex	
Level 1 headlines (`<h1>`)	Trebuchet	16pt	orange	255,153,0	#FF9900	bold
Level 2 headlines (`<h2>`)	Trebuchet	14pt	yellow	255,255,204	#FFFFCC	bold
Paragraph text (`<p>`) and block quotes (`<blockquotes>`)	Trebuchet	10pt	black	0,0,0	#000000	n/a

Table 12-2   Sample Details from a Style Guide

Review Site Logs

Another form of documentation for a web site is the site log or traffic report. Site logs are often used to help measure a site's success, in terms of hits, click-throughs, and traffic records. Because such reports can involve significant amounts of numerical data, many people find them confusing and difficult to interpret. The good news is the companies creating the reports know this and are finding ways to make them easier to understand.

Most site logs show information about the geographic location of users, the frequency of their visits, the length of average visits, and their computer types, to name a few. While the actual information you can gather from a user depends in part on what operating system your server is running, the following list includes the most common items gathered in site logs:

- Date and time user accessed the site

- Which file(s) were accessed

- Who accessed them—user's ISP, IP address, and login name (if applicable), as well as what operating system and browser is used

- Which site the user was visiting just before accessing yours—called the referrer

- Amount of content (in bytes) transferred

Site logs can be e-mailed to you (like the one shown in Figure 12–5) or accessed with a special user name and password online. Figure 12–5's log is primarily text, but others, like the one shown in Figure 12–6, translate the data into charts to ease viewing and interpretation. In the case of Figure 12–6, a popular tool called Google Analytics (**www.google.com/analytics**) is used to handle the site logs.

TIP
Google Analytics is a free tool, so you have no excuse not to track how your site is performing. You simply add a bit of custom code to the pages you want to track, and then watch the results with Google's browser-based reporting tool.

The best use of site logs is to identify what's working and what's not. For example, if your site logs shows the majority of your users leave the site from a certain page, you might reevaluate that page's content. Perhaps a link to an external site is drawing many

Hourly Summary

(**Go To**: Top: General Summary: Daily Summary: Hourly Summary: Domain Report: Directory Report: File Type Report: File Size Report: Status Code Report: Request Report: Referrer Report: Failed Referrer Report: Browser Summary)

Each unit (▬) represents 20 requests for pages, or part thereof.

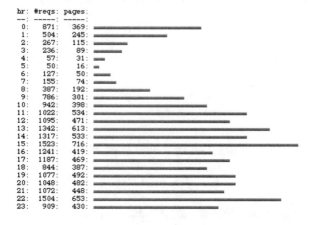

```
hr: #reqs: pages:
--: -----: -----:
 0:   871:   369: ▬▬▬▬▬▬▬▬▬▬▬▬▬▬▬▬▬▬▬
 1:   504:   245: ▬▬▬▬▬▬▬▬▬▬▬▬▬
 2:   267:   115: ▬▬▬▬▬▬
 3:   236:    89: ▬▬▬▬▬
 4:    57:    31: ▬▬
 5:    50:    16: ▬
 6:   127:    50: ▬▬▬
 7:   155:    74: ▬▬▬▬
 8:   387:   192: ▬▬▬▬▬▬▬▬▬▬
 9:   786:   301: ▬▬▬▬▬▬▬▬▬▬▬▬▬▬▬▬
10:   942:   398: ▬▬▬▬▬▬▬▬▬▬▬▬▬▬▬▬▬▬▬▬
11:  1022:   534: ▬▬▬▬▬▬▬▬▬▬▬▬▬▬▬▬▬▬▬▬▬▬▬▬▬▬▬
12:  1095:   471: ▬▬▬▬▬▬▬▬▬▬▬▬▬▬▬▬▬▬▬▬▬▬▬▬
13:  1342:   613: ▬▬▬▬▬▬▬▬▬▬▬▬▬▬▬▬▬▬▬▬▬▬▬▬▬▬▬▬▬▬▬▬
14:  1317:   533: ▬▬▬▬▬▬▬▬▬▬▬▬▬▬▬▬▬▬▬▬▬▬▬▬▬▬▬
15:  1523:   716: ▬▬▬▬▬▬▬▬▬▬▬▬▬▬▬▬▬▬▬▬▬▬▬▬▬▬▬▬▬▬▬▬▬▬▬▬
16:  1241:   419: ▬▬▬▬▬▬▬▬▬▬▬▬▬▬▬▬▬▬▬▬▬
17:  1187:   469: ▬▬▬▬▬▬▬▬▬▬▬▬▬▬▬▬▬▬▬▬▬▬▬
18:   844:   387: ▬▬▬▬▬▬▬▬▬▬▬▬▬▬▬▬▬▬▬
19:  1077:   492: ▬▬▬▬▬▬▬▬▬▬▬▬▬▬▬▬▬▬▬▬▬▬▬▬▬
20:  1048:   482: ▬▬▬▬▬▬▬▬▬▬▬▬▬▬▬▬▬▬▬▬▬▬▬▬
21:  1072:   448: ▬▬▬▬▬▬▬▬▬▬▬▬▬▬▬▬▬▬▬▬▬▬
22:  1504:   653: ▬▬▬▬▬▬▬▬▬▬▬▬▬▬▬▬▬▬▬▬▬▬▬▬▬▬▬▬▬▬▬▬▬▬
23:   909:   430: ▬▬▬▬▬▬▬▬▬▬▬▬▬▬▬▬▬▬▬▬▬▬
```

Domain Report

(**Go To**: Top: General Summary: Daily Summary: Hourly Summary: Domain Report: Directory Report: File Type Report: File Size Report: Status Code Report: Request Report: Referrer Report: Failed Referrer Report: Browser Summary)

Listing domains, sorted by the amount of traffic.

```
#reqs: %bytes: domain
-----: ------: ------
 8023: 30.07%: .com (Commercial)
  385: 26.37%: .au (Australia)
 7721: 21.28%: .net (Network)
 2331: 19.20%: [unresolved numerical addresses]
  627:  1.03%: .us (United States)
  134:  0.84%: .edu (USA Educational)
   44:  0.47%: .uk (United Kingdom)
  213:  0.25%: .ca (Canada)
   19:  0.14%: .mil (USA Military)
   32:  0.11%: .nz (New Zealand)
   13:  0.06%: .es (Spain)
    9:  0.05%: .ru (Russia)
    3:  0.03%: .ee (Estonia)
    3:  0.03%: .jp (Japan)
    3:  0.03%: .br (Brazil)
    3:  0.03%: .it (Italy)
```

Figure 12-5   This example of part of a basic site log shows the hourly summary for page views over the course of a week, as well as the domains from which users accessed the pages.

people away. Maybe the content on that page is so outdated that users leave in search of newer material. Regardless of the reason, examining site logs can at least give you some clues in the right direction.

Figure 12-6 This example shows a screen capture from the Google Analytics browser-based reporting tool.

Maintenance and Upgrades

All web sites require maintenance and upgrades at some point in their lifecycle. In fact, the better web sites undergo frequent maintenance to keep the content current and effective. When dealing with maintenance requests for my projects, I typically offer my clients the following options:

- I can develop a web-based maintenance solution that doesn't require them to purchase and study additional programs or to learn HTML (typically through the use of a content management system or even a blog tool).

- I can train their staff to use a commercial product, such as Adobe Contribute, or even to learn some basic HTML. I could also offer recommendations for other training options, such as self-paced study or classroom-based learning.

- I can set up a monthly maintenance contract, where they pay me by the hour to maintain the site.

If you're transferring the site to a client who doesn't know HTML, there are several ways to maintain a site without dealing with the HTML. First, you can use a WYSIWYG editor, such as Adobe Contribute, to make changes to a site. Contribute is a great tool built to work with Adobe Dreamweaver. This means you can build the site with Dreamweaver, and then set up clients with Contribute to maintain it.

You might think of Contribute as a scaled down version of Dreamweaver, where users can edit only those pages (or even aspects of pages) that the original designer deemed editable. So if you specify a Contribute user can edit only two paragraphs of text on a particular page of a site, he will have access only to those two paragraphs. This prevents unwanted changes from being made that might inadvertently break the site. Check out **www.adobe.com/products/contribute** for more information about using Contribute.

NOTE

Remember WYSIWYG means What-You-See-Is-What-You-Get and refers to how you can edit a web page without editing the code. When you open pages that weren't originally created in these types of editors, however, certain aspects of the page may change unexpectedly. To avoid causing permanent damage to a page, I recommend always making a backup copy of a page before maintaining it with a WYSIWYG editor.

You could alternatively set up the site using a content management system or blog tool that requires no knowledge of HTML. This was discussed in earlier chapters, since you must start off a project with such a tool and cannot add it at the end of a project. However, what happens if you get this far and only now realize the need for such a maintenance tool? Consider discussing a new project altogether (maybe Phase 2?) where you rearchitect the site to fit into whatever content management system is selected.

Summary

Congratulations! If you've successfully uploaded your pages to a server and made them live, and they match the original specifications, you certainly should be proud. The final chapter discusses search engine optimization and a bit about online advertising.

Chapter 13

Advertising Your Site

Key Skills & Concepts

- Understand how search engines work.

- Identify ways to improve a site's ranking in the top search engines.

- Recognize the differences between the design of pages to be displayed in web browsers and those displayed in e-mail readers.

- Become familiar with ways to design and code for e-mail readers.

After the web site is designed, coded, tested, and finalized, you're job is finished, right? Not necessarily. Web designers can be particularly helpful to business owners in two key areas, even after a web site is made live.

The first area—search engine optimization—involves not only preparing the site to be indexed by the search engines, but also being proactive about bringing new customers to the site through those same search engines. Often, this later task comes in the form of sponsored search advertising.

The second area—e-mail design—has become quite fruitful for many designers (myself included). Large numbers of businesses are finding online advertising (through ads and e-mails) to be more cost-effective than traditional print advertising. For this reason, many of those same businesses are switching some of their print budget over to online advertising. E-mail design seems to have grown exponentially as a result.

This chapter seeks to introduce you to what's involved with each of these tasks and to provide additional resources where you can learn more.

Helping Searchers Find Your Site

As a web designer, one of the most common questions I hear from business owners is this: How can I increase my ranking in Google? Search engine optimization (SEO) is the process of making a web site easy to find in search engines, using key words and phrases likely to be used by those in the site's target audience. Indeed, SEO should be a large part of any modern web site project. Unfortunately, many people are of the mindset that "if you build it, they will come." Because of that, SEO is left by the wayside and clients don't really understand its importance until they realize no one is visiting their site.

It's your job, as a web professional, to educate clients about the importance of SEO. If a site is built with SEO in mind from the beginning, it will be easier to increase the site's presence in the major search engines.

So what is search engine optimization all about? The next few sections help clarify this issue.

How Search Engines Work

Traditional search engines rank pages according to the number of times a key word or search term appears on the page. In the past, this has caused some less-than-honorable people to repeat key words over and over in an effort to increase their ranking. The search engines caught on to that little practice, however, and started banning sites that repeated key words in an unreasonable (that is, underhanded) manner.

Google, the most popular search engine, takes a slightly different approach. According to Google's web site, their process works like this:

> We use more than 200 signals, including our patented PageRank™ algorithm, to examine the entire link structure of the web and determine which pages are most important. We then conduct hypertext-matching analysis to determine which pages are relevant to the specific search being conducted. By combining overall importance and query-specific relevance, we're able to put the most relevant and reliable results first.

In essence, Google examines not just the page, but the whole web site, to evaluate the relationships between the pages and therefore the importance of the content within them. This means a key word used in a headline could indicate that it is of greater importance than a key word used only within the body copy.

Google is often referred to as a "crawler-based" search engine, because its systems "crawl" or "spider" the web to find relevant data. By contrast, some search engines are directory based and merely provide an index of sites, but they don't necessarily seek out related data. Each search engine has its own way of indexing data, in an effort to increase speed and efficiency.

TIP

Search engines don't just index static web pages. As this book was going to press, Bing and Google both released "real-time search" capabilities integrating Twitter and Facebook data, as well as blog and news service feeds, into regular search results.

As of August 2009, the top three search engines garnered a whopping 91 percent of the market share, according to Search Engine Watch (**http://searchenginewatch.com**). Google comes in first with just under 65 percent, followed by Yahoo at 16 percent, and Bing with just under 11 percent. Why is this important? Simple: You really only need to be listed in these three search engines to reach the vast majority of search engine users. With that in mind, I'm going to focus on these three search engines for the rest of this discussion.

Search Engines Look for Key Words

When someone starts a web search, the popular search engines evaluate key words and phrases found throughout your pages to find the best matches. Of course, content is king, so the best way to get your site found by the search engines is to include relevant content. But it is also important to repeat your site's key words in specific places.

Here are a few places where search engines looks for key words and phrases:

- **The address** A site whose address is www.marylandflorist.com will probably rank higher than the same site with an address like www.flowersbywendy.com. For this reason, many companies register multiple domains: one with the business name and at least one other that describes what the business does.

- **Headlines** Many designers don't use the heading tags (h1, h2, and so on) because they don't see the need. I argue that these tags are quite valuable, because the words contained within them signify importance to search engines as well as users. Using relevant headlines can go a long way toward increasing the usability and searchability of your site.

- **Body copy** This one can't be emphasized enough. If you are building a web site for a florist, the site surely needs to include content about flowers as well as the products and services offered. Avoid "getting off on a tangent" because it not only dilutes your message but also lowers the page's importance in search engines.

- **Images** No, search engines can't "see" your images, but they can read the alternate text associated with them. Unfortunately, a lot of people neglect to include `alt` attributes with their `img` tags. This is really a wasted opportunity to enhance the searchability of your site. I strongly encourage you to attach alternate text to every image on your pages. Here's an example: `<img src="image.jpg" alt="Photo of ABC Company CEO, James Rile" />`.

- **Links** Don't forget about your links. HTML provides for the `title` attribute to be included with a tags, as a way to attach a readable title to each link. Here's an example: `<a href="link.html" title="Click to find about more about ABC Company's swimming pool products and services">`. Without those titles, the resulting link address is usually a bunch of numbers and letters that make little sense to the user or a search engine. However, if you can control your folder and filenames and use relevant, readable text strings for each, you'll definitely increase the usability and searchability of your site.

- **Page title**   The title at the top of the page may seem insignificant, but it's typically the first thing a search engine user reads from your site, so make it count. A title like "Company Home Page" isn't nearly as effective as something like "ABC Company – Your Source for Swimming Pool Service and Installation".

- **Meta tags**   I've listed these last, as a way to identify their importance when it comes to search engine optimization. While it's true there are specific meta tags for transferring the description and key words to search engines, the other places I've just listed garner greater importance among modern search engines. So it's still good to include relevant meta tags, but you shouldn't rely on them as the only way to get the information to search engines.

NOTE
Remember that the content of meta tags isn't displayed on your web pages but is visible only to search engines and browsers. Refer to the section "Meta Data" in Chapter 7 for details.

Search Engines Consider Popularity
This is one case where a popularity contest counts, at least to a certain extent. Some search engines, such as Google, consider how many related sites link to a particular page. For example, suppose a user searches for "real estate Maryland". Google will first show sites that appear to be popular for those search terms. How does it determine what's popular? Two ways:

- Incoming links
- User input

When complementary web sites link to yours, Google considers that to be a sign of your site's value or worth. So in the case of a real estate office's web site in Baltimore, a site that has links from community organizations and local banks might be considered more valuable than sites without such incoming links.

Similarly, those pages that other searchers have "promoted" rise to the top of the search results faster than those not promoted. Figure 13-1 shows how users can click the "promote" button next to a link in Google's search results to let Google know this particular page is relevant to the search terms.

Figure 13-1 Google allows users to identify which links are relevant.

Even search engines that don't allow users to promote certain links do consider user input. When you search for a phrase, the search engine tracks which links are actually clicked within the search results. It records that information and adjusts its results as needed, to ensure the most likely (that is, most popular) links display before those that are rarely clicked.

This results in a bit of the "chicken-and-egg" syndrome for many web site owners. I often hear, "How can I increase my ranking in the search engines if I'm showing up on page 30 of the results and no one ever gets the opportunity to click my link?" Keep reading….

How Sites Get Listed

For any web site owner, getting a site listed in the search engines is certainly an important task. All three of the top search engines provide free online forms used to recommend new or updated sites. Here are the forms to which I'm referring:

- Submit your site to Google: **www.google.com/addurl**
- Submit your site to Yahoo!: **http://siteexplorer.search.yahoo.com/submit**
- Submit your site to Bing: **www.bing.com/docs/submit.aspx**

Usually, just submitting your site using these free tools is enough to get you listed, but it's not enough to get you anywhere near the top of the search results. That, I'm afraid, is not free.

How Sites Increase Ranking

Remember that chicken-and-egg syndrome I mentioned? The best way to increase your site's visibility, popularity, and ultimately it's ranking in the search engines is to take advantage of pay-per-click (PPC) advertising. All the major search engines offer it, and if you've done any amount of searching you've definitely seen it. I'm referring to those "sponsored links" or "sponsored sites" that display on search results pages, as identified in the following illustration:

Here's the way it works:

1. *Identify the key words and/or phrases you want to sponsor.* Certain words and phrases are more popular than others and therefore cost more to sponsor.

2. *Create the ad.* All sponsored ads are text-based, with a limited number of characters.

3. *Place a bid, which is the amount of money you're willing to pay each time someone clicks your ad.* For example, if you bid $0.10 per click, and 100 people click your ad, you'll be charged $10.

4. *Set a daily, weekly, and/or monthly spending limit for your advertising campaign.* If you specify not to spend more than $100/day, your ad won't be shown after that budget is reached each day of the campaign.

That's it! PPC advertising on the major search engines is easy to set up, but be warned that it can quickly become a full-time job. The most successful search engine advertisers sponsor a variety of different search terms, using multiple ads and campaigns to see what works. Likewise, certain search terms are more popular than others and therefore cost more to sponsor. I suggest you try a variety of options for a short period of time and track the results of each.

Here are links to each of the top three search engine PPC advertising tools. While this might initially seem overwhelming, I encourage you to take a look through the documentation and try a few test campaigns to get the feel of it before you hire someone else to do it for you. Even if you do decide to hire a third-party SEO company, the experience of having used these tools will help as you work with the other company.

- **http://adwords.google.com**   Google AdWords
- **http://advertising.yahoo.com/smallbusiness/ysm**   Yahoo! Advertising
- **http://advertising.microsoft.com/search-advertising**   Microsoft Search Advertising

Ask the Expert

Q: I've received offers from companies that say they can guarantee my site will be listed in the top spot for relevant key word search results. Shouldn't I try one of those before I waste a lot of time and energy on tasks with which I have little experience?

A: I hate to answer a question with another question, but…if you and all your competitors called one of those companies, which one of you would end up in the top spot? Typically, these types of solicitations are nothing more than scams. No one can guarantee your site will be at the top of the search ranking.

With that said, you may find this process to be quite time-intensive. Many businesses do choose to outsource their search engine advertising to other companies that specialize in SEO. If you or your client decides to hire a third-party SEO contractor, do your homework and make sure your expert is, in fact, an expert. Unfortunately, a lot of scam artists prey on business owner's hopes of rising to the top of search engine results.

PPC advertising and SEO are huge online industries. In fact, thousands of books have been filled with content on these very topics. Thankfully, a slew of resources are online and offline to help you learn more. Here are a few reputable places to help you get started:

- **www.google.com/webmasters**   Google Webmaster Central
- **www.searchenginewatch.com**   Search Engine Watch
- **www.seologic.com/guide**   SEO Logic
- **www.websitegrader.com**   Website Grader
- *Search Engine Optimization: An Hour a Day*, by Jennifer Grappone and Gradiva Couzin (Wiley 2008)

Increasing Your Audience Through E-mail

Perhaps the greatest increase in business for web designers over the past decade has been in the area of e-mail design. In fact, a whopping 75 percent of my freelance work (as of this writing) is e-mail design. At this stage in the game, the majority of my clients already have functioning web sites. Any work I'm performing on those sites is predominantly maintenance in nature. However, companies never have enough customers, and this is where e-mail design comes in.

Ten years ago, your e-mail inbox was a lot less colorful (and most likely a lost less full). The rise of CSS, and its widespread support among e-mail readers, has brought about an influx of HTML- and CSS-based e-mail. This type of e-mail brings color, images, formatting, and much more interactivity than its plain-text counterparts. While most companies still provide plain-text e-mails to customers who request them, the vast bulk of business marketing and advertising e-mail now sent is HTML-based.

For the web designer, this brings about a whole new avenue of work opportunities, as well as new headaches. Why? The opportunities come because an HTML e-mail is essentially just a web page. So if you can design and code web pages, you can design and code HTML e-mail.

The reason for the headaches is this: Support for HTML and CSS is growing among e-mail readers (and is leaps and bounds beyond where it used to be), but it still lags behind on many fronts. In fact, coding HTML for e-mail in 2010 looks a bit like coding HTML for web browsers did in 1999—which means you'll spend a lot of time testing, testing, revising, and testing some more.

When you have a project that calls for HTML e-mail, you should consider a few things before you get started.

The Purpose of E-mail Is to Communicate

At the end of the day, we use e-mail to communicate with each other. While there certainly are many forms of communication, e-mail has traditionally used written language to communicate. All e-mail readers allow users to read written text, and this is the most basic requirement of any e-mail reader.

When you start styling that text with color and other formatting, you stop relying on the written word to communicate your message. Suppose, for example, you received an e-mail from a friend. In that e-mail your friend listed the menu for a bridal shower you were helping to throw next weekend, and then included the following line at the bottom: "Thanks for helping with the party! I highlighted the items I still need. Can you help with any of them?"

If your e-mail program is set to read e-mail as text-only, there won't be any highlighted text in that e-mail. In instances like this, the communication method moves from the written language only to include visual clues such as highlighting. Before you make the decision to send HTML e-mails, you need to determine what will be the specific message of the e-mails being sent and how any extra formatting will affect that message.

The End User Display Is Unknown

Unlike web browsers, which have become much more uniform in their display and support of HTML, e-mail readers are plentiful and vastly different from one another. Consider all the ways you read e-mail. If you have a Yahoo!, Hotmail/Live Mail, or Gmail account, you probably read your e-mail in a web browser.

But you still have the option of reading your e-mail in a stand-alone e-mail program such as Outlook or MacMail. And if you are like a growing number of people, you might also check your e-mail on a mobile phone such as a Blackberry or iPhone. I just named off seven different ways to read an e-mail, and I'm only getting started!

It is virtually impossible to know how your HTML e-mails will display when read by the end user. Testing in as many of the popular e-mail readers as possible is certainly important, but ultimately you must make smart design decisions that ensure the widest possible audience can still glean the message being communicated. Keep this in mind when you're deciding whether HTML is the best delivery method for a particular e-mail.

Plain-Text E-mail Is Safer and Smaller

Due to the proliferation of HTML e-mail spam, the simple truth is that plain-text e-mail is more likely to get to the reader. This may mean that the most important e-mail communication with a customer—such as receipts—should be in plain text only.

For example, many e-mail readers block images and attachments from unknown senders or suspected spammers. One reason this happens is because anything attached to an e-mail is capable of harboring viruses and other malicious code. Also, when you send HTML e-mail with images stored on a web server, you can tell whether an e-mail was opened by simply reviewing the site's access logs to see if the images were displayed. This allows spammers to differentiate between active e-mail addresses and bad e-mail addresses.

In fact, HTML e-mails are more likely to be tagged as spam simply for having embedded images. That means your beautifully designed HTML e-mail may end up in a customer's spam bucket and eventually in the trash without the customer even knowing it.

Another reason HTML e-mail might not make it to the target destination is size. If you get a little crazy with large images and hefty attachments, you can cause someone's e-mail system to slow down drastically or even crash.

HTML E-mail Is More Visually Appealing

Now that I've given you several reasons why HTML e-mail might not be appropriate, I must state the obvious: HTML e-mail can definitely be more appealing than plain-text e-mail. Let's face it: most of us react more quickly to an image of a double-dip chocolate ice cream cone on a hot summer day than we might to those words mixed in with other text in a crowded paragraph. As the saying goes, "a picture is worth a thousand words."

The simple truth is that when done right, HTML e-mail marketing works. Here are a few of the reasons why:

- **Cost effective** Advertisers who used to rely on expensive print-mail campaigns are largely embracing HTML e-mail as an efficient way to get their message in front of customers more quickly and less expensively. While design costs might be similar, the cost of sending 1000 e-mails is significantly less than the cost to print and snail-mail 1000 postcards to customers.

- **Targeted** While most companies do target certain ZIP codes when sending snail-mail ads, e-mail advertising allows them to target very specific demographics and behaviors. For example, suppose you are a customer of a certain grocery store who has recently started offering delivery. Being interested in the service, you viewed a page on a company's web site describing this new service, but you never actually purchased it. Because you were logged in to your account with this company at the time you viewed the delivery page, the company decided to send you a targeted e-mail ad offering free delivery on your next order. Such targeted e-mails tend to be highly successful.

- **Timely** E-mail advertisements can be sent within seconds of an event's occurrence. Wake up to a snow day? Why not send a special "snow day savings" e-mail to parents of elementary school students? Customers could be reading your HTML e-mail (and making purchasing decisions) before a snail-mail equivalent even reaches the printer.

- **Fosters relationships** Companies have long known that loyal customers are often the best ones. If you can keep a customer happy, you stand a good chance at keeping her a customer. E-mail—particularly HTML e-mail with some interactivity—provides an effective tool for building and maintaining customer relationships.

At the end of the day, you can measure the success of any e-mail marketing campaign with the right software. Businesses can tell how many people opened the messages, what links were clicked, who saw which versions (HTML or plain text), and even the revenue each generated. So it is relatively easy to stop sending out campaigns that aren't working and to try something new.

Don't Send Spam

Before you start writing your HTML e-mails, you must know about the audience. From a legal standpoint, the most important thing to know about your audience is whether you have permission to contact them in this manner and for this purpose. In short, *spam is any e-mail sent without the permission of the recipient.*

E-mail the Right People

So how do you gain permission from recipients? Here are a few guidelines in that regard:

- *You can send e-mail to current customers.* Most people consider anyone who has purchased from a company within the last two years to be a "current" customer.

- *You can send e-mail to people who request information from you, either in person or online.* Keep in mind that you can send them e-mail about relevant topics only. In other words, if someone responds to a job posting on a company's web site but isn't hired, you can't start sending him marketing e-mail about your products.

This means you can't harvest e-mail addresses off e-mail forwards, or those found on the Internet. Just because I post my e-mail address on my personal web site, that doesn't mean I want to receive marketing e-mail from any business that visits my web site.

While it might be tempting to send mass e-mails to strangers, in the hopes that one might become a new customer, it is much more effective to target people who have already expressed an interest in your business or product.

TIP
If you're working with a client who is unsure whether their marketing list is legal, consider giving them a free "Permission Guidelines Handout" from Campaign Monitor: **www.campaignmonitor.com/downloads/permission-guidelines-handout/**.

Always Provide a Way to Opt Out

After you've decided to create and send HTML e-mail, you need to keep a few things in mind to make sure your beautiful creations don't break the law.

Federal guidelines require that you always provide a way for someone to tell you he no longer wishes to receive your e-mails. At a bare minimum, this means you must provide a valid return address to which users can send a "please remove me" e-mail. Most reputable e-mail systems offer efficient unsubscribe mechanisms that allow recipients to opt out through an online form linked from all e-mails.

Federal guidelines further require that you to keep such unsubscribe methods available for at least 30 days after e-mails are sent. After receiving an unsubscribe request, companies have 10 days to stop sending the recipient e-mail.

Adhere to Other FTC Rules

To avoid your e-mail being considered spam, you must also use legitimate headers and subject lines. In other words, you can't send an e-mail with a subject of "Free delivery on your next order" unless the offer is valid and indeed available to recipients. The from and reply-to e-mail addresses must also be active. The sender's business name and physical mailing address must also be visible in the e-mail.

TIP

Check out **www.ftc.gov/bcp/edu/pubs/business/ecommerce/bus61.shtm** for more information about the Federal Trade Commission's CAN-SPAM laws.

Identify the Necessary Tools for the Task

You've already learned that you can type HTML code in just about any text editor, but in order to be viewed by a web browser, it must be saved with a certain file extension (such as .html or .htm). Similarly, you can type HTML code into an e-mail, but it will just look like a bunch of code unless you send it through the proper channel.

Send Live Web Pages with a Personal E-mail Account

As I mentioned, an HTML e-mail is really just a web page. Have you ever wanted to e-mail a web page to someone? How you do this depends on your e-mail software. If you have Apple's Safari browser, you simply navigate to the page you want to send and choose File | Mail Contents Of This Page. Next, the page will display in an e-mail in MacMail. Simply address it and send it off!

Here are the steps you'd follow to send a live web page with Outlook 2007:

1. In Outlook, choose View | Toolbars | Web.

2. Enter the URL of the page you want to send.

3. Next, choose Actions | New Mail Message.

4. The new message will contain the web page you just viewed. Address it and click Send.

You can also use Internet Explorer 7+ to send a web page via e-mail. If you use the web-based Hotmail/Live Mail, choose Page | E-mail With Windows Live. If you don't use web-based e-mail but have Outlook or some other e-mail software installed and set up on your system, choose Page | Send By E-mail. (This option is grayed out if you don't have an e-mail account currently set up on your system.)

These methods are useful when you want to share a web page with family or friends. However, you wouldn't use these methods to send out mass business e-mails for several reasons. First, most Internet service providers (ISPs) limit the amount of bandwidth you can use on a daily or monthly basis. Sending lots and lots of HTML e-mail will likely have your ISP hounding you pretty quickly. In addition, sending bulk e-mail through your business or personal server runs you the risk of having *all* your e-mail blocked as spam.

Using an E-mail Service Provider

The best method for sending bulk HTML e-mail is to use an e-mail service provider (ESP). Similar to an ISP, an ESP handles all aspects of bulk e-mail delivery, from managing the recipient lists (both subscribe and unsubscribe features), to tracking the number of times each e-mail is opened and clicked.

Just as there are hundreds of ISPs out there, you also have your choice of quite a few ESPs. As a freelancer, I have used a fair number of ESPs for different businesses. Each has its pros and cons, depending on the business and its audience.

When researching ESPs, here are a few things to look for:

- Contact management tools to handle your subscriber list
- E-mail creation tools to help format and lay out the content
- E-mail sending tools to help you test your e-mails
- Design services to help with graphic design and creative support (if you need it)
- E-mail reporting tools to help you track things such as click-throughs, opens, and conversations
- Ease of use
- Support

As with any software, I encourage you to try before you buy. ESPs typically charge either a monthly fee or per-e-mail/per-recipient fees (or a combination of both). Many also offer rebranding tools to allow designers to create their clients' e-mails, and then give the clients the tools to send and manage them. Following are a few of the most popular ESPs:

- BlueHornet (**www.bluehornet.com**)
- CampaignMonitor (**www.campaignmonitor.com**)
- Constant Contact (**www.constantcontact.com**)
- Emma (**www.myemma.com**)
- iContact (**www.icontact.com**)
- Lyris (**www.lyris.com**)
- MailChimp (**www.mailchimp.com**)

NOTE
If you are considering sending bulk mail, run (don't walk) toward these ESPs as fast as you can. I strongly discourage you from using your personal e-mail account and e-mail software to send *any* amount of bulk mail. The risks are just too great, and the benefits too small, to justify it.

Design and Code for E-mail Readers

Finally, when you make the jump to e-mail design, always design and code your pages according to the method by which they will be viewed: an e-mail reader. According to several sources, the most popular e-mail clients are Microsoft Outlook, Yahoo! Mail, and Hotmail. While Outlook is a desktop program, Yahoo! Mail and Hotmail are both web-based services in which users access e-mail through the web browser.

TIP
Check out **www.campaignmonitor.com/stats/e-mail-clients** for updated stats on the most popular e-mail clients.

Ultimately, you must determine which e-mail clients to target in terms of your project's target audience. And just as with traditional web pages, you must test as much as possible within your target e-mail clients. As a designer who frequently creates HTML e-mail for clients, I have set up e-mail accounts in all the top five e-mail clients specifically to use for testing HTML e-mail.

Designing e-mail means you must take a different approach than you do for much of what I've already discussed about web design. A different set of guidelines exists for e-mail design. Here's an outline to get you started off on the right foot:

- *Web site navigation is unnecessary.* Unlike web sites, which typically include many different pages that need to be linked, an e-mail is meant to be a self-contained piece of information. Obviously you can, and should, provide inline links to relevant information, but it is a waste of space to include the web site's complete navigation within a marketing e-mail.

- *Images may not be seen.* Image blocking is much more common in e-mail readers than web browsers. In fact, some e-mail programs (such as Outlook, AOL, and Gmail) have default settings that block images in e-mail from unapproved senders. So you shouldn't depend on images to get your point across unless you also provide a text-only alternative. Also, images that are broken into pieces and then put back together with a table in HTML tend to fall apart in certain e-mail readers. For this reason, it's best to keep images whole and avoid slicing them into smaller pieces.

- *Images must be stored on a web server.* You can't attach the images to your e-mail when sending bulk mail. Instead, you must store the images on a web server and use complete, absolute references when linking to them. In other words, you must use a link like this, `<img src="http://www.wendywillard.com/e-mail/header.jpg">`, instead of this, `<img src="header.jpg">`.

- *"Teaser" text can increase your open rate.* In many e-mail readers, the user is presented with the first two lines of text before ever seeing the rest of the message. Often times, readers decide whether to open the e-mail based on that teaser text. Take advantage of this and explain why readers should bother to open your message.

- *Keep page widths around 600 pixels.* While it's true people seem to be using larger and larger monitors, that doesn't mean you can create e-mails to fill those screens. Most e-mail readers use a paneled approach, where the list of mailboxes might run down the left side, with the list of messages above the actual message area in the space on the right. This means your e-mail needs to fit in a small portion of the overall e-mail reader window, because the majority of your audience won't scroll horizontally to read an e-mail.

Figure 13-2 shows an example of a typical HTML e-mail. Notice that this message is not text heavy, but instead gets the message across in two or three sentences. The rest of the message is photographic in nature, to be visually appealing and attention-getting. There is a link at the top of the page for readers who can't see the images in their e-mail programs. That link takes users to their web browser, where another copy of the e-mail is stored online.

I've marked a few other aspects of the design, to point out other ways this e-mail design is different from a traditional web page.

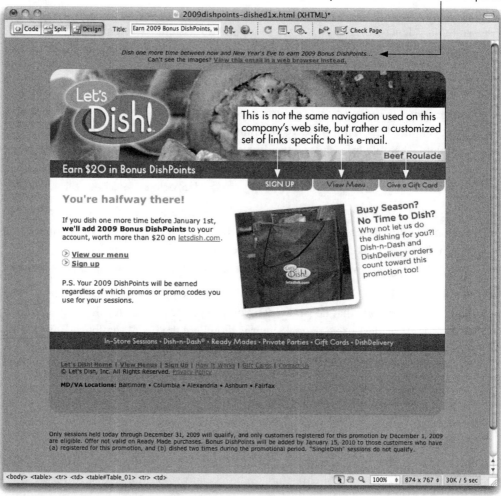

Here's my teaser text, telling readers what they can expect to find when this e-mail is opened.

This is not the same navigation used on this company's web site, but rather a customized set of links specific to this e-mail.

Figure 13-2 Sample HTML e-mail

CSS Support

Throughout this book, I've told you to separate structure and style for web pages. With e-mail, it's the complete opposite. Because you're sending a single page to an e-mail reader, you actually need to combine structure and style as much as possible.

Some CSS is not supported at all. In fact, many designers use HTML tables for page layout in e-mail design, because CSS positioning just doesn't work in most e-mail readers. Those aspects of CSS that are supported must be embedded within the HTML of the page in order to be recognized. I know this is counter to what I've already told you, but trust me on this one. Until the e-mail readers get up to speed on CSS support, your best bet is to go light on the styles.

In the meantime, refer to **www.campaignmonitor.com** for up-to-date resources on everything, from which CSS properties are supported by which e-mail readers, to how well Flash and video formats play in e-mail.

Testing

After you've designed and coded your HTML e-mail, the fun really begins. While we've come to the point where web pages that work in Firefox and Internet Explorer are considered "safe" for the Web at large, HTML e-mail still requires extensive testing in multiple clients.

Thankfully, many ESPs offer services to make this process easier. For example, Campaign Monitor provides screenshots to show how your e-mail will look in more than 15 of the most popular e-mail clients, including Outlook, Yahoo!, Gmail, and Lotus Notes. Visit **www.campaignmonitor.com/testing** to learn more. Figures 13-3, 13-4, and 13-5 show how the same test e-mail displays differently depending on the e-mail client. These screen shots are samples taken using Campaign Monitor's testing tool.

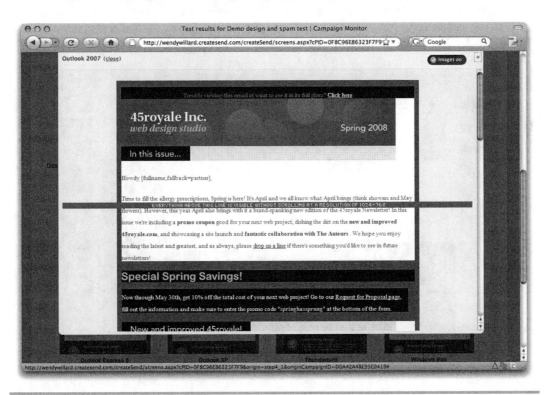

Figure 13-3   The sample e-mail, as it displays in Outlook 2007

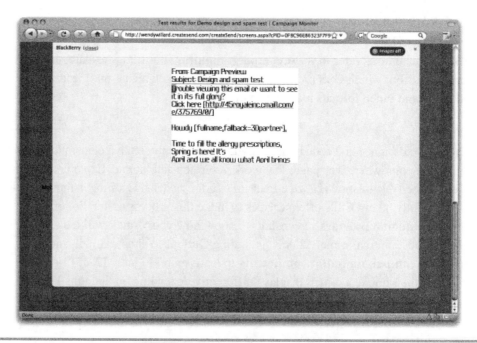

Figure 13-4 The sample e-mail, as it displays on a Blackberry

Figure 13-5 The sample e-mail, as it displays in Yahoo! Mail

Another great option is a standalone testing tool such as Litmus. Billing itself as the "advanced testing tool for web professionals," Litmus offers testing for both standard web pages and HTML e-mail. Litmus's basic account offers up to 50 tests per month in Internet Explorer, Firefox, Outlook, and Gmail. Additional fee-based options allow testing in 23 web browsers and 16 e-mail clients. Visit **http://litmusapp.com** for details.

Spam Test

One of the unique aspects you can test is the likelihood of your e-mail being flagged as spam. Many of the popular ESPs offer this testing with their e-mail messaging services. (If yours does not, you can download other tools to test HTML e-mail locally. MailingCheck, available from **www.mailingcheck.com**, is a free Windows-based spam checker.)

SpamAssassin is the most widely used spam filter used to process e-mail received by ISPs. If your e-mail gets blacklisted by SpamAssassin, you'll have a hard time getting your content in front of any of your subscribers. Refer to **http://spamassassin.apache.org** to learn more.

Wondering what might cause an e-mail to be flagged as spam? Here are just a few of the many reasons SpamAssassin might give you a higher "spam score." (And in this case, higher is not better.)

- HTML link text says "click here" (I warned you not to do this!)
- A WHOLE LINE OF YELLING DETECTED
- Messages that include "Dear Friend" or "Dear (Name)"
- Message that contains "call" or "dial" or "toll free" followed by 800, 888, 877, 866, 855, 844, 833, or 822 (For example, "Call 1-877-555-5555 for your offer now!")
- Messages with the phrase "risk free"
- HTML title contains "Untitled" (Always title your web pages, even if they're being e-mailed!)

TIP

Want to know more about how spam filters work? Check out **www.mailchimp.com/ resources/how_spam_filters_think.phtml**.

HTML e-mail is a whole different breed. While web browsers are fairly uniform in their display of HTML pages, e-mail readers still have a long way to go. Designing HTML e-mail involves lots of patience as you design, test, and redesign.

Ready for more practice? I encourage you to sign up for a free test account with one of the ESPs mentioned in this chapter. Then, try re-creating your sample marketing e-mail using their web-based creation tools. Each ESP offers different options, but all provide the messaging services necessary to send bulk HTML e-mail safely and securely.

Summary

This final chapter discussed two ways to extend your role as a web designer, beyond traditional web page design, by introducing SEO and e-mail design. Each of these topics easily fills their own books, which is why many designers have chosen to focus solely on one or the other. If you find yourself particularly intrigued by SEO and/or e-mail design, I hope you will research the additional resources mentioned throughout the chapter to learn more.

Appendix A

HTML/CSS
Reference Table

This appendix offers a reference table for the tags and properties learned in this book. It is organized alphabetically, with HTML tags and CSS properties included together for easy comparison. Because the scope of this book is at a beginner's level, I decided not to discuss a few advanced tags and properties. If you come across something not listed here or in the index, try visiting an online reference library such as the following:

- **http://webdesign.about.com/od/htmltags/a/bl_index.htm**
- **www.w3schools.com/css/css_reference.asp**

NOTE
The latest version of the HTML specifications can be found on W3C's web site at **www.w3.org**.

Generic Attributes

The following groups of attributes can be used by a large number of tags in HTML. In the following tables, a code is listed in the attribute column on a particular tag if it accepts any of the following groups of generic attributes.

- Core attributes (*core) provide rendering and accessibility information to elements.
- Event handlers (*events) provide a way of triggering an action when an event occurs on a page. Note that not all event handlers are listed.
- International attributes (*intl) provide a way of rendering documents using multiple language or character sets.

Group Type: Core

Attribute	Uses
accesskey	Assigns a keyboard shortcut to the element
class	Assigns a category label to an element
ID	Assigns a unique identifier to an element
style	Gives instructions on how to render an element
tabindex	Assigns the tab order of an element
title	Gives a brief description of an element

Group Type: Events

Attribute	Uses
onClick	Triggers an event when the element is clicked
onDblClick	Triggers an event when the element is double-clicked
onMouseDown	Triggers an event when the pointer is clicked over an element
onMouseUp	Triggers an event when the pointer is released over an element
onMouseOver	Triggers an event when the mouse pointer is passed over an element
onMouseOut	Triggers an event when the mouse pointer moves away from an element
onKeyPress	Triggers an event when a key is pressed and released immediately
onKeyDown	Triggers an event when a key is pressed and held down
onKeyUp	Triggers an event when a key that was pressed is now released

Group Type: Intl

Attribute	Uses
dir	Indicates the direction of the content flow
lang	Indicates the language of the content

HTML Tags

The following table provides a reference for the HTML tags discussed in this book. Although I have removed most of the deprecated (outdated) tags from this table, some deprecated attributes remain. Those are marked with a (D) to help make them easily recognizable. In most cases, these have been deprecated in favor of style sheets.

One additional note—some attributes are deprecated only in certain cases. For example, while it is not acceptable to use the align attribute with the p tag, it is okay to use it within a table (such as in the colgroup or tr tag).

HTML Tag	Attributes	Uses
`<!--...-->`	n/a	Inserts comments into the page that aren't seen when the page is viewed in the browser
`<!DOCTYPE>`	n/a	Indicates the version of X/HTML used; must be placed on the first line of the document
`<a></a>`	*core, *events, *intl	Creates links and anchors
	`coords`	Defines the size of a hot spot in an image map
	`href`	Specifies the location (URL) of the link
	`name`	Identifies an anchor
	`shape`	Defines the shape of a hot spot in an image map
	`target`	Identifies the target window where the link will be displayed
`<abbr></abbr>`	*core, *intl	Indicates the content is an abbreviation
`<acronym></acronym>`	*core, *events, *intl	Specifies an acronym
`<address></address>`	*core, *events, *intl	Formats the contact information for a page
`<area />`	n/a	Defines links and anchors within an image map
	`coords`	Specifies the size of the hot spot
	`href`	Specifies the location (URL) of the link
	`nohref`	Specifies that a hot spot isn't linked
	`shape`	Defines the shape of a hot spot in an image map
	`target`	Identifies the target window where the link will be displayed
`<b></b>`	*core, *events, *intl	Makes text boldface
`<base />`	n/a	Identifies the default path for links specified within the document
	`href`	Defines the location (URL) of the link
	`target`	Specifies the window in which the URL should open
`<big></big>`	*core, *events, *intl	Formats the text as one size larger than the default size

HTML Tag	Attributes	Uses
`<blockquote>` `</blockquote>` (D)	*core, *events, *intl	Sets off a block of text, indenting it on both sides
`<body></body>`	*core, *events, *intl	Encloses the content of the document
	`alink` (D)	Specifies the default color of an active link on the page (use the `color` CSS property instead)
	`background` (D)	Defines a background image for the page (use the `background-image` CSS property instead)
	`bgcolor`	Specifies the default background color of the page
	`link` (D)	Specifies the default color of the links on the page (use the `color` CSS property instead)
	`text` (D)	Specifies the default color of the visited links on the page (use the `color` CSS property instead)
	`vlink` (D)	Specifies the default color of the visited links on the page (use the `color` CSS property instead)
	`topmargin, leftmargin marginheight, marginwidth`	Specifies the size in pixels of the top and left margins (not in the official HTML specification; browser support varies)
` `	*core, *events, *intl	Causes a line break
	`clear` (D)	Causes text to stop wrapping around an image and start again on the next line (use the `clear` CSS property instead)
`<button></button>`	*core, *events, *intl	Creates a button
	`name`	Defines the name of the button
	`value`	Specifies the value or type of button
`<caption></caption>`	*core, *events, *intl	Defines a table caption
`<cite></cite>`	*core, *events, *intl	Formats a short quote or reference
`<code></code>`	*core, *events, *intl	Formats text as code (usually in a monospace font)
`<col />`	*core, *events, *intl	Specifies subgroups of columns within a column group, to allow them to share attributes

HTML Tag	Attributes	Uses
`<col />`	`align`	Aligns the subcolumn group horizontally
	`span`	Specifies the number of columns the subcolumn group spans
	`valign`	Aligns the subcolumn group vertically
	`width`	Specifies the width of the columns using percentages or pixels
`<colgroup></colgroup>`	*core, *events, *intl	Defines a group of columns
	`align`	Aligns the column group horizontally
	`span`	Specifies the number of columns the group spans
	`valign`	Aligns the column group vertically
	`width`	Specifies the width of the columns using percentages or pixels
`<dd></dd>`	*core, *events, *intl	Defines the description of a term in a definition list
`<del></del>`	*core, *events, *intl	Formats the text as deleted by marking a line through it
	`cite`	References another document with a URL
	`datetime`	Identifies the date and time of the deletion
`<dfn></dfn>`	*core, *events, *intl	Specifies a definition
`<div></div>`	*core, *events, *intl	Identifies a section (or division) of the page
`<dl></dl>`	*core, *events, *intl	Creates a definition list
`<dt></dt>`	*core, *events, *intl	Defines a term in a definition list
`<em></em>`	*core, *events, *intl	Gives emphasis to text (usually by making it italic)
`<fieldset></fieldset>`	*core, *events, *intl	Creates a group of form controls
`<form></form>`	*core, *events, *intl	Creates a form where users can enter information
	`action`	Specifies the location (URL) of the script to process the form
	`enctype`	Specifies the MIME type used to encode the content of the form
	`method`	Defines how the form will be processed (`get` or `post`)

HTML Tag	Attributes	Uses
`<frame />`	`id`, `class`, `title`, `style`	Creates frames
	`frameborder`	Specifies whether the border(s) between frames are visible
	`longdesc`	Defines a location (URL) of the long description for the frame contents, for browsers that do not support frames
	`marginheight`	Defines the size of the frame's top and bottom margins
	`marginwidth`	Defines the size of the frame's left and right margins
	`name`	Defines a name for the frame so that it can be used as a target window
	`noresize`	Specifies that the user cannot alter the frame's size
	`scrolling`	Defines when the scroll bars appear in the frame (`yes`, `no`, or `auto`)
	`src`	Defines the initial document (URL) that should be loaded into the frame
`<frameset></frameset>`	`id`, `class`, `title`, `style`	Creates a layout for a set of frames
	`cols`	Defines the number and size of the columns in the frameset
	`rows`	Defines the number and size of the rows in the frameset
`<h1></h1>`	*core, *events, *intl	Creates six levels of headline (h1 being the largest and most important; h6 being the smallest and least important)
`<head></head>`	*intl	Contains the header information for the page (such as the title and information for search engines)
`<hr />`	*core, *events	Separates sections with a horizontal rule
`<html></html>`	*intl	Contains and identifies the document
`<i></i>` (D)	*core, *events, *intl	Formats text as italic
`<iframe></iframe>`	`id`, `class`, `title`, `style`	Creates an inline, floating frame
	`align` (D)	Aligns the frame in the page (use the `text-align` or `float` CSS property or other CSS positioning properties instead)

HTML Tag	Attributes	Uses
`<iframe></iframe>`	`frameborder`	Defines whether the frame's border is visible
	`height`	Defines the height of the frame in pixels or percentages
	`longdesc`	Contains the link (URL) to a long description of the frame contents
	`marginheight`	Defines the top and bottom margins of the frame
	`marginwidth`	Defines the left and right margins of the frame
	`name`	Defines the name of the frame
	`scrolling`	Defines when the scroll bars appear in the frame (`yes`, `no`, or `auto`)
	`src`	Defines the initial document (URL) that should be loaded into the frame
	`width`	Defines the width of the frame in pixels or percentages
`<img></img>`	*core, *events, *intl	Embeds an image in a page
	`alt`	Specifies a text description of the image (required)
	`height`	Defines the height of the image in pixels
	`longdesc`	Defines the location (URL) of a longer text description of the image
	`src`	Defines the location of the image file
	`usemap`	Defines the image as a client-side image map and specifies the location (URL) of the map properties
	`width`	Defines the width of the image in pixels
`<input />`	*core, *events, *intl	Creates types of form input controls for users
	`accept`	Defines the file types allowed in a file upload control
	`alt`	Defines an alternative text description
	`checked`	Specifies that the input control should be checked by default when the page is loaded

HTML Tag	Attributes	Uses
`<input />`	`disabled`	Specifies that the input control cannot be used
	`maxlength`	Defines the maximum number of characters a user can enter in a text field or password box
	`name`	Defines the name of the input control, used when processing the form
	`readonly`	Specifies that a user can read, but not edit, an input control
	`size`	Defines the size of a text field or password box
	`src`	Defines the location (URL) of an image used in an input control
	`type`	Identifies the type of input control (text, checkbox, radio button, and so forth)
	`usemap`	Identifies the control as a client-side image map and specifies the location (URL) of the map properties
	`value`	Defines the initial value of an input control
`<ins></ins>`	*core, *events, *intl	Formats text as inserted since the last change
	`cite`	References another document with a URL
	`datetime`	Identifies the date and time of the insertion
`<kbd></kbd>`	*core, *events, *intl	Formats text as something the user should type on the keyboard
`<label></label>`	*core, *events, *intl	Specifies a label for a form input control
	`for`	Identifies to which input control the label belongs
`<li></li>`	*core, *events, *intl	Defines an item in an ordered or unordered list
	`type` (D)	Specifies the style of the list (replaced by the `list-style-type` CSS property)
	`value`	Specifies the initial value of the first item in the list

HTML Tag	Attributes	Uses
`<link></link>`	*core, *events, *intl	Indicates a relationship between the current document and another resource (such as a style sheet)
	`href`	Specifies the location of the resource
	`rel`	Specifies the type of resource
	`type`	Defines the MIME type
`<map></map>`	*core	Defines the properties of a client-size image map
	`name`	Names the map so that it can be referenced by other aspects of the page
`<meta />`	*intl	Gives information about the document
	`content`	Contains specified information
	`http-equiv`	Assigns a header field, which then can be used to transfer the user to another page or otherwise process the document
	`name`	Defines what type of information the content attribute specifies
`<noframes></noframes>`	*core	Provides alternative content for non-frames–capable browsers
`<noscript></noscript>`	*core	Defines the content displayed in browsers that don't support scripts
`<object></object>`	*core, *events, *intl	Embeds an object in the page
	`classid codebase`	Defines a URL indicating how the object should be implemented
	`codetype type`	Specifies the MIME type of the code referenced by the `classid` attribute
	`height`	Defines the height, in pixels, of the object
	`name`	Defines the name of an object
	`standby`	Defines the message to show while the object is loading
	`usemap`	Identifies the object as a client-side image map and specifies the location (URL) of the map properties
	`width`	Defines the width, in pixels, of the object

HTML Tag	Attributes	Uses
`<ol></ol>`	*core, *events, *intl	Creates an ordered list
	`type` (D)	Specifies the style of the list (use the `list-style-type` CSS property instead)
	`value`	Specifies the initial value of the first item in the list
`<option></option>`	*core, *events, *intl	Creates choices in a form select menu
	`disabled`	Specifies the specific option as viewable, but not selectable
	`selected`	Defines the option as selected by default when the page is loaded
	`value`	Defines the initial value of the option, used when processing the form
`<p></p>`	*core, *events, *intl	Specifies a paragraph of text (inserts a blank line by default above the paragraph)
`<param />`	`id`	Contains parameters for an object
	`name`	Defines the parameter's unique name
	`value`	Defines the parameter's value
	`valuetype`	Defines the MIME type of the value
`<pre></pre>`	*core, *events, *intl	Identifies text as preformatted (usually displayed in a monospace font)
`<q></q>`	*core, *events, *intl	Formats a short quotation
`<samp></samp>`	*core, *events, *intl	Formats text as a sample computer output, usually in a monospace font
`<script></script>`	`n/a`	Contains scripts, such as those written in JavaScript, executed in the page by the browser
	`defer`	Indicates the script will not generate any document content and the browser can continue drawing the page
	`src`	References an external script by giving its location (URL)
	`type`	Specifies the MIME type of the script (required)
`<select></select>`	*core, *events, *intl	Creates a form menu with choices (using the `option` tag) users can select

HTML Tag	Attributes	Uses
`<select></select>`	`disabled`	Specifies the menu as viewable, but not usable
	`multiple`	Enables users to select multiple choices
	`name`	Identifies the name of the menu, used when processing the form
	`size`	Defines the number of choices visible in the menu when the page loads
`<small></small>`	*core, *events, *intl	Formats the text as one size smaller than the default size
`<span></span>`	*core, *events, *intl	Defines a section of content
`<strong></strong>`	*core, *events, *intl	Gives stronger emphasis to text, usually by making it boldface
`<style></style>`	*intl	Adds an internal style sheet to a page
	`media`	Specifies the destination medium for the style information (such as print, screen, all, and so forth)
	`type`	Defines the MIME type of the content (required)
`<sub></sub>`	*core, *events, *intl	Formats the text as subscript
`<sup></sup>`	*core, *events, *intl	Formats the text as superscript
`<table></table>`	*core, *events, *intl	Creates a table
	`align` **(D)**	Aligns the table on the page (use the `text-align` or `float` CSS property or other CSS positioning instead)
	`bgcolor` **(D)**	Specifies the background color of the table (use the `background-color` CSS property instead)
	`border`	Specifies the thickness, in pixels, of the border around the table
	`cellpadding`	Specifies the amount of space around the content within the cells
	`cellspacing`	Specifies the amount of space between the cells
	`cols`	Identifies the number of columns
	`frame`	Defines which of the table's edges are visible

HTML Tag	Attributes	Uses
`<table></table>`	`height`	Specifies the height of the table, in pixels or percentages
	`rules`	Defines which of the table's interior seams are visible
	`summary`	Specifies a summary of the table for speech-synthesizing or nonvisual browsers
	`width`	Specifies the width of the table in pixels or percentages
`<textarea></textarea>`	*core, *events, *intl	Creates a form input control where users can enter multiple lines of text
	`cols`	Defines the height of the text area in the number of character columns visible
	`disabled`	Prevents users from entering text in the area
	`name`	Identifies the name of the text area, used when processing the form
	`readonly`	Specifies the text area as viewable, but not editable
	`rows`	Defines the width of the text area in the number of character rows visible
`<tbody></tbody>`	*core, *events, *intl	Defines the table's body (must be used with `tfoot` and `thead`)
	`align`	Aligns the cell contents horizontally
	`valign`	Aligns the cell contents vertically
`<td></td>` `<th></th>`	*core, *events, *intl	Defines an individual cell (`td`) or header cell (`th`)
	`align` (D)	Aligns the cell's contents horizontally (replaced with the `text-align` CSS property)
	`bgcolor` (D)	Defines the cell's background color (replaced with the `background-color` CSS property)
	`colspan`	Defines how many columns the cell spans
	`height` (D)	Defines the height of the cell in pixels or percentages (replaced by the `height` CSS property)

HTML Tag	Attributes	Uses
`<td></td>` `<th></th>`	`nowrap` (D)	Specifies that the content of the cell should stay on a single line (replaced by the `white-space` CSS property)
	`rowspan`	Defines how many rows the cell spans
	`valign` (D)	Aligns the cell's contents vertically (replaced with the `vertical-align` CSS property)
	`width` (D)	Defines the width of the cell, in pixels or percentages (replaced by the `width` CSS property)
`<tfoot></tfoot>`	*core, *events, *intl	Defines the table's footer (must be used with `thead` and `tbody`)
	`align`	Aligns the cell contents horizontally
	`valign`	Aligns the cell contents vertically
`<thead></thead>`	*core, *events, *intl	Defines the table's header (must be used with `tbody` and `tfoot`)
	`align`	Aligns the cell contents horizontally
	`valign`	Aligns the cell contents vertically
`<title></title>`	*intl	Gives a name to your page that will be displayed in the title bar of the browser
`<tr></tr>`	*core, *events, *intl	Defines a table row
	`align`	Aligns the contents of the row's cells horizontally
	`bgcolor` (D)	Specifies a background color for the row (use the `background-color` CSS property instead)
	`valign`	Aligns the contents of the row's cells vertically
`<u></u>` (D)	*core, *events, *intl	Underlines text
`<ul></ul>`	*core, *events, *intl	Creates an unordered list
	`type` (D)	Specifies the style of the list. (can also be accomplished with the `list-type-style` CSS property)

CSS Properties

This table acts as a reference for the style sheet properties used throughout this book. Because this is a beginner's guide, this table does not include every possible CSS property.

When listing values, those within brackets, such as `<length>`, indicate value concepts as opposed to actual values. For example, when a value is listed as `<length>`, you might use a pixel dimension, as in 10px. By contrast, a value of `left` is an actual value term, as in `float:left`. Here are a few more tips regarding value concepts:

- Length units take two-letter abbreviations, with no space between number and unit, as in `width: 100px` or `padding-top: 2cm`.

- Percentage units are calculated with regard to their default size.

- Color units can be specified by hexadecimal code: color: `#ffffff`; RGB value: `color: rgb(255, 255, 255)`; or name: `color: white`.

- URLs are relative to the style sheet, *not the HTML document*, and are defined like this: `list-style-image: url(star.gif)`.

Property	Use	Values	Default Value
background	*Shorthand for any of the background properties.*		
background-attachment	Defines whether a background image scrolls when the page is scrolled or remains fixed in its original location	scroll fixed	scroll
background-color	Defines the background color of an element	`<color>` transparent	transparent
background-image	Defines an image to be used as the background pattern	`<URL>` none	none

background-position	Defines the starting position of the background color or image	`<percentage>`
		`<length>`
		top
		center
		bottom
		left
		center
		right
			0% 0%

background-repeat	Specifies how a background image repeats	repeat no-repeat repeat-x repeat-y	repeat

Property	Use	Values	Default Value
`border`	*Shorthand for all the border properties.*		
`border-collapse`	Specifies whether the borders of each table cell are merged or separated from one another; applies to table elements	`collapse` `separate`	`collapse`
`border-color`	Defines an element's border color; can be specified for each side individually (as in `border-top-color`)	`<color>` `transparent`	*Varies*
`border-style`	Defines an element's border style; can be specified for each side individually (as in `border-top-style`)	`none` `hidden` `dotted` `dashed` `solid` `double` `groove` `ridge` `inset` `outset`	`none`
`border-width`	Defines an element's border width; can be specified for each side individually (as in `border-top-width`)	`thin` `medium` `thick` `<length>`	`medium`
`bottom`	Specifies the location of the bottom of positioned elements	`<length>` `<percentage>` `auto`	`auto`
`caption-side`	Specifies the location of a table caption	`top` `bottom` `left` `right`	`top`
`clear`	Specifies whether an element can have floating elements around it	`none` `left` `right` `both`	`none`
`color`	Specifies the color of the element by hexadecimal code, RGB values, or keyword	`<color>`	*Varies*

Property	Use	Values	Default Value

cursor	Changes the display of the cursor	`<URL>`
		`auto`
		`crosshair`
		`default`
		`pointer`
		`move`
		`e-resize`
		`ne-resize`
		`nw-resize`
		`n-resize`
		`se-resize`
		`sw-resize`
		`s-resize`
		`w-resize`
		`text`
		`wait`
		`help`
			`auto`

direction	Specifies in which direction the text flows	`ltr` `rtl`	`ltr` (left to right)

display	Specifies how the item should be displayed within the page flow	`inline`
		`block`
		`list-item`
		`run-in`
		`compact`
		`marker`
		`table`
		`inline-table`
		`table-row-group`
		`table-header-group`
		`table-footer-group`
		`table-row`
		`table-column-group`
		`table-column`
		`table-cell`
		`table-caption`
		`none`
			`inline`

empty-cells	Specifies whether to display empty table cells	`show` `hide`	`show`

float	Pushes an element to the left or right of other page elements; can be applied to any element that is not absolutely or relatively positioned	`left`
		`right`
		`none`
			`none`

Property	Use	Values	Default Value
`font`	*Shorthand for all font properties.*		
`font-family`	Changes the font family in which text is displayed:	`<family name>` `<generic family>`	*Varies*
`font-size`	Changes the font size in which the text is displayed: absolute sizes include pixels, ems, points, and picas; relative sizes are keywords such as small, medium, and large	`<absolute size>` `<relative size>` `<length>` `<percentage>`	`medium`
`font-size-adjust`	Adjusts the font size up or down, relative to the current font size	`<number>` `none`	`none`
`font-stretch`	Changes the horizontal width of the font	`normal` `wider` `narrower` `ultra-condensed` `extra-condensed` `condensed` `semi-condensed` `semi-expanded` `expanded` `extra-expanded` `ultra-expanded`	`normal`
`font-style`	Adjusts whether text is italicized	`normal` `italic` `oblique`	`normal`
`font-variant`	Adjusts whether text is displayed in small-caps	`normal` `small-caps`	`normal`
`font-weight`	Adjust the heaviness of the text	`normal` `bold` `bolder` `lighter` `100` `200` `300` `400` `500` `600` `700` `800` `900`	`normal`

Property	Use	Values	Default Value

height	Specifies the height of an element (does not apply to table columns or column groups)	`<length>`
		`<percentage>`
		`auto`
			`auto`

left	Specifies the location of the left edge of positioned elements	`<length>`
		`<percentage>`
		`auto`
			`auto`

letter-spacing	Adjusts the amount of space between letters	`normal` `<length>`	`normal`
line-height	Adjusts the amount of space between lines of text	`<length>` `<percentage>`	`normal`
list-style	*Shorthand for all list-style properties.*		
list-style-image	Uses an image before each item in a list	`<URL>` `none`	`none`
list-style-position	Specifies whether items in a list display inside or outside of the "bullet"	`inside` `outside`	`outside`

list-style-type	Specifies the type of "bullet" that precedes items in a list	`disc`
		`circle`
		`square`
		`decimal`
		`decimal-leading-zero`
		`lower-roman`
		`upper-roman`
		`lower-greek`
		`lower-alpha`
		`upper-alpha`
		`upper-latin`
		`lower-latin`
		`Hebrew`
		`Armenian`
		`Georgian`
		`cjk-ideographic`
		`kiragana`
		`katakana`
		`hiragana-iroha`
		`katakana-iroha`
		`none`
			`disc`

margin	*Shorthand for all margin properties.*		
margin-top margin-right margin-bottom margin-left	Defines the amount of blank space around the outside of an element's box	`<margin width>`	0

Property	Use	Values	Default Value

max-height
min-height
	Defines the maximum and minimum allowable height of an element (does not apply to table elements)	`<length>`
		`<percentage>`
		`none`
			none

max-width
min-width
	Defines the maximum and minimum allowable width of an element (does not apply to table elements)	`<length>`
		`<percentage>`
		`none`
			0

overflow	Defines how to handle content that does not fit within a particular block-level box	`visible`
		`hidden`
		`scroll`
		`auto`
			visible

padding	*Shorthand for all padding properties.*		
padding-top padding-right padding-bottom padding-left	Specifies the amount of blank space around the content, within a box	`<padding width>`	0

position	Specifies how an element is positioned on the page	`static`
		`relative`
		`absolute`
		`fixed`
			static

right	Defines the location of the right edge of a positioned element	`<length>`
		`<percentage>`
		`auto`
			auto

text-align	Defines the horizontal alignment of text and block-level elements	`left`
		`right`
		`center`
		`justify`
		`<string>`
			Varies

text-decoration	Adds lines above, below, or through text	`none`
		`underline`
		`overline`
		`line-through`
		`blink`
			none

text-indent	Specifies the amount text is indented	`<length>` `<percentage>`	0

text-transform	Changes the case of text	`capitalize`
		`uppercase`
		`lowercase`
		`none`
			none

top	Defines the location of the top edge of a positioned element	`<length>`
		`<percentage>`
		`auto`
			auto

Property	Use	Values	Default Value
vertical-align	Specifies the vertical alignment of text and inline-level elements (including table cells)	baseline sub super top text-top middle bottom text-bottom <percentage> <length>	baseline
visibility	Specifies whether/how an element is displayed on the page when it first loads	visible hidden collapse	inherit (the default value is inherited from the parent element)
white-space	Defines how white space is handled within block-level elements	normal pre nowrap	normal
width	Defines the width of an element (does not apply to table rows or row groups)	<length> <percentage> auto	auto
word-spacing	Defines the amount of space displayed between words	normal <length>	normal
z-index	Specifies the stacking order of the element (applies only to absolutely or relatively positioned elements)	auto <integer>	auto

NOTE

All these properties can also have a value of inherit, which tells the browser to use whichever value has already been assigned to the element's parent/container object.

Index

properties
  box, 240–243
  fonts, 224–225, 227
  list, 230
  styling image rollovers, 257–258
  table of CSS, 347–353
proposals. *See also* RFPs
  audience's connection, platform, and
    browser in, 35–41
  considering domain names, 46–47
  content for site, 51–55
  defined, 30–31
  defining scope and statement of
    work, 33–34
  documenting navigation, 54
  identifying conditions and
    assumptions, 34–35
  key components of, 32–33
  planning site hosting, 42–46
  pricing of project, 47–48
  schedules in, 48
  site maps in, 48–51
  stating project purpose, 33
  team biographies in, 48
pt (points), 225
publishing content, 292–309
pull-quotes
  adding border around, 241–243
  centering text in, 244
  using float property with, 246
px (pixels), 225

Q

questions
  asking clients, 15
  How, 22–27
  What, 20–21
  When, 21
  Where, 21
  Who, 5–20
  Why, 13–14
QuickTime parameters for object tag,
  266, 269

R

radio buttons, 207, 209
raster applications, 62
Real Media object tag parameters, 266, 267
Really Simple Syndication (RSS),
  278–279
reference navigation, 89
relative links, 213–214
relative positioning, 247, 251
remote sites, 300
resolution
  file, 121–122
  monitor, 39, 66–68
resources
  blogging, 43, 282, 283, 284
  color schemes, 106

CSS layout templates, 249
designing with fonts, 84
documentation, 31
domain name, 46–47
embedding Flash, 269
ESP, 325
Flash, 165, 167, 169
free FTP program, 302
free script, 212
FTC spam laws, 323–324
hosting, 46
JavaScript and DHTML, 277–278
navigation idea, 91–92
positioning content, 260
PPC advertising and SEO
  industry, 319
principles of color, 136–137
rollover, 258
sharing project communications, 110
sites for inspiration, 86–87, 94
social networking, 47–48
stock media, 108–109
styling forms, 235
usability testing, 57
web design organizations, 47
web development!, 51
reviewing site logs, 42, 306–308
RFPs (Request for Proposals)
  checking progress against,
    100, 304
  defined, 30
  formal, 13
  informal, 13
  proposal responding to, 32–48
robots meta tag, 188, 189
rollover effects. *See* image rollovers
rows
  rows attribute, 209
  tagging table, 204
RSS (Really Simple Syndication),
  278–279

S

Save Optimized As dialog box
  (Photoshop), 157
saving
  GIF images, 126, 142–144
  JPEG images, 145–146
  Photoshop output settings, 161
  PNG files, 146–147
  Word and WordPad HTML files, 181
scheduling
  about, 21
  including in proposal, 48
screen area
  dealing with inconsistent, 69–73
  defined, 38
  detecting and providing different
    page versions, 72–73
  resolution of, 66–68
  size of, 40, 66–68

testing size of, 70, 73
using liquid pages for changing,
  71–72, 73
viewing different sizes of, 38–39
scripts
  about, 190–191
  ActionScript, 27
  adding date to page with, 273–274
  adding to header content, 191
  client-side, 24–25
  creating dynamic navigation bar,
    274–277
  finding free, 212
  resources for JavaScript and
    DHTML, 277–278
  scripting hidden layers, 275, 277
  searching for existing, 271
  server-side, 23–24
  using JavaScript, 271–273
scrolling background image with
  page, 253
search engine optimization (SEO)
  about, 312–313
  hiring companies for, 318, 319
  how search engines work, 313–317
  ignoring meta tags, 189
  key words and phrases for, 314–315
  optimizing sites for searches, 312
  site popularity factor, 315–317
Search Engine Watch, 314
search engines. *See also* search engine
  optimization
  adding site to, 20
  finding audience information with, 11
  how they work, 313–317
  listing site on, 317
Search site map model, 51
secondary navigation, 87, 88, 89
security with passwords, 209
select menus
  coding, 210–211
  illustrated, 207
selectors
  combining, 223
  custom, 222–223
  defined, 221
  descendent, 223
  overwriting, 223–224
  using tag, 221–222
semicolons (;), 192
server-side scripting, 23–24
shadows, 254–255
shortcut links, 89
single-line text fields
  about, 208
  creating, 208–209
  illustrated, 207
site documentation. *See* documentation
site maps, 48–55
  All-in-One model, 49
  Flat model, 49
  Hub-and-spoke model, 50